Praise for

WHAT TO DO
WHEN THINGS
GO WRONG

Most people that watch the Super Bowl are only aware of the spectacle that kicks off at 6:30 PM EST the first Sunday in February. As former chairmen of the Super Bowl XLVII Host Committee, we have some understanding of the complexity and logistical difficulties in putting on not only the game itself but also the host/owner parties, the halftime shows and the extensive infrastructure prep for each host city.

Together we've been through countless political campaigns (domestic and international), The White House and raising two daughters. Each had its unique challenges. We wish we would've had this book through it all. It's genuinely applicable for every conceivable crisis; how to manage them, but more importantly how to avoid them. We've never seen anyone cooler under fire than Frank Supovitz. He has the ability to immediately adapt to his circumstances while instilling confidence in everyone working around him. Simply put, Frank Supovitz is the best and *What to Do When Things Go Wrong* should be required reading for all business leaders and college students who aspire to be.

—James Carville and Mary Matalin,
renowned political strategists and media personalities

In governing, managing major projects, and life, things will inevitably go wrong. Those best prepared for adjusting to the unexpected can not only recover but come out ahead. Very few people understand this better than Frank Supovitz. I watched firsthand how he handled major events like the Super Bowl and found this book to be a great entry point for people in business, event planning, or even politics. *What to Do When Things Go Wrong* is full of insight to help you in your own journey toward success.

—Mitch Landrieu, Mayor,
City of New Orleans (2010–2018)

Supovitz's breezy, personable, and often provocative storytelling style brings to life the more sobering and valuable lessons of avoiding and planning for crises, and then managing them when they happen anyway. *What to Do When Things Go Wrong* is a necessary read for anyone managing projects or people.

—**Paul Tagliabue,** Commissioner,
National Football League (1989-2006)

To you, Super Bowl Sunday may be a chance to gorge on guacamole. To Frank Supovitz, the Big Game is 1,327 disasters waiting to happen. In *What to Do When Things Go Wrong*, the NFL's former Super Bowl Czar takes you behind the scenes at the world's biggest sporting event. You get to laugh at Frank's stories, learn from his mistakes, and most of all, develop the planning and management skills that will help you keep your next looming disaster at bay.

—**Allen St. John,** award-winning journalist
and *New York Times* Best-selling author of
Newton's Football and *The Billion Dollar Game*

What to Do When Things Go Wrong is a seminal training tool for mitigating risk. Supovitz takes readers on a roller coaster ride of both glamour and potential disaster with storytelling techniques and memorable scenes that everyone can relate to. Like a disaster happening before your eyes or a Lifetime romance movie, the book is gripping, keeping readers wanting to know what's next, as the relatable content draws out personal experiences, sentiments, and insecurities from the reader.

What to Do When Things Go Wrong could be one of the classic business books that everyone who has ever managed anything needs to read and digest. It is a business lifesaving manual.

—**David Adler,** CEO and Founder,
BizBash Media

Frank's book provides a comprehensive treatment involving crisis management, with a strategic understanding of how to resolve unique and complex situations. In my years in the industry, I have never seen a treatment that focuses on all of these issues with an easy-to-understand and -implement message. It is a "must have" for those in business, and "in the business."

—**Rick Horrow,** author of *The Sport Business Handbook: Insights from 100+ Leaders Who Shaped 50 Years of the Industry,* and Visiting Expert on Sports Business at Harvard Law School

Frank Supovitz has great experience in successfully managing massive projects that cater to expansive live audiences and are broadcast to the world stage. In his book, *What to Do When Things Go Wrong*, Frank draws from his experience to guide the reader on how to imagine, prepare, execute, respond, and evaluate challenging situations that do and will go wrong. His use of personal experiences, procedures, protocols, and outcomes offer actionable processes that everyone can use to avoid and deal with uncomfortable situations that will arise in their own personal lifetimes.

—**Brad Mayne,** President & CEO,
International Association of Venue Managers

When things inevitably go wrong at an event, no matter how big or small, there is no one I'd rather have handle the response than Frank Supovitz. That's because he's prepared for anything. *What to Do When Things Go Wrong* should be required reading for every project manager whether they are in the sports world or not and should be placed right alongside any planning document they hold dear. As Frank notes, communication is key in a crisis and trust is a common denominator in making a plan flow flawlessly. After reading *What to Do When Things Go Wrong*, your team will be able to communicate through any problem and come away with a plan to trust when inevitable problems arise.

—**Jason Gewirtz,** Editor, *SportsTravel* magazine

What to Do When Things Go Wrong should be required reading for anyone in business, or life, looking for a roadmap on how to handle the evitable challenges we all face. Delivered in an entertaining and engaging manner, Frank Supovitz marries his incredible experiences leading some of the world's biggest events with a truly impressive series of lessons that can make us all better. I highly recommend it!

—**Ed Horne,** President, Endeavor Global Marketing

Most managers will never have a project with the number of variables that Frank Supovitz faced every year staging the Super Bowl for the NFL. The lessons he learned about planning, innovation, communication, time management, and preparing for every possible scenario—regardless how low the probability—are here for professionals in any business, not just sports.

—**Dennis Deninger,** Syracuse University sport
management professor and author, *Sports on Television:
The How and Why Behind What You See*

What to Do When Things Go Wrong is as practical, timely, and insightful for business professionals as it is for students who want to learn more about embracing unanticipated realities and dealing with unplanned outcomes. Supovitz provides readers with an inside look into event operations and crisis management at the NFL Super Bowl and leverages his professional experiences to offer readers countless practical and actionable strategies to manage and overcome the unexpected. The straightforward and witty tone makes *What to Do When Things Go Wrong* an easy-to-digest and essential read for project managers, event planners, and all college students.

> **—Scott Bukstein,** director, Undergraduate Sport Business Program,
> associate director, DeVos Graduate Sport Business Program,
> University of Central Florida, College of Business

There's this adage which has come to be known as Murphy's Law: anything that can go wrong will. It is as important for business leaders and project managers as it is for event planners in the sports and entertainment industry to keep this in mind. Following Frank's recommendations, our industry now has a blueprint on how to handle these event crises, and professionals from any industry can similarly benefit from Frank's real-life experiences and wisdom. Readers are getting a gift from the best in the business.

> **—Dr. Lou Marciani,** director, National Center for
> Spectator Sports Safety and Security (NCS4),
> The University of Southern Mississippi

What to Do

WHEN THINGS GO WRONG

A Five-Step Guide to
Planning for and Surviving
the Inevitable—And
Coming Out Ahead

FRANK SUPOVITZ

New York   Chicago   San Francisco   Athens   London   Madrid
Mexico City   Milan   New Delhi   Singapore   Sydney   Toronto

1 2 3 4 5 6 7 8 9   LCR   24 23 22 21 20 19

ISBN: 978-1-260-44158-1
MHID: 1-260-44158-X

e-ISBN: 978-1-260-44158-8
e-MHID: 1-260-44159-8

This publication is designed to provide accurate and authoritative information in regard to the subject matter covered. It is sold with the understanding that neither the author nor the publisher is engaged in rendering legal, accounting, securities trading, or other professional services. If legal advice or other expert assistance is required, the services of a competent professional person should be sought.

> —*From a Declaration of Principles Jointly Adopted by a Committee of the American Bar Association and a Committee of Publishers and Associations*

McGraw-Hill Education books are available at special quantity discounts to use as premiums and sales promotions or for use in corporate training programs. To contact a representative, please visit the Contact Us pages at www.mhprofessional.com.

Dedicated to

Catherine, Matt, Ethan, Jake, Amy, & Madison

who always make life go right

CONTENTS

STEP THREE **EXECUTE**

STEP FOUR **RESPOND**

STEP FIVE **EVALUATE**

ACKNOWLEDGEMENTS

A lifetime of errors, omissions, blunders, and bruises would not seem to be a very promising platform from which to guide other leaders, project managers, and other aspiring mess-ups on what to do when things go wrong. What I eventually did get right was to occasionally learn from my own fumbles, and more often from the wise counsel, trust, and friendship from countless mentors, bosses, teammates, and partners.

I met Allen St. John while he was writing *The Billion Dollar Game*, an intimate behind-the-scenes look at the Super Bowl. An event most often thought about only in terms of numbers and statistics, Allen discovered that there were real people under real pressure not only on the gridiron, but off the field as well. Allen and I reconnected many times over the years to talk about plans and planning, and about things that went wrong. His encouragement and deft preparation of the proposal for *What to Do When Things Go Wrong* helped to attract the interest of Alec Shane at Writers House, and through him to my talented and enthusiastic editor at McGraw-Hill, Cheryl Ringer. My profound thanks to Alec and Cheryl for their untiring support for the project.

Things could not have possibly gone wrong as often if I hadn't been blessed with dozens of people who trusted me with their company's brands and projects, including Bob Jani, Dick Evans, Chuck Cone, Mike Walker and Barnett Lipton at Radio City Music Hall; Gary Bettman, Steve Ryan, Steve Flatow, Steve Solomon, and Jon Litner at the National Hockey League; and Paul Tagliabue, Roger Goodell, and Eric Grubman at the National Football League. Nor could things have gone wrong as infamously without Alan B. Goldberg, Armen Keteyian, or Clem Taylor, who so capably and accurately documented the Super Bowl blackout and other preparations for *60 Minutes Sports*. Another shout-out is due to Howard Katz at NFL Films, who convinced truTV to shadow a dozen of us around for a year documenting how the league managed events for *NFL Full Contact*. Watching some of the finished episodes helped to remind me of a multitude of things that went wrong over the course of that year, but thankfully, there were far fewer viewers for that show than when the lights went out in New Orleans.

A hearty thanks to the experts who allowed me to include a small sample of their prodigious wisdom, including former NHL IT guru Chris Barbieri, Kevin Catlin of Insight Strategies, Inc., crisis communications expert Ivy Cohen of Ivy Cohen Corporate Communications, entertainment insurance specialist Paul Evans at Marsh, Inc., talent development consultant and executive coach Nancy Gill, Robert Krumbine of Charlotte Center City Partners, Kevin Kruse of LEADx, former Pennsylvania State Police Commissioner and current head of security for the Kansas City Chiefs Jeffrey Miller, and Noah Sarff of The Basement.

The number of teammates who have journeyed with me over the years from right to wrong and back again is a list too populous to mention in its entirety, and most will be grateful I left them out. A special thank-you, however, is due to those who came along in this book, as named or unnamed co-conspirators, including Jerry Anderson, Mike Arnold, Todd Barnes, Lance Barrow, Jack Budgell, Sherri Caraccia, Sammy Choi, Dan Donovan, Bob Hast, Ric Martinez, Brian McCarthy, Bill McConnell, Allison Melangton, Mark Miles, Phil Pritchard, Bruce Rodgers, Joan Ryan-Canu, Mike Signora, "Skippy," Doug Thornton, and Mike Witte. Thank you all for your contributions to the eventual recoveries from all that went wrong.

FOREWORD

Minutes after Beyonce blew up Super Bowl XLVII with an electrifying halftime performance the game went from blowout to blackout. Ninety-eight seconds into the second half with the Baltimore Ravens leading the San Francisco 49ers 28 – 6, fully half of the stadium lights inside the Superdome in New Orleans went dark. You may remember the moment.

At that very moment I was standing next to the author of this book. Frank's official title at the time was senior vice president of Events for the NFL. In his words, he was "the ringmaster" of the biggest sporting event on the planet, the man in charge of everything from broadcast operations to communications to transportation to game day operations and more. Much more. As I later wrote, "the sum total of a thousand parts broken down into a million pieces."

For the better part of two months I'd observed Frank in a number of different settings, relative to his job. I'd seen him stand in front of some 300 high-level employees and quickly and efficiently lay out the groundwork and ground rules for the game. I watched him tool around the vast confines of the stadium in his souped-up Segway, double-checking power cords and party preparations. But you never really know how a leader operates until things go wrong.

And, in Frank's case, I mean *really wrong*.

Franks came out of nowhere—as they so often do—inside NFL Control, the league's nerve center wedged into a section high above the field of play. As part of what would become a 33-minute behind-the-scenes feature for *60 Minutes Sports*, I was conducting an interview with Frank when out of the corner of my eye I noticed an entire bank of stadium lights snap off. Then another. Then another.

"Oh, oh," I uttered aloud. "That's not good."

Think about this scene for a second: More than a *billion people* watching around the world; more than 80,000 people crammed into an indoor facility, with the only escape route up aisles potentially packed with panic; all communications cut off, and the NFL's command post completely in the dark. I must admit my first reaction was equally as dark as half the park: *Is this some kind of terrorist attack?* As those thoughts were running through my head, Frank turned his, and like a powerful mainframe computer assessing faulty code, calmly and directly began the search for answers.

"Frank," responded one of his colleagues. "We lost the A feed."

It was not a time for guesswork. Or pretending to know more than he did.

"What does that mean?" Frank said.

"It means about a 20-minute delay."

I'd like to report during several other critical exchanges over the next few minutes a hint of hesitation or uncertainty crept into Frank's voice. But that would not be accurate. There simply wasn't. Not once.

No, instead what our crew witnessed (and captured on video) was a cool, collected leader assessing information. Actually applying the principles on which so much of this book is based.

"Do we have PA?" Frank asked at one point, citing the stadium's public address system.

Yes, he was told.

"Let's give people the PA"

Meaning, let's tell the stressed-out crowd exactly what we know and why. Tell them they're safe.

As the delay stretched into what would become 34 of the most surreal minutes in NFL history, Frank made one clear-eyed decision after another.

"Everybody, listen up, this is important," he said as power began to trickle back. "We're not going to start again until I know all systems are up."

More than once over the last six years Alan Goldberg, the lead producer of that *60 Minutes Sports* piece, and I have marveled at how Frank acted that night. In honor, Alan even came up with a nickname Frank has come to enjoy.

In part because of the events of February 3, 2013, we have become good friends and dinner companions. I dare say after reading this book you'll find yourself wanting to sit down with Frank and discuss the invaluable wisdom herein. And if the lights ever go out, or something else goes wrong, rest assured.

You're in good hands with The Cog.

Armen Keteyian

CAN THIS DAY GET ANY WORSE?

We've all been there. A personal or professional crisis suddenly strikes, and the stakes are high. Your heart beats faster. Your blood pressure rises. You alternately feel overheated and chilled; beads of sweat are erupting on your forehead. Things look like they are rapidly heading south, or maybe they have already traversed the equator. You have that hollow feeling in the pit of your stomach and you wonder what you might be doing for a living tomorrow. Your boss and your company are counting on you to make things right. Your family is counting on you to make things right. Your daughter's orthodontist, ballet instructor, and hockey coach are all counting on you, too.

It might be entirely up to you to make things right and make them right fast. Or, you may be a member of the team that is suddenly catapulted into a murky and unforeseen reality that needs to be navigated to get things back on the right track. Whether you are leading, being led, or totally on your own, the pressure is on and tempers are rising. Things are beginning to look awfully dark, indeed.

If you've been so uncommonly lucky that nothing has gone so seriously wrong, as any of the above, for you in your professional, academic, or personal life, let me provide you with a level of confident assurance. It will, and you need to read this book even more quickly and urgently than the rest of us. I guarantee that if nothing has gone seriously wrong for you at least once so far, something is going to go terribly, horribly, and spectacularly wrong sometime, somewhere, and somehow, despite your very best intentions, your painstaking and expert planning, and your unfailingly optimistic worldview. And, when you get past the first thing that goes terribly, horribly, and spectacularly wrong, guess what? There's another crisis coming, and when it arrives things will look dark all over again, and very possibly even worse.

And, I'm an optimist.

I've had days when things looked particularly dark. If you were among the more than 108 million Americans watching Super Bowl XLVII on February 3, 2013, my own encounter with something going terribly, horribly, and spectacularly wrong probably looked pretty dark to you as well. That was when the second power failure of the night hit the Mercedes-Benz Superdome in New Orleans. When the first power failure hit, the San Francisco 49ers defense had already played 30 minutes of football.

What was that moment like, and what were we feeling? Well, imagine the very worst moment you have ever had at the office. If you are very, very lucky, only you or perhaps a handful of customers or clients will notice what went wrong. Imagine, instead, that 80,000 of your best, highest-paying customers are not only keenly aware that things are not going very well, but that every one of them are right outside your door expecting you to make things right. Watching them watch you are more than 3,000 accredited members of the press tweeting, posting, and postulating in real time on the confusion around them in the eerie indoor twilight while you are searching for a solution to a pretty noticeable problem.

Now, imagine tens of millions of TV viewers across America licking Buffalo sauce off their fingers so they can tap their neighbors on the shoulder without leaving greasy, red memories on their jerseys, too. Roughly 18 million more viewers experienced the worst TV moment in Super Bowl history than the pointedly unscheduled guest appearance at a notorious halftime show nine years before.

It couldn't get any worse, right? No, it's not a sundae without a cherry. So, let's top it all off with an award-winning TV journalist and documentary crew from *60 Minutes* standing right next to you, with cameras rolling for an ad hoc interview at the very moment you suddenly needed a change of underwear. A little pressure? Yes, you would think, with a generous helping of heart palpitations, cold sweats, and a side of acid reflux.

I'm happy to report that from this point things didn't get any worse that night. But, they could have. In fact, we may have been mere seconds from what could have instead been an irrevocable, unrecoverable, premature ending to what was then the third most widely-viewed TV program in American broadcast history. Thanks to the quick-thinking team of well-prepared professionals in the Super Bowl's event control center and throughout the Superdome, things got a lot better. After what Armen Keteyian termed "34 of the most surreal minutes in NFL history," Super Bowl XLVII resumed to a brighter, if somewhat controversial conclusion, ripe for conspiracy theorists hypothesizing on what exactly went wrong, why, and at who's behest.

The moment the lights went out in New Orleans was stressful for a lot of people. I felt more than a little of that pressure because I was the NFL's senior executive in charge of events at the time, and managing the Super Bowl was one of my chief responsibilities. My game-day office was a specially-constructed booth perched high above the crowd called "NFL Control," the nerve center for Super Bowl operations. From there, every aspect of the game-day experience could be monitored and managed, from football operations and officiating to stadium operations and transportation. Law enforcement and public safety, security, broadcasting, social media, public relations, transportation, medical services, hospitality, and more were all in our team's hands. NFL Control was well-named because every part of the game-day plan was timed to the second, planned to the square inch, and closely monitored from the beehive of activity in the booth. When something went wrong, NFL Control was either the first to know, or the next to find out. And, the first person to take the heat, well, that was me.

If you manage a project, department, brand, company, or heaven forbid, an event, you've been there, too. Things go wrong all the time and you have to make them right when they do. Maybe you're a team member, project coordinator, customer service representative, or a salesperson. No matter the role, when something goes wrong, you will likely feel some share of the stress generated by the specter of impending failure and what that may mean for your coworkers, friends, or even your own livelihood.

This book will not solve your crisis when something goes wrong. **You** will. But, this book will give you the tools to help you avoid, forestall, and manage crises when they happen. This book is not designed to turn us into courageous peace officers, fearless soldiers, or brave firefighters. Not in the literal sense, anyway. This book will not turn you into the next airline Captain Chesley "Sully" Sullenberger, Apollo 13 Commander James A. Lovell, Jr., or Pakistani activist Malala Yousafzai. Fortunately, the vast majority of things that go wrong will not suddenly plop you in the improbable position of being thrust onto the world stage.

Unfortunately, however, there are a vast number of things that can and will go wrong. You won't require superhuman Spider-sense, the reaction time of The Flash, or Bondian savoir faire to cope with the challenges you face. But you will need to think ahead, act fast, and stay cool when they do go wrong.

What to Do When Things Go Wrong is about preparing regular people like us, whether we are accomplished in our fields, working our way up, or just starting our career journey, to find effective solutions in a productive and timely manner when we are faced with a challenge to our success. It is a prescriptive playbook designed to prepare us for the blips, bloops, blunders, crises, and disasters we will inevitably encounter, illustrated by real-life stories drawn from the experiences of project managers from sports, live events, business, and life in general, including my own.

THE FIVE PHASES OF CRISIS MANAGEMENT

What to Do When Things Go Wrong will explore the five critical phases of crisis mitigation and management. While not everything that goes wrong is a crisis, many small problems become bigger ones if they are not handled thoughtfully, quickly, and correctly. It is not easy to be thoughtful, quick, and correct all at the same time. So, it is way better to start being thoughtful *before* something goes wrong than after it has already happened.

1. Imagine
The first step is to **Imagine**. You can call it brainstorming, or ideation, or "blue-skying"—whatever business buzzword you'd like to apply. Imagining is *not* the same as planning. Imagining happens before and

inspires better planning, but continues throughout the preparation process, and even as planning matures and shifts into execution.

When you start a project, you will almost certainly know your desired outcomes and why they are important. You may have identified some of the strategies that will guide your thinking. You might even have a very good sense of the tactics you will employ to reach your goals. That process—identifying your objectives, developing your strategies, and outlining your tactics—is the well-worn roadmap to success. Great managers are laser-focused on crafting excruciatingly detailed planning documents, schedules, Gantt bar charts, PERT (Program Evaluation Review Technique) flowcharts, and runs of show, which are the tools of the trade to keep projects moving forward. Developing these plans takes experience and expertise, and if everything clicks along just as it should, the desired result is almost certain to be achieved.

Having applied a vivid imagination comes in very handy, however, when things don't click along. Before that happens, you need to have taken off your rose-colored glasses, put on a pair of shades, and imagined all the things that could go wrong. You don't have to be Stephen King to perceive the monsters under your bed. Even a child can do it.

2. Prepare

The second step of attenuating the effects of the limitless things that can go wrong, and managing them when they do, is to **Prepare**. This involves applying all those dark imaginings and analyzing how those scenarios might destroy your expertly crafted plan. Simply, it is planning for the unplanned. You will, no doubt, have a finite amount of resources, ranging from time and money to staff and materials. You will have to decide how to deploy them in ways that are most likely to prevent problems, large and small. In my mind, when I'm thinking about what could go wrong, "prevent" and "prepare" are essentially interchangeable.

3. Execute

The third step is to **Execute**. Planning and preparation are over. The time to roll out your most ambitious project yet is now. Or, maybe you are facing something less dramatic, but equally important: the day of your big presentation in front of the C-suite suits or the opening of your new bank branch. Execution is putting your impressively meticulous plan into action, all the while remaining vigilant and at the ready to deal with those monsters if they peek their heads out from between your slippers. In many ways, the thing that distinguishes the execution phase of a project is the fact that time becomes both the most *important* force and the most *precious* resource. Your roadmap has been set, and your project has been faithfully following the route you've laid out, but suddenly, something happens that requires a detour.

4. Respond

What you do when you discover that the bridge is out on the route you intended to follow is the fourth step: **Respond.** Your imagination helped you develop some clever, foolproof contingency plans. You did all your homework and took every reasonable, and perhaps even a few unreasonable, precautions. You prepared yourself. You prepared your team. And despite all that, something went wrong. Why? It doesn't really matter right now. That's a conversation for later. But don't take it personally; it's often just a law-of-averages thing. The world is complex and sometimes something out of your control simply goes wrong, for instance, a power outage at the Super Bowl. You must make it right and you have to do it fast because the clock is ticking, and if you don't . . . well, who knows what might happen. Make the right decision, and you're back on the road to recovery. Make the wrong decision, and you might just turn a smaller problem into a full-blown disaster. Sometimes making the right decision takes just a little longer than making the wrong one, but that doesn't mean that time is on your side.

5. Evaluate

The process to candidly **evaluate** the results of your planning, execution, and response begins soon after the project has concluded, and may continue for weeks or even months. Most efforts are measured against numbers-driven key performance indicators, like net income, sales growth, performance versus budget, attendance, broadcast ratings, or changes in consumer sentiment. Whether things went wrong or flawlessly from an operational perspective, these important metrics can spell disappointment or distress if they are not accomplished to the company's expectations. The evaluation process should also include a frank assessment of the intangibles that do not always show up on a spreadsheet or in a box score, including what went wrong along the way and why, because fixing them can improve efficiency, delivery, and the bottom line in the future. Then, it's time to start imagining all over again.

• • •

I know that all of this sounds pretty gloomy, and that I'm someone who looks at the glass half-empty. But it's quite the contrary. When I manage a project, I'm optimistic that all the planning, experience, and education my team and I have accumulated will either drive the desired outcomes or help us manage the situation if those outcomes prove elusive. In order to remain confident, however, I have to play the role of a pessimist and force myself to imagine and prepare for the worst.

How does having managed nine Super Bowls qualify me to help? By itself, it doesn't. But, when you spend three decades managing more than 200 high-profile sports and entertainment events across the globe for high-profile brands—including the National Football League, the National Hockey League, and Radio City Music Hall— you are bound to encounter a few glitches. More likely hundreds of glitches, in every size, shape, severity, and variety. I've learned that the problems don't always follow patterns, but the solutions often do.

ONE OF THE WORLD'S MOST COMPLEX AND VISIBLE PROJECTS

At their core, events are just projects. They are often very visible, very complex, and very interesting projects, but planning an event is very much like crafting a business plan to start a new company. You identify your objectives, develop a strategy to achieve them, create a budget that allocates your available resources, and focus your team of dedicated subject experts on executing the tactics required to generate the optimal result. Managing events is also very much like overseeing a project to develop a new product, formulate a new marketing plan, expand into new territories, or install a new telecommunications system. All these efforts require meticulous planning and an imagination that can visualize the damage if deadlines are not met, an accident occurs, or a failure unfolds due to either human error or simple bad luck.

The number of things that can go wrong at a "mega-event," like the Super Bowl, is dizzying. All for a single football game on a Sunday evening, it requires the conversion of the host stadium to accommodate thousands of media, domestic and international broadcast facilities, hospitality pavilions, fan activities, and operational compounds, inside a hardened security perimeter that can require as much as 2½ miles of barricades and fencing. Beyond the sports match, event day includes hours of pregame broadcasts on multiple networks, a 10,000-guest pregame Tailgate Party, and a famously spectacular and highly produced halftime show. Outside of the stadium, the Super Bowl devours tens of thousands of hotel rooms for fans, business partners, and workers; gobbles up convention centers, theaters, and public plazas for a week-long schedule of fan festivals, broadcasts, awards dinners, concerts, and galas; and a dizzying number of parties hosted by the league, business partners, media outlets, charities, and other organizations. Arrangements must be made for indoor and outdoor training facilities for the competing teams, hundreds of charter buses and private planes, hundreds of thousands of square feet of temporary offices, media workrooms, security and law enforcement command posts, and storage facilities dotted across the region.

By game day, as many as 20,000 people—most of them local—will have received credentials as full-time, hourly, volunteer, media, or contractor staff to service the needs of the event, fans, guests, or partner companies of the NFL. Even if the program of activities was exactly the same each year, the process of acquiring and managing all of these assets and coordinating the diverse schedule of events that they support requires an enormous planning effort because the Super Bowl moves to a different location each year. As a result, the Super Bowl occupies an entirely different footprint annually based on the size, layout, opportunities, challenges, and the political vagaries of each host region. The Super Bowl is truly a "mega-event" composed of millions of details, and as anyone who has worked on a mega-event will tell you, it is inevitable that something, somewhere, sometime, will go wrong every time. Hopefully they are small, largely unnoticed problems, but sometimes, they are large, and very noticed. But, with so many moving parts, it is impossible to avoid the occurrence of at least some of those blips, bloops, and blunders.

LEARNING FROM THE THINGS THAT GO WRONG

Looking after Super Bowls, as well as many other mega-events over my career, I've had my share of uncomfortable moments that generated some combination of annoyance, frustration, anxiety, and stress. They often produced disappointment, anger, nausea, and self-doubt. But, as they inevitably piled up over more than 25 years of managing major sports events, I started to notice a number of consistent truths, and those led to learning how to plan better and how to more capably manage when things went wrong.

It is often said that you learn more from things that go wrong than from things that go right. I heartily agree. But between you and me, I would rather learn from things that went wrong for someone else. That's the priceless opportunity that this book gives you: to learn from my mistakes.

Some of the things that have gone wrong for me have been predictable and avoidable, and some of them have been solvable. But, not everything is. Sometimes, a problem can't be solved, but it still must be managed. All things that have gone wrong can teach us something, once we've gotten past the pain and the bruises to our egos. And if we handle them the right way, we can turn a really bad day into one that was not so bad after all.

Chances are you won't manage something as complex or as exposed as the Super Bowl. But whatever project you're overseeing, or whatever presentation, meeting, or important customer interaction you're engaged in, if that activity is important to your company or livelihood, then that's *YOUR* Super Bowl.

My hope is that when you've finished this book, your sleeping will have improved because you are better prepared. And when things do go south—because they just will—you'll be able to identify, evaluate, prioritize, and respond to the challenges as they pop up on your virtual radar screen. What to do when things go wrong? In many ways, that's life's ultimate question. With this book, you'll be able to answer it. Even if *60 Minutes* just so happens to be standing beside you when it does.

STEP ONE
IMAGINE

DEFINING DISASTER

et's talk about crisis-proofing your project. But, before we do, let's agree on what a crisis is. Not everything that goes wrong is a crisis, of course, but let's consider the worst possibilities first, and we can scale down from there. The way I see it, there are four distinct levels of crisis, differentiated by what is truly at stake. Each demands a different level of urgency, focus, and priority of response.

RISK LEVELS

Level 1—Safety and Security Risk

First, do the circumstances put people at risk? When a crisis unfolds, safety should always come first, second, and third. Whenever the potential for physical danger exists, cost considerations should factor well behind. In the event world, safety takes precedence not only for the audience, but for the staff, athletes, performers, contractors, media, and anyone else at the venue. Note that what I am *not* referring to is *inconvenience*. I'll take an upset, inconvenienced customer all day long over one who has a chance of being bandaged by EMTs, sped to a hospital, or hunched over a porcelain plumbing fixture.

You've probably personally experienced this protocol put in practice dozens of times. Have you ever had a flight delayed because "there's an indicator light on in the cockpit, and nothing seems to be wrong, but we're going to have maintenance come take a look?" I hate being inconvenienced by flight delays but I'm totally okay being 100 percent sure that my plane is more likely to stay in the air for as long as it takes to get to my scheduled destination. Whenever steam rises from my forehead after that announcement, I imagine how I would feel if the pilot instead said: "There's an indicator light on in the cockpit, but whenever that happens it usually turns out to be nothing, so we're going to go ahead and taxi out to the runway. Flight attendants prepare the cabin for departure and thank you for flying with us." I'm a comfortable flyer because not only do I know I will never hear that, but I also know the pilot won't take off without making certain every indicator light of any color, shape, or size has been taken care of.

You are the pilot of your business, project, and problem. The singular imperative to protect the lives and health of our customers, clients, colleagues, and staff is one of the major reasons why companies managing a crisis have endured significant financial loss, customer inconvenience, and sometimes even public ridicule, but they still declare recalls on potentially contaminated food, dysfunctional airbags, and imperfectly designed juvenile furniture. You would be well within your rights to argue that companies first respond to challenges in ways that reduce their exposure to legal penalties and subsequent litigation. I would agree with you, but putting that skepticism aside, let's also agree that the protection of human life is paramount, and when making decisions, whether in the planning phase or in the heat of a crisis, the best and most important outcome is that "no one got sick, hurt, or killed." When presented with any situation that requires a decision that directly or indirectly increases or decreases risk to life or health, it's an easy decision. You go with decreasing risk. Always.

Level 2—Brand Risk

The next level of crisis puts a brand at risk. The objectives of the sports brands I worked for included: (1) staging competitions of the highest caliber; (2) officiating them with unquestionable impartiality; and (3) presenting them in an entertaining package, which added value to the fan's experience, regardless of the outcome. (I recognize that if you are a fan of the team that gets pummeled, it may be among the worst three hours of your life, during which you will question all these objectives.) Change the delivery of any one of these three variables, and the brands will suffer to some degree.

If the games aren't competitive, they are less compelling and less exciting. If the officiating seems inequitable, we start to wonder about the motivations of the league or the referee, whether our concerns are intellectually justifiable or not. And, if we are not entertained or we do not feel valued, we begin to evaluate whether the cost and inconvenience of attending a game is worth our money.

These examples are crises of confidence that can build over time, and if they become chronic, they can create a host of other problems. Fans will stop buying tickets, sponsors will stop sponsoring, and broadcasters will stop broadcasting. Trust in the brand, established over the course of years, will begin to dissipate and suddenly, the entire economic system of the organization will be under stress.

Great organizations monitor the deterioration of brand perception over time to try to course-correct, resurrect consumer trust in the brand, and keep from doing long-term damage to the company. However, the company may not be as prepared as it should for the decisive responses required when a crisis emerges because something went wrong *very* suddenly.

On April 9, 2017, a passenger was badly injured by security guards on a commercial flight at O'Hare International Airport in Chicago, and dragged, apparently unconscious, down the aisle and off the plane. Moments later, footage of the incident hit social media and the airline had a brand crisis on its hands. The next morning, United Airlines CEO Oscar Munoz responded with a public statement that explained the company's standard practice of "re-accommodating" passengers, but by then, outrage had spread like a major contagion. Negative opinion further metastasized when an e-mail to the airline's employees surfaced that seemed to defend the treatment of this particular "belligerent" passenger as in keeping with company procedure. Notwithstanding the withering social and traditional media firestorm, yet another day would pass before United Airlines issued a public apology for the treatment of the injured passenger.

I am not aware of whether United Airlines had a plan on how to respond if an allegedly disruptive passenger refused to be re-accommodated, but I am reasonably sure that if they did, this wasn't it. The assault on the airline's brand continued to mount when an official apology was issued two days later, which no matter how genuine, made it appear that the company was responding not to the problem that occurred on their plane, but to the resulting public outrage.

This example also illustrates that more than one level of risk can be in play at any one time. At first, United Airlines simply faced a passenger who refused to be removed from his flight. By forcibly removing him, the level of the issue was escalated by one broken nose, two missing teeth, and a concussion. One of the individuals involved in the altercation contended that the actions of the passenger caused his own injuries while resisting removal, but that's really immaterial. The plan should have been to take every effort to avoid injuries, regardless of the cause, and if an injury somehow did occur anyway, how that situation should be handled.

Level 3—Product Risk

The next level of crisis can put a product, project, or activity at risk. My projects are events, but yours might be protecting the food supply chain, designing top-performing airbags, opening a new restaurant, introducing a new web application, or simply keeping the trains running on time every single day. The food supply chain may be entirely free of E. coli and other nasty contaminants, but the food supply chain could be disrupted by a distribution center worker's strike, a crop-damaging freeze, or a truck-stopping fuel shortage. Your airbags may need an inflator made by a subcontractor that suddenly goes bankrupt. Or, the new wonder drug may be stuck in regulatory purgatory. The construction of your new restaurant may be delayed, the web application doesn't function optimally on certain types of phones, or the trains can't move because the tunnel running under the river has flooded over the third rail.

This level of crisis can be significant to the product and might even result in some amount of financial loss, customer inconvenience, or reputational damage. Product risk has the potential to evolve into brand risk if not skillfully managed and thoughtfully responded to. Only true pessimists strictly adhere to *Murphy's Law*, which popularly states that "anything that can go wrong will go wrong." But I do believe in the greater truth of *Murphy's First Corollary*, which observes: "Left to themselves, things tend to go from bad to worse."

When things are going badly, you simply can't leave them to themselves. You must step in to keep product risk from growing into brand risk, or worse, safety risk. The revelation that Apple Inc. programmed software updates that purposefully drained batteries faster on older model iPhones, for instance, created a product risk, which resulted in numerous incensed customers. The company rapidly responded by lowering the price of replacement batteries.

In the sports world, we have to work fast because not much escapes notice and nearly every product issue can become a brand crisis. That's because the product is so visible, the consumers—our fans—are so passionate and knowledgeable about the product, and the media are always ready to provide the uncompromising depth of analysis that fans demand. Nevertheless, making a fast decision is not as important as making the right decision; proper and thorough contingency planning can help reduce the amount of time required to get there.

What About Financial Risk?

Financial exposure is certainly implicit in each of the first three levels of risk. A shortfall of revenue or expense overruns can either be or result from the crisis itself. The costs of fixing things that went wrong, implementing longer-term corrective actions to ensure they go right in the future, and regulatory or legal impacts flowing from the crisis can also produce direct and profound financial implications. Future revenues can be impacted by the reaction of the marketplace to the crisis and the company's response, and damage to the brand or product. Financial risk is omnipresent at every level, save the next one.

Level 4—Personal Brand Risk

When something goes wrong, many of us think about what it means to us personally. It's only human. We wonder what people will think of us while the crisis is unfolding, or after it has passed. Will our bosses or customers trust us to solve the problem or deal with the aftermath? Will we undergo a painful investigation or demoralizing corporate scrutiny? Will our colleagues think poorly of us? Will the failure become a news story within the company, the industry, or the general public? Will we be demoted, or lose our year-end bonus? Worst of all possibilities, will we lose our job and have a hard time finding another? This risk usually follows an incident that fits into one of the first three levels of crisis. Forget it completely and focus entirely on solving the game-time crises first. I am not suggesting being a saint or a martyr. When something goes wrong, focusing on resolving or managing the issue can reduce the negative impact on your personal brand. It rarely works the other way around.

CRISIS TRIAGE

Why should I bother you with a philosophy lesson on levels of risks and wrongness? To help you with triage when something does go badly and time is not on your side. Triage is simply a fancy word for a system of prioritizing.

When you visit a hospital emergency room, you are usually quite lucky if you have to wait three, four, or five maddening hours to be seen by a treatment team. The minutes drip away in interminable slow motion because the triage team has determined that you are unlikely to die while waiting. Meanwhile, the emergency room staff has given fast passes to life-threatening injuries, illnesses, gunshot wounds, and heart attacks past the room filled with the miseries of broken wrists, hernia-inducing coughs, and lacerations from careless bagel cutting. If you are managing a crisis, or drafting plans to avoid one, you will need to evaluate the issue with the same cool, calculated objectivity as the seemingly emotionless triage nurse, who is in actuality trying to evaluate which crisis is the one that needs to be treated soonest.

Like the emergency room, it is not uncommon for more than one thing to go wrong simultaneously, or for the first malady to cause a chain reaction of other problems. As counterintuitive as it may sound, our first task at the Superdome was not getting the power restored and the game re-started. It was to be sure that no one was likely to get hurt (a Level 1 risk) as a result of the blackout.

Our initial response was to take steps to avoid panic and fans trampling each other as they rushed for the doors. If the blackout was an equipment failure, one that could be corrected with a minimum of inconvenience, the safest advice we could provide to fans was to stay inside. If, on the other hand, it was a fire in the building that caused the outage, or a fire was ignited because of it, we would need to implement a quick evacuation. Perhaps the blackout was a deliberate act connected with a larger, more insidious situation—a terrorist incident, a cyberattack, or a disaster outside the building. In order to make the decision whether or not to evacuate the building, we needed more information, and quickly. If the failure originated from a fire inside the stadium or immediately outside, we would need to direct fans away from those locations. If there was an active shooter waiting for fans to come pouring out of the stadium—as sadly later occurred at the Ariana Grande concert in Manchester, England—keeping people inside would be the obvious course.

Knowing that we could communicate with 71,024 fans and thousands more workers and media, and identifying what to tell them, was way more important than figuring out how to get the lights back on. I concentrated on that while law enforcement officials, NFL security, and the stadium management team evaluated the frightening possibilities of the foregoing paragraph.

Crisis triage will always focus first on actions that alleviate physical dangers. You will be thinking of a great many things if, and when, something goes wrong. Always start with "are people safe, and if they are, what do we have to do to make sure they stay that way?"

To me, the greatest moment in halftime history was Prince performing *Purple Rain* in the rain at Super Bowl XLI on February 4, 2007. When the stormfront, which was forecast to pass quickly across the Miami area, seemed to stall over Dolphin Stadium, I wasn't focused on how emotional, poignant, and theatrically spectacular that performance would be. I was concerned whether there was any possibility that the electronic gear—lighting, audio, or even his famously iconic electric guitar—could injure the star or any of the hundreds of support cast or crew.

After protecting the safety and health of our customers, clients, and staff, we then consider brand risks, which are the issues that can do the most profound and long-term reputational or financial damage to the health of our business. As time is often of the essence, a number of smaller, easier-to-solve problems may have to wait or be delegated to others while the greater, more impactful, and potentially existential issues are addressed. Regrettably, sliding one problem ahead of another can create controversy, unhappiness, and dissatisfaction among those impacted by other important, but less imperative, issues, like when you have to wait in the emergency room for someone to X-ray your broken shoulder because a head trauma patient was wheeled through those swinging double doors ahead of you. Your shoulder will still be fractured, but probably won't get any more broken while the more severely injured individual is being stabilized. But that time could have been devastatingly more important to the head trauma patient if your shoulder was examined first.

Your broken shoulder represents a product risk in which something goes wrong that is unlikely to have a serious, long-term impact on your overall health. Your shoulder may hurt, it may keep you from typing with two hands for a while, and it may require months of excruciating physical therapy to reestablish its previously glorious contribution to your backswing. But you will return to being a high-functioning human with the proper amount of time, treatment, and effort.

When your product, project, or activity "breaks its shoulder" and is unlikely to have a serious, long-term impact on the health of your company or brand, you may have time to be more thoughtful about the response if the product risk doesn't escalate into a brand risk. You should prioritize next for action those product risks that have this potential. Problems that will likely never elevate to this level of significance can be addressed after the more important things are handled.

If you stay true to your mission by planning wisely to reduce or forestall disaster, or managing the response to a crisis once things go wrong anyway, the reflection on your own personal brand will often take care of itself. Where we as emotionally fragile and egocentric humans fail is when we allow the threat to our personal reputation to motivate our thinking. Solving problems intelligently, in the right order, can help restore the luster to our brands. Eventually.

The truth is that it is impossible to completely crisis-proof our projects, companies, or products. But we can make them more crisis-resistant and we can apply a triage decision-making framework that will help us prioritize responses when something goes wrong anyway. Simply, we have to do everything we can to keep a crisis from happening in the first place, and if it does, we will need a plan on how to respond. First, apply a dark and fertile imagination to visualize as many potential threats to our success as possible. Then, we can spend the time, money, and energy to keep all those monsters securely UNDER the bed.

ANYTHING THAT CAN GO WRONG

never had the opportunity to meet Captain Edward A. Murphy, but he was my kind of guy. He was the actual Murphy behind *Murphy's Law*. There are many versions of the origins of his eponymous law that "anything that can go wrong will go wrong." Like many famous attributions, it is questionable whether he was the first to say it, or whether he ever said it at all. After learning a little bit about Captain Murphy, it appeared to me that *Murphy's Law* was not based on a sense of dark, foreboding pessimism, which spawned an industry of T-shirts, posters, and websites bursting with corollaries, extensions, and addenda applicable to a wide variety of subjects and disciplines. *Murphy's Law* was based on an unflagging quest for perfection. Perfection was particularly important to Captain Murphy because of his work as a U.S. Air Force engineer; he was tasked with overseeing projects that tested the limits of human endurance under particularly stressful conditions.

THE MAN BEHIND MURPHY'S LAW

In 1949, Captain Murphy was an engineer at Edwards Air Force Base, overseeing a project to determine how much *sudden deceleration* a human body could withstand and survive. The tests measured the effects of physical forces on the human body when a fast-moving vehicle abruptly stops moving, but the brain, internal organs, and skeleton wanted to keep going. A mistake could be awfully messy.

Murphy's engineering team assembled a simulator, which was essentially a rocket sled on rails. A test pilot was to climb aboard, strap-in, and take a very fast but relatively short ride ending with a very sudden stop. It was part of a multiyear series of studies entitled "Effects of Deceleration Forces of High Magnitude on Man," or Air Force Test MX981. So, if you are ever offered a friendly ride in a vehicle with that model number, I suggest you call an Uber. Understanding this test would require precision performance of the rocket sled, Murphy inspected the device and discovered that it was incorrectly wired by one of his subordinates. In his frustration, Murphy reportedly muttered: "If there is any way to do it wrong, he'll find it."

After Murphy's team repaired the error, Dr. John Paul Stapp, an Air Force doctor, took a seat on the device and rode, or more appropriately, stopped into history, withstanding a bone-jarring horizontal force of 40 g. For the physics-challenged among us, a force of 40 g is 40 times the force of gravity. At the press conference held shortly after the test, Dr. Stapp credited the project's safety record to the engineering team's dedicated fight against "Murphy's Law," and before long, an entirely new treasure trove of sarcastic wisdom started oozing into the public consciousness. It is not known how many of the biting, popularly quoted observations that comprise the many variations of *Murphy's Law* were ever written, spoken, or otherwise invoked by Captain Murphy himself. One account suggests that he considered the multitude of Murphy-isms "ridiculous, trivial, and erroneous."

DEFENSIVE DESIGN

What was more important to Captain Murphy than crafting laws was the principle of *defensive design*—ensuring that plans, tests, and experiments are developed with contingencies that take all possibilities into account. Colonel Stapp himself is credited with Stapp's *Ironical Paradox*, which observes: "The universal aptitude for ineptitude makes any human accomplishment an incredible miracle." I'm not big on believing the worst in people, but Dr. Stapp had a point. People mess up all the time. We must be vigilant to make sure we don't do that too often or in situations that can have profoundly serious impacts.

One observation that Captain Murphy may have appreciated was put forward by Northrop's project manager, George E. Nichols, who's no-nonsense "Fourth Law" instructs us to: "Avoid any action with an unacceptable outcome."

Thanks more to Captain Murphy's vigilance than his sardonic wit, Dr. Stapp survived the test and beat his own record five years later, surviving a peak acceleration of 46.2 g. The greatest nonfatal g-force ever measured occurred more than a half-century later at the Texas Motor Speedway, after Kenny Bräck's car made wheel-to-wheel contact with another vehicle. The contact caused him to lose control of his car and impact the fence at an estimated 214 g during the final race of the 2003 IndyCar Racing Series.

THE GREAT EQUALIZERS

I arrived anonymously in Jacksonville, Florida, a week before Super Bowl XXXIX in 2005. Every row of seats on the shuttle bus from the airport was filled with the NFL staff who needed to be on-site for the last few remaining days, rather than the three or four weeks that the event team had been in town. The buzz onboard was a lesson in how much one can learn when you keep your ears open and your mouth shut, and no one knows who you are. My real orientation on all things Super Bowl began on that ride—as opinions, perspectives, and analysis on everything, everyone, and everywhere on the bus went around and around. I recognized that I was experiencing perhaps the only unfiltered fly-on-the-wall insights I would ever get on the job.

It was my first working NFL experience in 17 years. In 1988, I was Radio City Music Hall's associate producer for the Super Bowl XXII halftime show in San Diego, California. The Super Bowl was big in 1988, but since then, it had taken Murphy's rocket sled to growth, and didn't appear to be likely to stop any time soon. The Super Bowl had grown into an event that invaded a city, occupied every available hotel, gobbled up every usable venue, and consumed every available resource.

Notwithstanding my having been involved with big events for many years, I felt the g-forces of a sudden zero-to-100 mph acceleration. From my hotel window, I could see the stadium and many of the sites around downtown Jacksonville, which had been activated for the Super Bowl. As the week went on, masses of Philadelphia Eagles and New England Patriots jerseys filled every café, restaurant, and public space in between. Although I wouldn't characterize myself as growing anxious, I was definitely mindful that I would soon be leading the team responsible for pulling off the event. "It's just so big," I remember saying every night when I phoned my wife, Cathy.

I walked along the St. Johns Riverwalk the next morning with my boss, NFL COO Roger Goodell (currently commissioner of the NFL), heading to a meeting with Detroit Super Bowl XL Host Committee Chairman Roger Penske and Host Committee CEO Susan Sherer on Penske's yacht. Super Bowl XL was going to be held the following year in the Motor City, and it was important to make a good impression on Roger Penske. My predecessor in the Special Events Department, Jim Steeg, who had overseen the Super Bowl's remarkable expansion for more than two decades, was leaving the NFL for the San Diego Chargers, and I'm sure this was of great concern to him.

On the drizzly walk along the St. Johns riverbank, Goodell tried pumping up my confidence. "You are going to take the Super Bowl to an entirely new level," he said. I felt the speeding rocket sled screech to a sudden halt. "What level is *that*, exactly?" I remember wondering. "The Super Bowl is already on its own level."

There was no choice in the matter. The pressure was definitely on, and the expectations were stratospheric. I had to immediately start gathering the information and perspectives of league insiders, establishing the relationships, and understanding the playing field (literally and figuratively)—all the critical inputs I would need to start imagining how to ensure that Super Bowl XL would measure up to the expectations of an "entirely new level." Oh, great. XL is not only "40" in Roman numerals. It also means "extra-large." Any more pressure you want to put on me, guys?

Goodell and I walked up the gangway to the ship. It was not easy to push aside the thought of it being a walk off of a gangplank, even though the boat was in front of, and not behind, me. We both took off our shoes at the request of the steward before walking into the yacht's commodious living room on the bare, stunningly perfect hardwood floor.

Up until then, there was absolutely nothing that wasn't intimidating about my first day on the job. Until I noticed the fruit bowl on the credenza. It was a strikingly beautiful, brilliantly colored, thick-walled glass Swedish Kosta Boda bowl. It's not that I'm an expert on Swedish bowls. It's just that I used to buy one of these same vividly colored bowls on my way back from the annual National Hockey League (NHL) International Series preseason games in Sweden. I have four or five of them, and they cost me about $25 each from the duty-free shop. I'm pretty certain that Roger Penske didn't personally buy his glass Kosta Boda bowl in a duty-free shop, or anywhere else, for that matter. Someone else probably bought it to decorate this magnificent boat. This one insignificant detail made me feel a whole lot less intimidated. I had the same bowl as Roger Penske!

Once I started working with this incredible, very real individual, I realized that Roger Penske would never have intended to intimidate me. Any such feeling would have been totally imagined by me, conjured up entirely by my perspective of his fame and prodigious accomplishments. He had an awesome yacht, and he earned every plank and brass fitting. It was a simple bowl, the same kind that was on my own coffee table, which connected me on some common level to the titan of industry before me. That is still probably where any similarity between Roger Penske and me ends, but I glanced at that bowl a few times during our meeting when I felt any creeping nervousness. Its familiarity equalized any anxiety.

The Merriam-Webster dictionary definition of *intimidate* is "to frighten into submission," and "implies inducing fear or a sense of inferiority into another." Roger Penske was not intimidating me, and neither was the Super Bowl. I was inducing fear and a sense of inferiority into myself by imagining that I might not be up to the task in front of me. Starting a daunting, challenging project like managing and organizing a Super Bowl and feeling intimidated by it, or by the people involved, would not have been a good foundation for sound planning or competent execution. If something went wrong along the way, I would already be halfway to panic. If I imagined being outclassed by the job, I discovered I could apply the same imagination to finding ways of equalizing the playing field. This ability would come in handy later on when I started attending meetings with NFL owners.

The Super Bowl was still "just so big," but it didn't own a glass Kosta Boda bowl to make me feel more its peer. Something else would present an opportunity to equalize the intimidation I imagined. The

2005 Super Bowl in Jacksonville was the only one I ever experienced from the sidelines. I picked up a walkie-talkie the morning of the game and never pressed the "talk" button. I just listened to the incessant buzz of radio traffic. What I heard helped me to understand that all of the issues faced by the staff during a Super Bowl were familiar to me. There were just a lot more issues in any given minute. Someone had the wrong credential and couldn't get where he needed to go; a pipe burst in the locker room area; concessions were running out of food; queues were growing longer at the security checkpoints; traffic was tied up on the highway. There was nothing happening that I hadn't heard before. I felt better knowing that problems were handled at the Super Bowl just like they were at NHL All-Star Games, or at any event for that matter. Someone identified the problem and rectified it or called someone else for help.

When you feel intimidated by a new project, task, job, or event, search for your *great equalizers*, things and situations that are common and familiar to you. The practice of visualizing your great equalizers will come in handy during every step of the project management process. They may not be as simple as a Kosta Boda bowl, but if you are facing something entirely new, remember that you've faced other things for the first time, and you handled them well. If you didn't handle them well, you learned from when they went wrong. Imagining that something awful might happen? That's great. That's the time to imagine a plan to reduce or eliminate that possibility. Something went wrong anyway? Remember that things have gone wrong for you before and that you lived to tell about it. Or, if you prefer, remember some of the things that went wrong for others in this book. Feeling intimidated is a function of your own imagination. Repurpose that imagination by applying past experiences to conquer your anxiety.

A FRESH SET OF BRAIN CELLS

It was time to forget about Penske's Kosta Boda bowl and time to get to work imagining the "next level of Super Bowl." During the week, I made sure to: experience every major event, attend every production meeting, and visit every venue—from the media center, team practice facilities, and major hotels to party and charity event sites, fan festivals, and of course, every square inch of Alltel Stadium (now TIAA

Bank Field), the host stadium. I spent every night reading the meeting notes, production schedules, and bid documents, and I devoured the *Game Operations Manual*, the league's go-to resource that lays out every detail, guideline, and regulation pertaining to staging an NFL game. I still kept a low profile, but in truth, it was not to eavesdrop like I did on the shuttle bus. I knew the pressures everyone was under and did not want to be a distraction. There was a flipside to anonymity, of course. I was nearly thrown out of the stadium by security during Paul McCartney's halftime rehearsal because almost no one knew what I looked like.

As it turned out, having lots of event experience, but little familiarity with the Super Bowl beyond what America had seen on television, was not a disadvantage, but rather the best starting point of all. It was not a blank canvas, of course. There was something already stellar and very special about the Super Bowl, built on the hard work of hundreds of people at the League Office who had stewarded the event to prominence; the on-field greatness of Bart Starr, Joe Namath, Lynn Swann, and Roger Staubach; the innovative and insightful broadcasts of Dick Enberg, Pat Summerall, Curt Gowdy, and John Madden; and the passion, viewership, and support of the NFL's fans and partners. It gave me the opportunity to experience America's unofficial holiday with entirely new eyes, a fresh set of brain cells, and the imagination to enhance and add value to 39 years of the event's greatness.

Was the event big? Yes, enormous. Spectacular? Peerless. At the pinnacle of its potential? As I would discover, not then, not later, and not even now. When the game ended, I waited for the presentation of the Vince Lombardi Trophy. Television went to commercial, the crew began setting up the stage, and fans flooded the exits. By the time NFL Commissioner Paul Tagliabue presented the trophy to New England Patriots owner Robert Kraft, the stadium was nearly empty. The players, team personnel, and media on the field seemed to outnumber the fans in the stands. Having come from the NHL, where fans idolize the Stanley Cup and stay in the arena to experience its presentation—even to the opposing team—I thought it was incredibly strange that so few fans remained to witness the historic moment of what the winning team worked all season to achieve. I also thought back to how often I paid attention to the trophy ceremony when I watched the game on television. Not very often, I recalled.

I felt I had found perhaps the one thing that we could start to imagine differently. Something that elevated the Vince Lombardi Trophy presentation enough to get people to watch it, in the stadium and on television. What we developed for Super Bowl XL was a red-carpet entrance for a prominent football personality—fittingly, Super Bowl I and II MVP Bart Starr—carrying the trophy to the stage to a stirring, specially composed Vince Lombardi Trophy theme. Players lining the red carpet in future years spontaneously started reaching over to touch the trophy on its way to the stage, and a new tradition worth hanging out for was established.

Firing up your imagination before planning begins generates innovation. But as you will also see, it informs your planning process, and will even help you devise solutions when something goes wrong.

FILLING BIG SHOES

The real takeaway from my week in Jacksonville observing the Super Bowl was that there were thousands of details that needed to be developed from planning to management to execution. Because I was new to the organization, I was reliant on the team that was in place to help guide me through the process. What concerned me most was that Jim Steeg had been in his job for more than 20 years. Much of the growth of the Super Bowl into an American cultural experience happened under his watch. With that much experience and that long a tenure, Jim instinctively knew everything that needed to get done and how to go about doing it. He was far more familiar than I was with the intricacies of the game, the people, and the politics of the league, as well as the problems we should anticipate.

I knew a lot about managing major sports events, but little of those things. Nevertheless, I had to assume leadership over the NFL's most important events and earn the confidence of the owners, the Commissioner, and the executive staff. I had to lead a team that was understandably loyal to Jim, had no experience working with me, and in some cases might have been annoyed that I was hired from another league. I was disappointed, but probably should have expected it when several team members resigned within days of my arrival; some of them resigned before I found the coffee machine, the men's room, and my office on Park Avenue in New York.

As a result, I would not only have to immediately pick up the planning for Super Bowl XL in Detroit, but I would also have to hire and integrate new team members into what remained of the department. In fact, the first in a series of major planning meetings was only a few weeks away and we were already short on the institutional knowledge that the experienced staff took away with them. In the interim, our team would also have to manage the logistical details for the NFL Combine in Indianapolis, Indiana, and the NFL Annual Owner's Meeting in Maui, Hawaii. Most pressing, I discovered, was the need to quickly find a home for the 2005 NFL Draft to be held in April, just two months away. Time was a scarce commodity, to say the least.

I knew that Jim Steeg had details in his head on what to do to make things go right, and how to respond when things did not, more than anything in the memos, schedules, or manuals I had read. Whether during planning or during the event, if people expected something to happen just because it always did, I needed to disabuse them of those notions, or something would slip between the cracks for sure.

ASSUME NOTHING, DOUBLE-CHECK EVERYTHING

I started the first Super Bowl production meeting with a slide that said: *"Assume Nothing, Double Check Everything"* and told them why. I wasn't Jim. It was critical to our planning that everyone working on the Super Bowl, no matter how long they'd been working on it, imagined that none of the things that "just happened" and none of the things that were "just there" would happen or be there. This way, if something went wrong, it wasn't because we failed to provide the resources or physical assets they assumed would be there. It wasn't pushing potential blame for something that could go wrong from me to them. It was asking them to help ensure that when something did go wrong, it wasn't for that reason; that is, the assumption that I was handling all the details that Jim managed for decades.

I reinforced the concept by repeating the phrase at all remaining quarterly Super Bowl production meetings and the daily staff meetings leading up to game day. *"Assume Nothing, Double Check Everything"* would become the first of a series of annual "mantras"

29

with which we opened every meeting. Each mantra was designed to serve as a rallying cry for the year, one that in a few words would set expectations for, and of, everyone working on the event.

Looking back, this "mantra" could have been inspired by Captain Edward Murphy. In inspecting the rocket sled, he did not assume everything was wired correctly. I could be entirely wrong, but I'd like to think that he didn't really know ahead of time that the technician who wired it had done it wrong. Rather, that he was systematically and scientifically double checking and not assuming that the vehicle Dr. Stapp was about to ride into history was not going to make him history. Captain Murphy imagined the worst or imagined that the worst was not impossible. He was all about taking action *before* things went wrong, and he didn't think that *Murphy's Law* was a joke. According to his son, he was annoyed that people didn't take it more seriously. Murphy, Stapp, Nichols, and others were perfectionists. They had to be. People (including Stapp himself) could die if they weren't. They had to imagine the worst outcomes in order to be a little shy pressing the "LAUNCH" button without checking on things just one more time.

I imagine the worst when doing my job, and so should you. Not because we are pessimists, but because, like Captain Murphy, we are committed to having things go right. If we imagine all the ways things can go awry, we start to understand where we, our brands, or our products might be exposed to risk. Often, we imagine these things and how we could have, or should have, dealt with them after they have already happened. Although that's second best, it does sharpen our senses to be on guard for similar failures the next time around.

When the 1996 NHL All-Star Game was held in Boston, we could have hired the Boston Bruins' eager and enthusiastic anthem singer, Rene Rancourt, to perform *The Star-Spangled Banner* and *O Canada*. We instead booked a nationally renowned, operatically talented television personality to deliver the traditional opening. One of our production team members had deep connections to the hard-to-reach celebrity community through his network of personal assistants. Rather than slog through the slow and labyrinthine bureaucracy of agencies and management companies, we connected with the actor's personal assistant, and appealing to his sports-loving nature, secured his agreement to join us in Boston. So, we had only ourselves to blame.

We arranged for a first-class ticket for the actor on a flight from Miami that would arrive at Logan International Airport with plenty of time to get him to the arena for a sound check and rehearsal before the doors opened to fans. A production assistant waiting to meet the flight called us 45 minutes after the scheduled landing to let us know that there was no sign of our celebrity. He was on the manifest as a ticketed passenger, but he had not boarded in Miami. We thought that perhaps he missed the plane and there was another flight scheduled to take off soon, which would still give us room to get him to the arena in time for the performance, but not for a rehearsal. Rehearsing is always a good thing when a performer is going to step onto a thin rubber-backed carpet on a freshly minted sheet of ice.

Once the cabin door was closed, the airline could tell us whether he was on the flight or not. He wasn't. At the risk of being humiliated, we asked the Bruins to call Rene Rancourt. Having the night off, Rene had planned to host a dinner party at his home. He could have been a jerk and enjoyed making us squirm, but, as I would come to appreciate, that wasn't Rene. He grabbed his tuxedo, sped to the arena, belted out two goosebumps-worthy national anthems, finished them off with his iconic and enthusiastic fist pump, and then returned to his guests. He saved our lives just like he saved the life of another event organizer when Kate Smith canceled her anthem performance just before Game 6 of the 1975 World Series. What really happened to our celebrity friend? We actually worried that something awful had happened to him, but when we read nothing about it in the media, we stopped worrying.

After that night, I could vividly imagine an anthem singer not showing up. Or, having the flu. Or, being abducted by aliens hiding in his luggage. Okay, maybe not that, but I could imagine a lot of things. So, although our team kept booking celebrity anthem singers for the NHL All-Star Game, we also invited the host team's favorite performer to be our guest at every game thereafter, with the understanding that he or she might be asked to leap into action at the last possible moment. Captain Murphy would have certified this plan as "defensive design," the notion that contingencies are built into the system. I call it sleeping better the night before the game.

Having a plan that covers only what to do when things run smoothly does not constitute adequate planning. It is creating a road map, and that might be fine 80 percent, 90 percent, or even 99 percent of the time. But it's that nasty issue that happens 20 percent, 10 percent, or 1 percent of the time that can sink your business, derail your project, or make an event memorable for all the wrong reasons. So, whatever you are planning, sit in a quiet space with your ears plugged and your eyes closed—if that's what works for you—and imagine the worst. Sales dry up. The warehouse floods. The lobby of your office building is suddenly a taped-off crime scene. Your freight elevator stops working. How do people get to work? How will your customers and clients be served?

You can't make up every solution on the spot and be successful. Using your dark imaginings to tease out contingencies should inform your overall planning strategy so that you can then incorporate potential solutions into your defensive design. Otherwise, you may not be able to overcome challenges that expose weaknesses in your plan or project as quickly.

If your imagination is vivid enough, you'll uncover a great number of things that can potentially go wrong, from the annoying to the simply inconvenient and cataclysmically catastrophic. The good news is there is no limit to your imagination. There is only a limit to your time, your team's expertise, and your money. You won't think of absolutely every potential issue. But, if you identify, prioritize, and account for the right contingencies in your planning, you are well on your way to deferring *Murphy's Law* to another day.

You will naturally prioritize based on the least improbable things that could go wrong and those that could do the most damage to your project, brand, or company. Why did I purposely use a double negative? Because if it is probable that something is going to go wrong, you should reassess the project, product, or event. I'm betting you've already gotten your project to the point where the odds of something going wrong is already reduced to the relatively improbable. But things that are the least improbable are, alas, still possible.

Applying our imaginations to building multiple contingency plans that reduce the risk of failure is truly a pain in the neck. Extra planning you may never put into action can take a lot of time and threaten deadlines. Resist your natural impulse to mentally, but not actually, diminish the probability of things going wrong because they would be expensive, time-consuming, complicated, or otherwise inconvenient to the planning process. It is also very easy to imagine your boss, best client, or some other exceedingly important stakeholder introducing a new variable that you hadn't planned on—for example, a new product feature, a different launch strategy, or an accelerated set of deadlines. That seems to happen all the time, so be sure to leave yourself enough time to calculate the impact and redraft your plans.

IT'S A MATTER
OF TIME

Mick Jagger was 100 percent wrong. Time is *not* on my side. No, it's not, and it's not on your side either. Whether you have a big budget or a small one, years of experience or just launching your career, work for a stately iconic brand or a brash entrepreneurial start-up, the amount of time that fits into an hour is 60 minutes. While what you do with that hour can move the ball toward your goal line, time will always be every project's most limiting factor. Welcome to the club.

I learned this important and most enduring lesson in Dr. Benny Barak's Consumer Behavior class at Bernard M. Baruch College of the City University of New York. For our term project, our study group had three weeks to create a mythical product for an existing company and develop a comprehensive business plan to launch our innovation to a selected target demographic. The four of us met one night at a Manhattan bar to start planning our campaign, but somehow, we could never get everyone back together to keep the momentum going. We all had full-time jobs, night classes, significant others, and a surprisingly more limited beer budget than we had anticipated. We struggled to do the research, share intelligence, and gather meaningful contributions from each member of the team. Somehow we produced a final product that was submitted on time; it had to be because it wouldn't have mattered how good it was if it was turned in late. It would have earned us a failing grade irrespective of our farsighted brilliance.

After handing in the paper, Dr. Barak asked the class for feedback about the assignment. I offered that I didn't feel we had enough time to do as good a job as we wanted. Consumer Behavior wasn't our only night class, after all, and everyone had different schedules. We had demanding jobs that often took priority over our academic pursuits, and three weeks was simply not enough time to perfect our plans.

Dr. Barak stroked his professorial salt-and-pepper beard. "Maybe so," he mused thoughtfully, "but as you advance in your careers, you will never have enough time. You will be forced to get things done in the time you have." He turned out to be as right as Mick was wrong.

Most of us don't get to pick our deadlines. The product will launch, the project will be presented, or the game will kick off when the company says it must, and whatever time we get is the time we have. Like my classmates, the colleagues we will count on will have different schedules, different priorities, and different commitments, both professional and personal. As project managers, we are stuck having to deal with all of those competing agendas, and the recognition that not everyone with whom we are working will place the same level of importance on the things that are of the highest priorities to us.

THE TIME YOU GET IS ALL THE TIME YOU HAVE

So whatever time you think you have to complete the mission, you should start by imagining that you have less time. You'll be glad you did when the unforeseen happens, for example, when you must throw away old plans and start over because new variables are introduced, new contingencies need to be developed, and colleagues are slow to respond.

Think of time as an airtight container, and your project as a gas. One of the properties of a gas is that it fills the container it occupies. Somehow, the work you have to do always fills the time you have to do it in, even if you started out earlier than you originally thought would be necessary. Increase the work to be done with the new details to be resolved and it is like pumping more gas into the container. The pressure increases. Now think about shrinking the container and the amount of time remaining to complete the project, instead. The pressure will rise again. Increase the work and shrink the time at the same time, and the pressure doubles. You may be headed for a blowout.

I don't like that kind of pressure in my life, so I always try to make my container bigger than is typically necessary. That is, when possible, I allot more time than might be required for just about any task so I can handle the pressure when the time gets shorter, or the workload gets heavier than I expected. I used to think that made me "time's bitch" because I always felt the pressure of time. I leave for the airport at least two hours before my flight boards even though a problem-free commute takes less than an hour. I imagine there may be even more New York traffic than normal, an accident on the route, a problem parking in the closest garage, or an extra-long line at the security checkpoint.

I'd rather grab a cup of coffee and work in the airline club than worry about catching my flight when a thunderstorm floods the Long Island Expressway and traffic slows to a crawl. So maybe, just maybe, I'm not "time's bitch" after all. Maybe I'm "time's boss" because imagining that I always need more time to get to the airport helps me stay more in control, more nimble, and less pressured when something goes wrong on my drive over. I've never missed a flight yet. Take that, time!

I'm not expecting or asking you to be as mindful of time as I am in everything you do. In fact, I recognize and accept that most people are not. Many of us default to getting to the airport at the latest possible moment or to the movies just as the lion starts to roar. Different strokes. But, sometimes our worlds collide . . .

SAVING HOURS ONE MINUTE AT A TIME

A lonely dawn had broken in Detroit as the Super Bowl XL event team straggled into the conference room at the Detroit Marriott at the Renaissance Center. Every day during the three weeks leading up to the game, we scheduled morning briefing meetings at our headquarters hotel before everyone dispersed to the stadium or to other meetings and event sites around town. The events team and at least one senior representative from each functional area participated, including: stadium operations, construction, security, media relations, broadcasting, transportation, accommodations, hospitality, team and medical services, and host city operations. Respecting the early hour and everyone's time, we usually set out a selection of breakfast pastries, fresh fruit, and several gallons of overpriced hotel coffee.

In Jacksonville, the year prior, two meetings were held daily, one first thing in the morning and one around 12 or 13 hours later. Neither started remotely on time, but the evening session was always the most delayed as staff in the field were often wrapped up in important work that delayed their arrival. Because the time between the end of the evening meeting and the follow-up meeting the next morning was rather uneventful, I decided to restructure the daily meetings. Our new plan was to host one meeting at the beginning of the day, which would start with updates on the status of any problems discussed the previous day and would be followed by a round-robin of reports from each area that surfaced new issues and announced changes to the plan.

On the first day of these newly structured meetings, I was in place at 7:00 a.m. with a small handful of our team at the folding tables arranged in the form of an elongated rectangle. Most of our team was either chatting collegially outside the room, just leaving their hotel rooms, or still detailing their hair into the perfectly coiffed uncoiffed coiffure. Apparently, the first subject of the first meeting, when it finally began at 7:10 a.m., was going to be the necessity of starting our meetings on time.

The next morning, there were five of us sitting around the table set for 30 people. At precisely 7:00 a.m., I closed the door and started the meeting with a handful of reasonably important announcements in a normal voice. Another half-dozen teammates—who were milling about in the room or were gathered at the coffee station right outside the door—quickly took their seats as we launched into follow-up items from the day before. The rest of the gang arrived over the next 10 to 15 minutes, many chattering to each other until they entered the room, surprised that they were interrupting a meeting in progress.

I grabbed a second cup of coffee a few minutes before 7:00 a.m. on Day 3, and noticed the urn was only half full. The vast majority of our team was already caffeinated, seated, and ready for the meeting.

A handful of sheepish stragglers entered quietly after the door was closed and took their places.

Day 4 and beyond, latecomers were the exception rather than the rule. Not only did we never start that meeting late or without the room filled with very nearly the entire complement of participants until game day, but the same could be said for the years that followed.

I sat in my usual spot ten minutes before the meeting, a steaming cup of black coffee within convenient reach, reading my notes from the previous day's briefing, and outlining additional topics to be covered. Magically, when everyone's iPhones approached 7:00 a.m., the din of conversation in the room diminished to silence all by itself. I could tell it was time to start without ever glancing at my watch. Assuming the meeting took the same amount of time, regardless of whether it started at 7:00 a.m. or 7:10 a.m., imagine how much productive time we added to the system across 30 colleagues? Thirty people, ten minutes at a time, every single day. That's a total of more than 100 people-hours over the course of three weeks.

It wasn't intended as a power trip (although I admit it did seem pretty effective), but rather a drive toward changing our department's culture by respecting not only our own time, but that of others, and wringing out all of the efficiency we could in the hour we were together. A 48-minute hour is simply less productive than a full 60-minute hour, and I'm not alone in thinking that way.

New York Giants former head coach Tom Coughlin's meeting policy was even tougher than mine. In 2004, the *New York Times* reported that two Giants players who had arrived a few minutes early to a team meeting were fined $1,000 each. On another occasion, defensive great Michael Strahan found the team's meeting room door closed two minutes before the scheduled start time and was also rewarded with a fine notice. Coach Coughlin, apparently, believed that "meetings start five minutes early." As for me, I'm good with "right on time."

LITTLE HAPPENS WITHOUT A DEADLINE

The start time of our meeting was essentially a deadline, the time for participants to be ready to start discussing how we as a team were delivering against every other deadline. We demonstrated the importance of meeting deadlines by making the start time definitive, reliable, and inviolate; missing that deadline was a stigma. In labor negotiations and congressional budget deliberations, there seems to be more posturing than progress until a deadline for action has nearly arrived. Often, little happens even when there is a deadline. The penalties for missing deadlines can include a disruptive work stoppage or a government shutdown, but the penalty during the American Civil War was far more severe. Diaries and news reports from that time describe a physical line or a ditch drawn around a prison camp—a "dead line"—as a physical boundary that a prisoner best not attempt to cross under the penalty of being shot. Most deadlines are not literally life-and-death, but I still try really, really hard not to cross them.

During my NFL career, the most sacrosanct deadline of all was on the first Sunday in February at 6:28:30 p.m. Eastern Time. That was usually the time for the opening kickoff of the Super Bowl, conceived so the broadcaster could generate the greatest viewing audience and the highest ratings in two half-hour segments, the one before and the one after 6:30 p.m. I wasn't one to argue against that strategy, as the game's stratospheric viewership ratings justified the $5 million NBC charged for a 30-second spot on the Super Bowl LII broadcast in 2018. Our collective job was to make sure everything we did, at every second of that day, led up to an on-time delivery.

Although most Super Bowl deadlines were less micro-precise, they were still important because, come hell or high water, it was nearly 100 percent certain that the game was going to be played on the first Sunday of February, not Monday or Tuesday, and not on the second Sunday of February. Every deadline for every task that was crucial to being ready for a kickoff at 6:28:30 p.m. was essential to identify and communicate to the team. For leaders, they were even more important to model and enforce. Set deadlines for yourself and respect them, and the others you count on will follow suit.

IMAGINING INNOVATION

Keeping things fresh, adjusting to the needs and demands of the marketplace, and progress are all good things. When I work on an event held annually, I always try to add things that are new or different to the product, or better ways of doing things than the year before. There is always room for improvement and growth, even for something already "on its own level."

Super Bowl XLIV, held on February 7, 2010, was originally scheduled to be staged in a new spectacular stadium to be built for the New York Jets on the west side of Manhattan. But the game was moved to South Florida when plans for building the new venue were abandoned after New York City failed in its bid to host the Olympics. The new site was a natural choice because it wasn't so new at all. It would be the region's tenth time in 44 years to host a Super Bowl; almost one-quarter of all Super Bowls ever played were played in South Florida. Also, it was just three years since the last time (ninth time) the region hosted a Super Bowl in 2007.

But, being just 36 months later, we didn't want to stage a repeat of the exact same experience. Instead of basing the majority of the non-game activities in Miami, 15 miles south of the stadium, we decided to move our base of operations and the focal point of non-game-day festivities to the neighboring beach city of Fort Lauderdale, 20 miles in the other direction. That decision resulted in having to set aside an enormous amount of additional time and human resources to re-imagine a new operations plan before real planning could begin. This was not unusual for the Super Bowl. It moves every year to a different place. But, it was definitely unusual to have the event in South Florida without being centered in Miami.

Of course, introducing innovation into a system doesn't have to involve moving an entire city's worth of events into a new neighborhood. It can be manifest in introducing a new size and type of product packaging, rolling out a new app, or setting up a new distribution system. Constantly injecting innovation into your product, service, system, or presentation is essential to the health of your project and the vitality of your brand. Every time you try something new to improve the system or unlock value, you will naturally be introducing new uncertainties and exposing your brand to new risks. Innovation, simply, takes a great deal more time—and well it should. You and your team will need every precious moment not only to develop and create new project features, but sufficient time to comprehensively imagine the implications of introducing something new and to develop the Plan B's if things don't go right.

Innovation is most often an evolving process. A new idea changes and is reshaped repeatedly to fit emerging challenges, and as it does, it consumes time and attention that wasn't required before. Imagine newness and opportunity whenever and wherever you can, but also consider the time you'll need to effect that change. If you think about how many times you can recall hearing the phrase "we'll put doing that off until next year," you know I'm right. Eventually, next year becomes this one.

Whether introducing innovation or just more fully exposing the risks that were already there, you can be sure that once you start imagining the things that could go wrong, you'll discover an unsettling sensitivity to imagined disasters that will continue throughout the planning process, and probably into execution. I apologize in advance for the loss of sleep. It's not to convince you of impending failure. It's to give you confidence that by investing the time into imagining the worst, you will more often come out ahead. With a growing repertoire of things that could possibly go wrong, where then do you begin to imagine how to make them go right?

LIVING IN THE LAND
OF THE LIKELY

Torii Hunter's leaping grab of a drive well over the wall in right-center field robbed Barry Bonds, of the San Francisco Giants, of a certain home run in the first inning. Yet, it did not win Hunter, of the Minnesota Twins, the Most Valuable Player (MVP) honors in the 2002 MLB All-Star Game, held on July 9, 2002, in Miller Park, Milwaukee, Wisconsin. Later, with two outs in the bottom of the third, Bonds posted a pair of runs, lining a pitch from Roy Halladay, of the Toronto Blue Jays, over the right field fence to give the National League an early 4 to 0 lead. Halladay was already the American League's third pitcher in as many innings. The four-run difference shrank as the score seesawed through the top of the eighth inning. With one man out, Omar Vizquel, of the Cleveland Indians, tripled into the right-field corner scoring Robert Fick of the Detroit Tigers from second base and tying the game.

Between the two leagues, only five pitchers remained of the 19 pitchers named to the All-Star Game rosters, and team managers Joe Torre and Bob Brenly faced the prospect of the game going into extra innings. As it was customary for All-Star team managers to use all of their players during the game, Torre sent two of his remaining relievers to the mound in the eighth and ninth innings, throwing only 11 and 14 pitches, respectively. Brenly pulled reliever John Smoltz, of the Atlanta Braves, for a pinch hitter after throwing only eight pitches in the ninth inning, leaving each team with just a single hurler to take the game into extra innings.

After the American League stranded a man on third base to finish the top of the 11th inning with the score still deadlocked at 7 to 7, the umpires walked to the front row of field-level seats to explain the dilemma to Commissioner Bud Selig. Neither team manager wanted to risk injury to their final two pitchers by having them throw for more than two innings in an exhibition game. Deliberations on how to finish the game were made in full view of the fans in the stadium and 14 million viewers on national television. As Captain Murphy would have predicted, the game ended three outs later in a reluctant tie, as had been decided during the awkward field-level meeting, amid fans booing and chanting "Let them play! Let them play!" There was no winner of the 2002 All-Star Game and no MVP was named for the game. But thanks to Hunter's spectacular catch in the first inning, the American League extended its undefeated All-Star streak.

Extra innings, of course, are not unknown in baseball. According to *The Washington Post*, there were 185 lengthened matches out of 2,428 games during a recent season, comprising 7.6 percent of the schedule. Of those, 63 (2.5 percent) lasted 12 innings or more. Of course, All-Star Games are not remotely like regular season games. But, knowing that a tie at the end of nine innings is not unheard of, and that even longer games are entirely possible, it is hard to understand why a rule was not in place well before Curt Schilling, of the Arizona Diamondbacks, unloosed the first pitch of the night.

A tied score after nine innings was 100 percent predictable, and a 12-inning game was totally within the realm of possibility. The first tied score in 73 years of All-Star Games was in 1961, when rain forced a premature end with the score deadlocked after nine innings. That All-Star teams had never run out of pitchers in the past was clearly no prognostication of the future, notwithstanding that a 15-inning game was played to a National League victory in Anaheim Stadium on July 11, 1967.

Smarting from fan criticism, Major League Baseball made good on its promise to ensure this would never happen again by initiating a rule that some position players, including pitchers, be held in reserve even at the risk of them never playing, and that certain players be permitted to re-enter the game even after they were replaced. A definitive conclusion to the game was particularly important in later years when baseball ruled that the top seed in the World Series would be determined by the winner of the All-Star Game, a rule that temporarily addressed the event's relevance to fans.

THE OUTCOME IS PREDICTABLE WHEN YOU DON'T PLAN FOR THE PREDICTABLE

What the 2002 All-Star Game teaches us is the importance of planning for the predictable. The probability of a game going into extra innings was reasonably high, and in baseball there is no telling how many innings it will take to break a stalemate. The notion that a team could run out of pitchers during a game was an entirely imaginable possibility. Several years before, the NHL had foreseen the possibility of a tie in their All-Star exhibition and instituted a rule to play one five-minute overtime, followed by a shootout to break a stubborn tie. As hockey fans know, ties used to be a common outcome in the regular season, but this is the format now used in the regular season as well.

It may sound silly, or at least overcautious, to have had a rain plan for an outdoor event in the desert city of Phoenix, Arizona, and before Super Bowl XLII on February 3, 2008, I would have agreed with you. The historical average monthly rainfall totals for the city in the month of January is 0.77 inches, but during the ten days of scheduled fan activities leading up to the game, we enjoyed about half the year's expected allotment of liquid sunshine. I left my hotel one afternoon in a torrential rainstorm and grabbed one of the gifts that had been graciously left in my room by the Phoenix Convention & Visitors Bureau when I checked in for the month. I didn't for a moment think about how strange it was that an umbrella was one of those gifts, but I was grateful it was there. I grabbed it out of the basket and set out for the convention center, where the NFL Experience and the Media Center were being set up. When I opened the umbrella, the inside a little too cleverly said: "If your meeting was in Phoenix, you wouldn't be needing this right now."

I'm sure you've listened to weather reports, heard a forecast of a 20 percent chance of showers, and thought that the best way to ensure that it doesn't rain is to bring an umbrella with you. You leave your umbrella home anyway because, after all, it's only a 20 percent chance. It may or may not rain, but here's what I know for sure: if you do leave your umbrella home and it does rain, you will get 100 percent wet. Even in Phoenix. The question is, how will that ruin your day, your project, or your event, and is it worth having a plan for when the unlikely happens?

Probability is just one key factor master planners consider when imagining what situations are worthy of the time and resources required to develop contingency plans. Safety considerations, of course, are paramount. Anything foreseeable going wrong that could result in physical danger should zoom to the top of any list. Another important factor is the damage that can be done reputationally and economically by an unlikely, but possible, occurrence. The potential impact on your brand or bottom line can escalate the need for a contingency plan for scenarios for which probability alone might not qualify.

Like Major League Baseball's All Star Game, probability seems to work against us when a project occurs annually or with regularity. Just ask Robert Krumbine, the chief creative officer for Charlotte Center City Partners (CCCP) in Charlotte, North Carolina. The mission of Krumbine's organization is to "envision and implement strategies and actions to drive the economic, social, and cultural development of Charlotte's Center City." Among many other programs, CCCP participated as the producer of the "Avenue of the Arts" component of a street festival called "Taste of Charlotte." The annual three-day event, running from Friday to Sunday, has been operating for decades and, of course, from time to time weather can dampen spirits and attendance. One recent edition experienced a bit more than that.

The festival opened on a sunny spring morning, as 125 local artists settled in to their tents, fussing over displays of their handiwork. Krumbine, as he always does, checked in regularly throughout the day with multiple weather resources to stay on top of any changes in the forecast. "Suddenly," he recalls, "we heard about storms brewing to our west." It wasn't an unusual occurrence in the spring. "We didn't necessarily think the worst. You may get a little bit of rain, a little bit of wind, and everybody just battens down the hatches for a few minutes." Krumbine kept his eyes open, and when he and his associates saw a purplish wall of clouds bearing down on the festival, he knew it was time to act, and fast. He jumped into a cart and started warning guests to seek shelter as soon as possible.

When the front hit, it was "like a train on a track right through the middle of the festival," destroying many of the artists' booths and wares. The winds lifted a 30- by 40-foot tent off its moorings and sent it smashing through a nearby office building's glass windows.

Krumbine saw more structures ready to rip away from their tethers, so he jumped off the cart, and with his team, physically held tents in place to reduce the extent of the damage to the artwork and the structures around them. In retrospect, holding metal tent poles in place during a severe thunderstorm "was not a very smart thing to do," he acknowledges. "It was a knee-jerk reaction." Happily, no one was injured during the fast-moving high-wind event, but the festival site was devastated. Krumbine, city agencies, and all the important stakeholders quickly gathered in the police department's mobile command center to assess the damage and decide what to do next. They determined that by suspending operations for the rest of the day and working through the night, they could get the festival site repaired and reopened for the following morning.

"It completely changed the way we think about contingencies now," Krumbine recalls. "Now, we spend so much more time looking for potential problems and how we are going to deal with life safety first. Where do people go during an emergency? Now, we use that overlay for other events we do."

It often goes that way. Something goes wrong and it changes how well you can imagine something similar happening again. Charlotte now requires a minimum standard for tented structures and a greater amount of ballasting for tents to keep them securely fastened to the ground. "The Taste of Charlotte" incident also teaches us the importance of having a place for senior officials to go to discuss important issues away from the limelight, and certainly away from the public and the media. So while you are imagining what can possibly go wrong, also imagine where you will rally the important stakeholders when you have to make difficult decisions and how you will gather them.

MAY THE ODDS BE EVER IN YOUR FAVOR

Whether it's rain or any other factor that could derail your project, a 20 percent chance of some single thing going wrong is actually a pretty high probability. It may sound that this means you have an 80 percent likelihood of success, but unless you truly believe that's the ONLY thing that can go wrong, think again. It simply means that you have an 80 percent chance of that one specific thing going right. There are still a lot of other things that can go wrong that can eat away at that 80 percent escape from disaster.

The more complex the project, the more likely something is going to go wrong somewhere, sometime, or somehow. Every time you imagine the possibility of something going wrong, you should add the probabilities together to determine how likely your project will be afflicted with just one of these failure factors (see Figure 5.1).

Let's say that in addition to the one thing that has a 20 percent probability of failure, you imagine something else that might have only a 5 percent likelihood of going wrong. That means if you escape the first problem, which by your own reckoning you will do 80 percent of the time, your likelihood of complete success goes down by another 5 percent. Now, the chance that you'll be free and clear of one of these two sources of anxiety is down to just 75 percent of the time. Add another factor that has a 5 percent probability of failure and the likelihood of enjoying a success—unencumbered by any one of those three issues—is now down to only 70 percent. Keep adding factors that can go wrong, and you can see that your likelihood of total, unequivocal success drops with every single one. The more complicated the process or project, the more details, the more factors in the equation, the more probability that at least something is not going to go well. Consider a project as complex as the Super Bowl, and you can imagine that plenty is going to go wrong on Super Bowl Sunday. Every time. The trick, of course, is to make sure that the things that don't go right are the least important, the least damaging, and the least visible. That, of course, was not always the case.

I wouldn't waste much of your precious planning time calculating your likelihood of complete escape from something going wrong. A total escape is near impossible. This is just an illustration of why it's important to imagine and eliminate from the system as many things likely to go wrong as possible, or to try to make them less likely. Few risk factors will be as high as that 20 percent likelihood of scattered showers. If you have many risk factors, your project already has real problems.

EXAMPLE 1: Probability of "A" or "B" going wrong: p(a) + p(b)

Two factors have probabilities of 20 percent and 5 percent:

A 20 percent failure rate is a 1 out of 5 chance, or 1/5

A 5 percent failure rate is a 1 out of 20 chance, or 1/20

1/5 + 1/20 = 4/20 + 1/20 = 5/20

5/20 = 0.25 = 25 percent

There is a 25-percent probability that one of these two things will go wrong.

EXAMPLE 2: Probability of "A," "B," or "C" going wrong: p(a) + p(b) + p(c)

Three factors have probabilities of 20 percent, 5 percent, and 5 percent:

1/5 + 1/20 + 1/20 = 4/20 + 1/20 + 1/20 = 6/20

6/20 = 0.30 = 30 percent

There is a 30 percent probability that one of these three things will go wrong.

FIGURE 5.1. **Calculating Partial Failure**

Your contingency planning framework will look a lot like a classical decision tree: "If this happens, we do that. If that happens, we do this." It will unquestionably save your project valuable time and resources, and result in better and more informed decision making if you are acting on a contingency plan rather than trying to figure out your response from scratch when the heat is on. You will have more time to gather more intelligence and opinions while also reasoning through all of the ramifications and potential consequences of any course of action if you imagine them ahead of time.

• • •

A few hours after the conclusion of Super Bowl XLVIII between the Seattle Seahawks and Denver Broncos, the temperature plummeted and by morning, eight inches of fresh snow had blanketed the New York metropolitan area, stranding many out-of-town fans and guests at area airports. If that snow had fallen just 12 hours earlier, the game would have been very different. It was an unusually brutal winter. Deep "polar-vortex" cold often dropped temperatures into the single digits. Heavy snows ahead of the game delayed construction and preparations at MetLife Stadium in East Rutherford, New Jersey. Snowfall in January and February in the northeast was, of course, predictable. What wasn't predictable was exactly when it would snow and how much. So, contingencies had to be built into the plan in case it snowed a lot and at the worst possible time.

The intrigue of canceling, postponing, or moving a Super Bowl made for irresistibly good news copy. New York *Daily News* journalist Bill Price sounded the alarm more than a year ahead of the game: "According to the new *Farmer's Almanac*, which will be printed soon, the weather on Feb. 2, 2014—the same day Super Bowl XLVIII is scheduled to be played at MetLife Stadium—will feature 'an intense storm, heavy rain, snow, and strong winds.'" He continued, "Not good news for organizers of the event, which will be played outdoors in a cold-weather city for the first time in history." He went on to explain that Pete Geiger, editor of the *Farmer's Almanac*, had told the Associated Press "This is going to be one for the ages."

I was repeatedly asked about the *Farmer's Almanac* forecast and whether it made me nervous. "We've been in cold-weather cities before," I told Bob Glauber, football columnist for *Newsday*. "We've been in situations where snow has fallen ahead of the Super Bowl. There are rescheduling scenarios for 256 regular-season games each year. Same thing for Super Bowls since the beginning of Super Bowls," I assured his readers. Of course, I was nervous. Not because of the *Farmer's Almanac* forecast, or any forecast made 13 months ahead of time. Besides, how much news would they have made if they predicted a beautiful Super Bowl Sunday? I was nervous because a major snowfall at a miserably unfortunate time was a very real possibility.

In the same article, Glauber went further in trying to reassure his readers: "One thing the league has going for it when it comes to being reasonably certain the game will go off as scheduled: Since the construction of Giants Stadium at the Meadowlands in 1976, no Jets or Giants game has ever been postponed because of weather." (Thanks for trying to make me feel better, Bob, but a happy weather history doesn't have any bearing on the likelihood of a future outcome.)

Throughout the processes of planning, execution, response, and evaluation, applying your imagination should never cease. But now that you've imagined enough challenges, let's get down to planning those contingencies!

STEP TWO
PREPARE

THE "BCD'S" OF CONTINGENCY PLANNING

Wouldn't you know it. The *Farmer's Almanac* was right about Super Bowl XLVIII, which was held at Met-Life Stadium in East Rutherford, New Jersey (as we just discussed in Chapter 5). The northeast winter of 2013–2014 would turn out to be among the coldest, snowiest, and most challenging in memory. Nearly five feet of snow blanketed the New York City area that year, 260 percent above the normal seasonal total of 19 inches. Little did NFL owners know when they met in 2010 to award the first-ever outdoor Super Bowl to a cold-winter city that the term "polar vortex" would be introduced that year to the region's common lexicon. For 28 days, daily high temperatures remained below freezing, seven of them were bitter cold days that never climbed above 10 degrees F. We expected tough weather conditions, and we rationalized that if surviving a deep-winter Green Bay Packers game at Lambeau Field is regarded as a bucket-list fan experience, so too could the first-ever Super Bowl played in extreme cold. Moreover, we postulated, New Yorkers consider themselves to be a rather tough bunch who could withstand just about anything.

Super Bowl Boulevard opened on Wednesday night in Manhattan, transforming 14 blocks of Broadway from Herald Square to Times Square into a free, three-quarter-mile-long football fan festival. The nighttime temperature dipped to 12 degrees as the Rockettes, the cast of *Jersey Boys*, and government dignitaries took to the stage—each taking their shivering, teeth-chattering turn for the official opening ceremony. We wondered if all those tough New Yorkers and resolute fans from Denver and Seattle would really brave the freezing temperatures as our event team huddled in the hollow shelter beneath the stage. We needn't have worried. A little cold didn't hold back the 1.5 million fans who jammed onto Super Bowl Boulevard as tightly as rush-hour subways for four days.

While warming ourselves beneath the stage, we were also monitoring the game-day forecast, which looked anything but good. Another snowstorm was heading our way and it could hit sometime on Sunday. That was really unwelcome news, but we were ready to roll out one or more of our contingency plans if it did.

PLANS B, C, AND D

Contingency planning is not about constructing our core project plan, or Plan A. No matter what we set out to achieve, it's crucial that we *articulate our goals and objectives*, *identify the strategy* that defines how we will achieve them, and *develop the tactics* we will employ to bring the strategy to life. Regardless of your business, industry, or profession, any project you undertake should start with those three activities and in that order. This is what you do every day, and you may very well be an expert on how to pilot a project in your field from conception to completion.

Let's assume you have forged a complete, robust, informed, and realistic Plan A for your business or project. Now reflect on all those potential challenges you imagined that could dull or destroy the effectiveness of your tactics, send your strategy off the guardrails, or push your goals even further away. Some might pose minor threats, some more major threats. Any number or combination are possible, so resist thinking that the planning process is over once you have your neat, new, and fully developed plan. It's hard, I know. Contingency planning is a disquieting undertaking because it messes with all our exacting, expertly developed, detail-laden Plan A's.

We all crave closure, the feeling that everything is ready and buttoned up, and as watertight as possible against threats. We want a perfectly crafted, infallible plan, but NFL coaching legend Vince Lombardi was speaking to us as leaders when he said: "Perfection is not attainable, but if we chase perfection we can catch excellence." Lombardi didn't use one play or one plan to win football games. He and his coaching staff developed a playbook chock-full of plans and contingencies for whatever the opposing team, injuries to his roster, or Mother Nature might throw at the Green Bay Packers. He won championships thanks to his foresight on all the things that could go wrong at the line of scrimmage, in the backfield, or deep in enemy territory.

Developing contingency plans is joining Lombardi's chase for perfection. When we consider all possibilities, we reduce the chances of failure, and as a consequence, we catch excellence more often. Our contingency plans may suggest undoing some of the great things we did when we made Plan A, and spending time, money, and energy developing Plans B, C, and D to deal with possibilities that will probably not go wrong the majority of the time.

Investing your finite resources in contingency planning is very much like buying insurance (which you should have too). When we spend money on insurance premiums, we hope we never have to file a claim, but if we suffer loss or damage, we are happy we had that safety net in place. Effective project leaders invest time and talent developing contingency plans that they truly hope, like an insurance policy, will turn out to be a colossal waste of time. But, having those plans can prove invaluable if something goes wrong and you need to work quickly to activate one or more of the plans.

HOW MUCH IS ENOUGH?

Effective contingency planning is rooted in believing the possibilities of your dark imaginings and the pragmatism of your problem-solving capabilities. Understanding how many, for which, and what kinds of imagined adversities we should plan for *always* starts with the things that have the greatest potential to go wrong, and those with the greatest safety, financial, and reputational implications. Plans B, C, and D may address different issues and varying levels of severity. You may need a Plan B to deal with a two-week delay in a product's launch date, a Plan C to address a three-month delay, a Plan D to identify expenses targeted for reduction when revenues are forecasted to fall short of expectations, and a Plan E to quickly reconfigure a marketing campaign threatened by the misbehavior of a hired spokesperson.

How many contingency plans should you develop? As many as you can afford to create, especially for circumstances that can significantly affect the success of your outcome. My advice, after you've considered every possibility, is to treat yourself to a beer or glass of wine. Then, get back to it, because you've only considered every possibility that you have imagined so far. How detailed and robust should those plans be? Those plans should be as detailed and robust as necessary to make them effective and actionable, because a contingency plan that does not address how severe a challenge can be is truly a wasted effort if that crisis strikes.

Contingency plans for Super Bowl XLV—held on February 6, 2011, at Cowboys Stadium (now AT&T Stadium), in Arlington, Texas—anticipated the possibility of snow and cold the way the Dallas-Fort Worth Metroplex usually experiences it. Frozen precipitation is certainly a possibility in February, but more often than not, whatever falls melts away within a day or two. If probabilities worked against us, it would choose to snow precisely on the morning of the event like it did the prior year, when more than 12 inches fell right before the NBA All-Star Game. But, for the preceding 24 years before 2010, no winter in Dallas saw a total as much as the 4.3 inches that blanketed the region the week of the Super Bowl. We were prepared for that, or so we thought.

Recognizing the possibility of wintry conditions descending during the hours and days leading up to the game, the North Texas Super Bowl Host Committee dedicated one of their key logistics experts to the task of developing a winter weather response plan. We did not need a plan that cleared frozen precipitation from the entire region, just the parking lots, major highways, and primary routes between key locations like the stadium, team hotels, practice facilities, media center, and headquarters hotels, shrinking the focus of snow-clearing activities to "just" 1,600 square miles.

Depots of snow melting materials and sawdust were established at strategic locations throughout the area and spreader trucks from other, more snow-susceptible cities in Texas were redeployed to the Dallas–Fort Worth area. A winter weather command center was established to coordinate clearing activities and detailed schedules were developed to prioritize which routes required the most urgent attention at any given hour on any given day.

For most of the month leading up to Super Bowl XLV, it looked like we and our host committee partners had invested time and talent on a wasted exercise. Then freezing rain, sleet, and snow began falling the Monday night of Super Bowl week. The winter weather command center was activated and began monitoring roadway conditions across the region. A fleet of trucks hit the roads to spread the stockpiled chemicals that were effective at temperatures above 20 degrees. Unfortunately, the mercury had plummeted overnight to the single digits and teens. By then, every asphalt surface was glazed with ice and nearly impassable, forcing the closure of schools and many businesses for a solid week.

I cautiously negotiated my car through a 19-mile labyrinth of stranded tractor-trailers and SUVs, their headlights pointing in every direction along Interstate 30. Tuesday was Super Bowl Media Day at Cowboys Stadium and, notwithstanding the hazards on the road, the two teams and the media had to likewise serpentine between the obstacles on the highways to the event. The media and the Green Bay Packers were staying in downtown Dallas; the Pittsburgh Steelers were lodged in downtown Fort Worth, 35 miles apart. With highways better suited to ice hockey than motor traffic, that proved to be a suboptimal strategy. Pittsburgh's buses crept with glacial deliberateness into the stadium parking lot, led by a truck spreading a superfluous carpet of sand before them. Steelers owner Art Rooney, Jr., was the first to alight from the bus and only the first to remark that "this was a bad plan."

We had a reasonably good contingency plan to deal with snow and ice as is occasionally experienced in North Texas, but not robust enough to cope with the sudden, unreasonably colder-than-normal temperatures we experienced for the week. Because of the materials we chose to deploy, our finely-detailed and expertly-crafted snow removal plan was essentially useless; our plan was an intricate and fully thought out half-measure in the unusually extreme conditions. We were confident in the plan that assembled an impressive fleet of spreaders and a massive quantity of materials. Not once did we ask ourselves "what if it's even colder and for even longer?"

PLANNING FOR THE PREDICTABLE

In the northeast, it is completely predictable that measurable snow will accumulate throughout the winter and if our plan for Super Bowl XLVIII had been to count on the sun to melt the ice, we could have been waiting until April. The Super Bowl had been staged in winter-weather cities before, but never in a stadium open to the elements. In Dallas, we only had to worry about how people would get to and around the city, but we were presented a whole new level of complexity at MetLife Stadium in East Rutherford, New Jersey. The weather could affect every aspect of the game itself, from the field and sidelines to the grandstand and concourses, and safety was our number one concern.

New Yorkers may complain loudly and often, but other than transforming our airports into some of the world's most hopeless and densely-populated dormitories, snow doesn't usually stop us. It just slows us down. Since accumulating snow was predictable at some point over the winter, we had to plan as though the *Farmer's Almanac* was even more right. What if a blizzard event actually did strike the region at the worst possible moment? Or, at a moment that was only a little better than the worst? If the storm smacked us on Super Bowl Sunday itself, crippled the region's roads and railroads, and rendered the stadium unsafe for fans or players, how and when would we be able to play the game? Monday Night Football was not unheard of. Tuesday night was also an option. What if the snowfall was so prodigious and the wind was so powerful that essential infrastructure and services were severely crippled, and first responders and equipment had to be redirected from game-day operations to emergency management duties?

Superstorm Sandy

The New York City Marathon faced such a situation in the wake of Superstorm Sandy, two years prior during late October 2012. This powerful storm struck the New York metropolitan area a week before the race, after leaving a trail of devastation stretching from the Caribbean and all along the Eastern Seaboard. Millions in the tristate region remained without power or heat when Mayor Michael Bloomberg announced the city's intention to host the race to give the region "something to cheer about." Instead, the potential diversion of emergency resources to a sports event generated enormous controversy. "Many were offended by the notion that the city would put resources in the form of police presence, water and food supplies, and electric generators toward the race while communities remain without basic services," wrote Meredith Melnick in *The Huffington Post*. "Some were so adamant that they created online campaigns to prevent the foot race." A few days later, the mayor reversed the decision. Mayor Bloomberg and then New York Road Runners (NYRR) president Mary Wittenberg released a joint statement saying: "While holding the race would not require diverting resources from the recovery effort, it is clear that it has become the source of controversy and division." The race was canceled for the first time in its 42-year history.

Rescheduling the Super Bowl from a Sunday?

Canceling the Super Bowl was simply not an option. But, if we faced a similar scenario, could we play the game the following Sunday, or two Sundays after? We had contingency plans for those possibilities. Rescheduling the Super Bowl would be a task of gargantuan complexity, so it was better to think through how to do that well before the weather forecast suggested we must.

NFL Commissioner Roger Goodell had an even more interesting twist to add to the plan. If the forecast called for a blizzard on Sunday, he asked, could we possibly stage the game on Saturday night and return everyone safely home before the storm began? We would need to create a plan that ensured that stadium employees, police officers, traffic and safety officials, railroad engineers, bus drivers, and the thousands of others we needed to stage the game would also be rescheduled if we had to activate this option. We determined that we would need to make that call no later than Thursday at noon. Once an announcement to play Saturday was made publicly, it would be so newsworthy that few would be caught unaware. The issue, really, was confirming how many of the thousands of people we relied on to make game day happen we would be able to mobilize on Saturday and we would only have about 36 hours to get that figured out.

The real risk inherent in making that decision, of course, was whether we would know enough on Thursday about the track and severity of a potential storm on Sunday. We all know how inaccurate weather forecasts can be that far ahead. We could well have moved heaven and earth on a Thursday to play the game on Saturday and later wake up to a crisp, but beautifully sunny Sunday afternoon in New Jersey. Meanwhile, we would have forced the cancellation of all those Saturday night Super Bowl parties booked by sponsors, charities, media companies, and others. The reputational and financial risks of that outcome were certainly significant, but the risk of looking foolish would have been overridden by concerns for public and player safety. Luckily, we never had to make that call.

Because we had a good handle on our contingencies, we were prepared with options and action plans well ahead of time. The number of productive human-hours planning the response was massive. Although we experienced record cold temperatures all season long, it was Super Bowl IX—played at Tulane University in New Orleans on January 12, 1975—that retained its claim as the coldest kickoff on record for the event, at 46 degrees.

For Super Bowl XLVIII, MetLife Stadium was an unexpectedly balmy 49 degrees when the Denver Broncos received the opening kick. The *Farmer's Almanac* forecast had missed by a hair. Snow began falling three hours after the time expired and by morning, enough fresh powder had dropped to cancel more than 45 percent of all the outbound flights on Monday.

CONTINGENCY PLANS: RE-IMAGINING PLAN A

Developing contingencies can inform the entire project management process and cause us to re-imagine Plan A while we still have time to do so. Focusing attention on contingency creation early in the planning process can help expose fatal flaws and potential weaknesses in our original plan, and encourage us to either fine-tune Plan A, or completely replace it with an entirely new strategy more likely to succeed. Provided that we have the time, we should not be shy about elevating a contingency idea to Plan A if we believe doing so can correct a deficiency in our preparations or improve our project's performance.

While true for entirely new initiatives, it is perhaps even more important to not overlook the importance of contingency planning for endeavors that are repeated throughout the year, annually, or in different markets. Even subtle shifts in the business environment, customer sentiment, and other variables can significantly impact outcomes. Or perhaps an underlying lack of preparation that could address a potential problem has simply not yet been exposed because things have always gone right in the past. That is why it is essential to avoid falling into the trap of "dusting off plans that have always worked before" without considering contingencies for yet-unexperienced challenges.

The First Halftime Show in an Outdoor Winter Environment

The Super Bowl XLVIII halftime show at MetLife Stadium was the first one to be held in an outdoor winter environment. In the past, the show's set-up and removal involved as many as 600 crew members who burst out of the tunnels at a literal run to set up the stage, sound equipment, and effects in the middle of the field in just eight minutes. Weighing as much as 10 tons, the stage is typically designed in 25 or more segments atop enormous wheels that are navigated from a huge tent in the parking lot and through the tunnels beneath the stadium onto the field. The pressure to set up the entire stage and all of its components within the time allotted, and its removal within seven minutes, is enormous and one of the great logistical spectacles that the television audience never sees. Unless, of course, something goes wrong.

We relied on speed and precision for the halftime setup, but safety is always the overriding concern. Our greatest fear was the possibility that one or more of the stage crew could slip on an icy field during those frantic, frenetic minutes, and possibly get caught under the truck-sized wheels. That prospect was unthinkable on so many levels that from the outset, we had to think about the annual halftime show very differently, as though ice or snow would surely glaze the field. We started doing just that almost three years before the game, long before anyone knew what the halftime show would actually be. Our stage designer, Bruce Rodgers, joined me for a chilly winter visit to MetLife Stadium to figure out what to do.

First, we considered building the stage in the stands so it would not have to be wheeled out at all, but there were a host of issues that made that option unattractive. For one, the stage would be a big empty platform most of the time. Getting the performers to it would mean walking them through the audience, certainly not ideal. And, we would need to remove somewhere between 200 and 500 seats, which would cost up to $750,000 in lost ticket revenue.

Bruce then explored the notion we ultimately embraced, building most of the halftime stage against the wall behind one of the team benches and leaving it there throughout the game. We decorated the front of the stage with the same banners that adorned the rest of the field-level walls, so the stage was essentially invisible until the teams left the benches after the first half. Bruce designed a retractable runway and two rolling arches of video screens, which could be wheeled over the player benches without touching any of the team's equipment, supplies, heating units, or game-time communications gear. He found a way to safely convert what looked like a decorated false wall into an effects-laden stage that would eventually host spectacular performances by Bruno Mars and the Red Hot Chili Peppers, without having to move very much across a potentially frozen field.

Our contingency planning process entirely changed a 48-year old Plan A, moving tons of equipment across a potentially slippery field, to creating a different way to achieve the same spectacle without adding physical risks. We were able to achieve this because we began crafting contingencies early in the planning process, with sufficient time to plot a different course that would almost entirely avoid the impact of winter weather instead of having to activate a Plan B based on approaching weather, or worse, a potential injury.

CONTINGENCY COSTS

The costs of developing contingency plans are most often expressed in human terms. That is, time and people are required to focus, imagine, and prepare for deviations from the standard procedure or the core plan. Often, time- and staff-constrained project leaders delegate some aspects of contingency planning to a third party, such as a security consultant, public relations agency, regulatory consultant, insurance broker, or even an event management company, depending on the size, scope, and nature of potential threats to success.

Planning contingencies, of course, often pales in comparison to actually executing those plans. Imagining that a snowstorm could greatly reduce the number of cars we could park at MetLife Stadium didn't actually cost very much at all. The real costs would be encountered in renting more off-site property to accommodate the parking spaces we would have lost. We did just that because there was no less expensive solution available, and perhaps no solution at all if we didn't act to acquire them months ahead of time. It was better for us to contract with land owners and set the real estate aside well in advance, while the leverage to strike a reasonable deal was still on our side and, frankly, having no solution to insufficient parking was not an option.

The best contingency plans, of course, require little expenditure of money until you need to act on them. Securing access to services and materials that might be required to mitigate the possibility of something going wrong can shrink your response time to an event, but not necessitate having to pay for those things unless you actually need them.

Good planners and budgeters always consider the unknown and include a contingency factor in their financial plans. Resist conflating the notion of a "miscellaneous" budget line and a "contingency." *Miscellaneous expenses* is a catch-all category to aggregate small expenditures that don't fit any specific expense line. A *contingency factor* is different. This is a set-aside amount for expenses that you simply didn't plan for.

When possible, I try to reserve 10 percent to 15 percent of any cost estimate for the unforeseeable. The greater the unknowns, the higher the allocation toward contingencies should be. How, you might ask, can we oxymoronically know there is a greater number of unknowns? Any number of factors can increase the likelihood of encountering unplanned costs, including the following:

- If the product, activity, or content is entirely new
- If the product, activity, or content relies on new, emerging, or unproven technologies
- If the product, activity, or content is subject to uncertainty due to regulatory review
- If the product, activity, or content is dependent on a new staff, a new facility, or a new vendor relationship

If you ultimately don't use the budget you set aside for contingencies, your profit and loss (P&L) statement will look better. If you need the contingency funds, but don't have them, be sure that your 401(k) is fully vested. Would you prefer to bet your project or career on the hope that everything will turn out just fine?

HOPE IS NOT A STRATEGY

It was a brutally cold day in January 1993, even for Montreal. Weeks-old banks of greyish snow were piled high at every intersection where a fresh, slick layer of translucent ice had been pounded into shiny, flat sheets better suited to skating than to steering. Can you think of a more appropriate setting for the NHL's All-Star Weekend? I led the league's events department and NHL Commissioner Gary Bettman had started his new job just four days before.

It was important to make a great impression on the new boss, but it was infinitely more important to make an impression on hockey fans because it was also the 100th year that the Stanley Cup was awarded. Some sports fans in North America may not know a thing about the "Great Frozen Game," but they do recognize the iconic shape of the Stanley Cup. Sir Frederick Arthur Stanley, Lord Stanley of Preston, the governor-general of Canada, donated a magnificent bowl of sterling silver in 1893 to be awarded to the dominant amateur hockey club in the Dominion of Canada. This was 24 years before the founding of the National Hockey League (NHL) in 1917, which sometime after its advent had convinced the Cup's trustees that awarding the trophy to the highest level of competition in professional hockey was the best way to promote the sport across North America.

There is only one real Stanley Cup. It's the one you see on the ice when a team wins the NHL championship; it's the one that the players kiss and hold above their heads as they skate around the arena at the end of the deciding game. There is a replica of the Stanley Cup that is exact in almost every detail, except for some deliberate features that enable the Hockey Hall of Fame to tell the two apart. If you see the Stanley Cup anywhere outside of the "temple" to the sport on Yonge and Front Streets in downtown Toronto, it is THE Stanley Cup. The replica never leaves the Hockey Hall of Fame and it is only displayed when the real Stanley Cup is on the road. Over the summer, each of the champion players take turns returning with the chalice to their hometowns around the world. When the NHL season gets started again in the fall, it is right back at the Hall of Fame, and you'll have to earn it all over if you want to see it again.

For the Stanley Cup's 100th birthday in Montreal, where ice hockey is a religion, we knew we had to do something really special. What better way to celebrate an All-Star Game during this auspicious anniversary year than to bring back three beloved Montreal Canadiens legends, with 23 Stanley Cup championships among them, and have them skate around the ice for one more time holding the trophy high above their heads?

ABANDON HOPE

It was a Saturday afternoon more frozen than the Montreal Forum ice as Maurice "The Rocket" Richard, Jean Béliveau, and Guy LaFleur donned skates and white Montreal Canadiens jerseys. The Forum atmosphere was electric, the air was abuzz with animated debates in French and English about the Canadiens' chances of winning another Stanley Cup that season (which they did). Three gods from the pantheon of Canadiens hockey waited just off the ice, hidden underneath the stands where the Zamboni was dumping its load of shavings after grooming the ice into a sheet as smooth as a baby's cheek. Our stage manager assigned to cue the entrance of the Cup went through his checklist when he arrived at the Zamboni gate.

"The Stanley Cup is not in the building," he determined.

I knew where it was supposed to have been earlier that afternoon. The president of NHL Enterprises was hosting a pregame brunch for the League's business partners at our headquarters hotel, and the Stanley Cup was the featured guest of honor. I honestly wasn't comfortable with that and I had told him that I would rather have the Cup at the Forum early, well before we needed it. I was assured that the trophy would be there in plenty of time.

If everything went as planned, there were about 90 minutes between the end of the brunch and the beginning of the event. I hoped it would be enough time, and when I got the radio call, there were still 15 minutes to go. "They're cutting it awfully close," I muttered to Jack Budgell, the game producer. "We could be really screwed," I said to myself.

The event was televised and subject to strict time constraints. We could not be late. We could either do it, or not do it. "Any sign of the Cup?" I asked the stage manager 10 minutes before we went to air. I asked myself, "How did I enjoy my first and only year at the NHL?"

We contacted the broadcast team in the production truck to let them know that we might have to dump the segment, and with less than five minutes to go, we put the call out that this highly anticipated moment was off. I had just finished sharing the disappointing news when a seemingly miraculous report came over the walkie-talkie: The Cup just entered the building. "Get it into Rocket's hands and let's go," I responded. "We're back on!"

It was one of those moments that we knew would start our event off with a bang. And, that's exactly the sound that a priceless, sterling silver, 100-year-old national treasure makes when it's dropped 8 feet to the ice. It slipped right out of Maurice Richard's hands and I still recall that sound with utter clarity because 16,000 hockey fans became totally silent at the very moment the Stanley Cup proved that gravity was still a law. Jack and I watched from the press level as Richard recovered both his poise and the trophy. He lifted it again over his head as he, Béliveau, and LaFleur skated around the ice to fans roaring with appreciation. We could see, even from the press box, that the Cup would require a skilled silversmith when the game was over. It was seriously dented, and we were, too.

The Stanley Cup had made it to the Montreal Forum just in time, but it might have been better if it hadn't. The ice storm had traffic gridlocked. The trophy had left the brunch as it ended, and was being escorted by Phil Pritchard, the Hockey Hall of Fame's "Cup Keeper." Both were sitting in the back of a taxi pointed toward the arena, but the taxi was getting nowhere fast. The Cup was nestled comfortably inside a foam-filled road box, which was visually unremarkable except for the "fragile" and "heavy" stickers wallpapering the outside. The Cup was heavy alright, and about to prove how fragile it really was.

Have you ever been stuck in traffic and wondered whether it would be faster to walk than to sit there? Phil Pritchard KNEW he could. So, he tugged Lord Stanley's box out of the cab, while he was still blocks from the Forum, and pushed the box across the ice coating Boulevard René Lévesque in the -24 °C (-11 °F) temperature. He couldn't tell us any of this because, alas, we did not possess the brick-sized phones available in 1993. When he arrived at the truck entrance to the Forum, Phil's face and extremities were red from the cold, but his hardy Canadian core was successfully warmed by the exertion, victorious over hypothermia. Lord Stanley, in his metallic glory, was not so lucky. All three dozen pounds of his gleaming, finely polished silver skin had cooled to the below-zero temperatures outside, so when it was quickly thrust into The Rocket's hands, it was simply too cold to handle. It fell from his grasp, pealed like a church bell, and lay sad and dented on the Forum ice.

No matter what would happen over the course of the day, it would be hard to get past having damaged the Stanley Cup. That's because the TV monitor, tuned to the live French-Canadian broadcast, treated viewers to repeated slow-motion replays of the moment of infamy from multiple camera angles, with close-ups on the looks of anguish by the players. Happy birthday, Lord Stanley!

DON'T BLAME IT ON THE BOSS

I fully acknowledge my slight tendency toward obsessive-compulsive behavior. Left to my own devices, I would have never planned to have the Stanley Cup show up a half-hour, or even an hour before we needed it. I'd have wanted to have it there at least two hours, maybe even three hours, before the event began. My boss needed it at his sponsor brunch, and I hoped all would go exactly as planned, and if it did, it would be there in time. Well, we all know how often everything goes exactly as planned.

It's hard to argue with bosses, especially in your first year on the job. But I have found that at least some of them are reasonable and willing to negotiate with you if you spell out the things that could go wrong and that could wind up embarrassing them along with your-self. It was incumbent on me to lay out the consequences of something going wrong and negotiating Lord Stanley's release before the end of the brunch. We could have even created a ceremony for its exit from the ballroom. I didn't do that, and I owned the problem as a result. The outcome was my fault, not his.

Truly, hope is not a strategy. I should have abandoned hope and instead articulated the ramifications of the Cup arriving late for myself and my boss. He may well have agreed that the risk was too great not to allow us to move the trophy to the arena before the brunch was over and the entire episode might have been avoided. It is equally possible that despite my diplomatic best, my boss would have chosen to not agree to cooperate. It would still be my fault, not his. I should have had contingency plans for that possibility, as well, long before we were faced with the necessity for last-minute, and ulti-mately flawed, decision-making.

In hindsight, I realize that a contingency plan was required, including the need to closely monitor the weather's effect on traffic and making another pitch to the boss when conditions favorable to gridlock were developing. Further, we should have had a plan on what to do if the trophy simply did not arrive at the arena by a certain time. We could have, for instance, had a plan that would have moved the presentation to an intermission, or during a break in the middle of the game.

We didn't have a contingency plan in place, so I made the decision to cancel the original plan and move on, and then hastily I un-canceled it after Phil's desperate dash to the arena. We were so relieved that the Cup had so miraculously appeared at the last moment that no one had considered its "too-cold-to-handle" condi-tion. At the potential cost of ignoring the centennial, and with no other plan ready to activate, we urgently put the Cup into the Rock-et's hands. Our entire plan fell apart because its underpinning was based purely on the hope that the Cup would be there. That wasn't the boss's responsibility. It was mine.

When we don't, or can't, win an argument with our boss, it's up to us to develop the contingency plans required to deal with the prob-lem should we end up being right and things go wrong as a result. Being right, but not prepared, will be no consolation.

"SUPERSTITION AIN'T THE WAY"

Coaches, athletes, event organizers, and normal humans frequently invest in a form of hope when they embrace *superstitions*, activities they believe will avoid or lead to certain outcomes. Some athletes refuse to shave or alter their pregame meal during the playoffs. Michael Jordan was thought to have worn his lucky University of North Carolina shorts under his Chicago Bulls uniform, inspiring the trend of players wearing longer shorts in the NBA. Baseball fans often join their home team's players, sporting their "rally caps" backwards and inside-out to encourage a come-from-behind shot at taking the lead. Do they work? Maybe a little bit in the locker room. As Yogi Berra is quoted as having said, "Baseball is 90 percent mental. The other half is physical." If athletic performance is dependent on mental and emotional preparedness in addition to the physical, then superstitious routines may help reinforce confidence to some degree. Any small competitive edge can make the difference between winning and losing.

I'm not sure the same holds true off the field. If performing a ritual superstition is a way to make yourself feel better, I suppose there's no harm in it. But if it's a way to "protect" yourself and your project, it's doing you no good at all. Perhaps quite the opposite.

Hawaiian Ti Leaves to Repel Evil and Bring Good Luck

I learned the event business at Radio City Music Hall from a mentor, genius, and certified crazy person, who oversaw all the shows the company produced outside the theater. He was as creative as they come. He was a perfectionist who demanded that every detail was addressed. While producing an event at the Waikiki Shell in Honolulu, Barnett Lipton noticed local stagehands carefully hiding Hawaiian Ti leaves around the site. Local tradition suggests that in the right hands, the Ti plant possesses properties that repel evil and bring good luck. One of the elements of luck that Barnett had most hoped for in this humid tropical environment was an evening under the stars without rain, and he was indeed blessed with just such an evening.

We find it easy to believe superstitions when they seem to "work" much of the time. For as long as I worked with Barnett, he insisted we find a local florist, in every city every time we staged an event, to procure a supply of Hawaiian Ti leaves. At first, I thought he was kidding, but he was deadly serious.

Back when the summer and winter Olympics were held the same year, the U.S. Olympic Committee staged an enormous multisport event just for American athletes during the three intervening years, called the U.S. Olympic Festival. Barnett produced the opening and closing ceremonies for the 1989 U.S. Olympic Festival in Norman, Oklahoma, and I was the associate producer in charge of talent. Part of my job was to manage the enormous number of rehearsals during the month leading up to the event. Some of the rehearsals were held at Memorial Stadium; others were held on football fields dotted throughout the area. One evening, we were rehearsing a segment that involved a few hundred local dancers when the skies to our south darkened ominously to a deep purple-black, punctuated by forks and brilliant flashes of lightning and deep rumbles of thunder. An open football field surrounded by metal grandstands is one of the last places you want to be in a thunderstorm, so we stopped the rehearsal and moved everyone to shelter. As powerful as nature's sound-and-light show was, the storm skittered off somewhere beyond the end zone and we never saw a drop of rain in the stadium. Rehearsals resumed after about 20 minutes. Afterwards, the two-mile drive back to the hotel was sobering. The state road running outside the University of Oklahoma was flooded with deep, nearly impassable ponds of rainwater and covered with thick, heavy tree branches.

Barnett was in the lobby waiting for me and looked relieved when I drove up. A severe microburst had ripped through the area dropping hail and torrential rain. At the stadium, however, we had already hidden Ti leaves at every entrance to the field, under the stage deck, and behind the speaker stacks. Even Barnett was impressed, and you can bet your lucky socks I made sure, without being asked, that there were Hawaiian Ti leaves ready for every event from then on.

I brought that hope with me when I went to work for the NHL, and there were Ti leaves hidden all over the Montreal Forum on the day when the Stanley Cup made its rapid descent to the ice. That was the day that I learned that although plants can do amazing things, like making their own food out of sunlight, at least in my hands they can't keep bad things from happening. I gave up investing any hope in superstitions, even ones that seemed to work sometimes. More importantly, I realized that the very notion of investing in hope itself is a counterproductive endeavor. I wouldn't say that giving up hope as a strategy helped me to sleep better. Quite the contrary, it kept me up nights more often. I recognized that *hoping* a reality into existence isn't the same as *helping* it into existence. We can't really affect the outcome with hope, or truly apply it to being totally prepared for everything that can go wrong—like a winter storm in Montreal or a torrential cloudburst in Oklahoma.

PREPARE FOR ANYTHING

Are your plans actionable for all you can foresee going wrong and not just plans that look good on paper? If you have committed to giving up on hope as a preparation strategy and you have begun developing the contingency plans that are most likely to be activated when things go wrong, it is time to start leveraging the essential tools that will inoculate you, your project, and your company when they do.

You and your team have been working around-the-clock, missing meals, and losing sleep over every detail of your core plan and everything you can imagine that could possibly go wrong. You have pored endlessly over the schedules, deadlines, processes, and formulas to move your project forward. You have identified potential weaknesses, flaws, delays, bottlenecks, and threats, and have developed contingencies that will guide your course of action should one or any combination of those things transpire. You believe you have plans that provide the framework for what you will do in case of a labor dispute, an engineering failure, a structural deficiency, a regulatory challenge, or the malfeasance of key staff members or spokespeople. But the work is far from over.

YEAH, WE'VE GOT THAT COVERED

Do we have that covered? Do we really? It is certainly tempting to think so.

Perceiving potential threats to success and drafting the responses we believe to be most appropriate to deal with them provide only the blueprints for contingency planning. We have not yet gone far enough to define a complete and viable course of action.

When architects design a building, their drawings and blueprints convey how the new structure will meet the functional and aesthetic objectives of the developer. They illustrate what the edifice will look like, how it will accommodate the needs of its tenant-customers, and how it will incorporate the requirements of building codes that keep occupants and visitors safe.

However, what blueprints do not do by themselves is tell the engineering and construction teams *how* to build the building. They tell the contractor exactly where the massive air conditioning unit should be mounted on the rooftop, but don't provide guidance on when, in the construction process, it should be installed, or how it will get up there.

Our project contingency plans are like that. We apply our training, intelligence, and skills to developing the right blueprint for handling various challenges. The preparation process, however, may not be complete until we have determined how we and our teams will put those plans into action. Until then, they may only look good on paper.

As the architects of our projects, we know how to develop plans that will define how our Plan A will be constructed. We are also the operations team that must analyze and evaluate the contingencies to make sure they will work when we need them. Chances are, our contingency plans will make intellectual sense. The question is, if they are the right ones, have we put enough thought into ensuring they are actionable? Allow me to illustrate.

The crowds of fans on the west side of Cowboys Stadium (now AT&T Stadium) were well in excess of what anyone expected. We had installed nearly 100 magnetometers, walk-through metal detectors, on the east side of the stadium, where all the major parking fields were located. Less than a third of that number were installed on the west side, where only NFL buses were expected to arrive.

The Super Bowl is designated as a National Special Security Event (NSSE) by the U.S. Department of Homeland Security, requiring extraordinary measures to protect attendees against potential acts of terrorism and criminal activity. What that means at the Super Bowl is the establishment of a hardened perimeter of concrete barricades and fencing extending no less than 300 feet around the stadium. It is almost always a great deal more than that. The NFL Tailgate Party, a massive pregame extravaganza for 10,000 of the league's closest friends and business partners, was most often located inside the perimeter, so the guests could be cleared through the magnetometers (mags) on their way to the pregame soiree and then head to their seats in the stadium without additional screening. Areas supporting operational compounds for broadcasting, law enforcement, and equipment storage are also enveloped by the barricades, increasing the amount of fencing to as much as 2 1/2 miles. It makes for a very large footprint.

Because parking permits at the Super Bowl can cost hundreds of dollars, they serve as a great revenue opportunity for the event and also a powerful incentive for fans to find parking somewhere else. As a result, hundreds of fans that year found spaces in cheaper lots west of the stadium, which were operated by pop-up entrepreneurs at fast-food joints, big-box stores, and in residential driveways. The entrance at the west gate was simply overwhelmed with many more people than we had ever expected to show up there. The queues grew to such a length that by the time the gates opened, waiting times for the earliest arrivals to get through security could be expressed in hours.

ASK NOT JUST "WHAT," BUT "HOW"

The notion that a set of gates could become overcrowded was totally foreseeable every year, and on paper, we had a plan for exactly WHAT we would do. We anticipated directing people away from overburdened gates to entries that were less crowded. When it came time to act, however, we quickly determined that we had no good plan for HOW we would accomplish that. As a result, we learned the hard way that it is essential to not only have a strategy (i.e., to move fans away from more crowded to less crowded gates), but also to have a fully thought out tactic (i.e., how we would move the fans to another gate).

Like Texas itself, Cowboys Stadium is a very big place and the security perimeter more than doubled its footprint. Even some of the streets surrounding the stadium were swallowed up by the perimeter, so any fan who wanted to walk from one side to the other would have to circumnavigate a very long, circuitous, unmarked route to get there.

We began instructing security guards along the queue to inform fans that the wait to enter was much shorter on the other side of the building. Unfortunately, there were no signs to follow or instructions to explain to the fans how they could get to the other side. Also, there was no staff to direct the fans along the way. So rather than abandon an endless, frustratingly slow queue to undertake a lengthy journey to an uncertain fate, fans stayed right where they were, simmering and rightfully unhappy.

Super Bowl XLV, held in 2011 in North Texas, unearthed a great many flaws in the way we planned, managed, and executed our events. We were reasonably skilled at identifying *what* contingencies we needed to consider, but it was equally important to visualize and develop a realistic plan that defined *how* we would execute them. Had we added the "how" tactic to our "what" strategy, we would have had a system to communicate wait times, signage to direct fans around the building from the west side to the east side, and staff assigned to assist them along the way. If we had better developed our "how" in this case, we would have also discovered that our blueprint that installed security gates only on two sides of the stadium was flawed and that the long and arduous route was far too long to be a reasonable alternative.

We feel better prepared when we have imagined a potential obstacle to our success and have developed a response to meet the challenge head on. It is certainly tempting at that point to "tick the box" and move on to the next challenge, but until you've fully thought through the course of action, the "how," you may only have a strategy, and not the tactic that defines a viable contingency plan.

PLANNING FOR THE UNPREDICTABLE

We now know that the first step in contingency planning, *identifying the most likely things that could go wrong,* and the second step, *having a strategy to address the issue if one or more of them do go wrong,* comprise an incomplete process without knowing exactly how you will realistically and reliably *execute the strategy.* But, can we, as counterintuitively as it sounds, develop strategies and tactics to also deal with the unforeseen and unpredictable? The answers are "yes" and "no."

The more complex our project or plan and the more unpredictability we face, the more things that can go wrong. We cannot have a plan for absolutely everything, but we can get closer to the ideal of a better-prepared system for things we can control, the things we can't, and even the things we will never see coming. What is unforeseeable to us can often be perceived by others who are not bogged down by the enormous investment of detail and planning that has consumed the core planning group. Fresh sets of experienced eyes, unbiased brain cells, and uninvested investigators can make our preparations stronger.

That is one of the reasons why we introduced a "tabletop" exercise into our Super Bowl planning. It wasn't until later that we realized we could also use it to pressure-test and validate our "hows." A *tabletop exercise* is essentially an operational rehearsal. We brought onboard a third-party facilitator about a month before the Super Bowl to review all of our plans that, by that point, had taken three years to create.

It's human nature to resist changing things after investing so much time and effort. I'm sure that's why many of our staff and contractors thought stadium security expert Dan Donovan was a pain in the ass. They had to press the pause button on the important work they were doing to provide him with time, documents, and answers to probing questions. What the staff perceived as a series of unproductive meetings, however, helped Dan understand the design of our plans, schedules, processes, and procedures, as well as our contingencies, our level of preparedness, and blind spots in our thinking.

About 10 days prior to the Super Bowl, Dan gathered everyone who would be located at NFL Control and most of the people in charge of various aspects of game day. Over the course of four hours, Dan would run through five or six crafted scenarios, all of which involved things that might not go well at the Super Bowl. He would set the scene in great detail and throw in something truly awful.

Ford Field—home of the Detroit Lions and the host of Super Bowl XL, held on February 5, 2006—is snuggled into a cozy corner at the intersection of two interstate highways. A few modest strips of parking and a garage are shoe-horned into the spaces between the stadium and the highways. The main entrance is directly across the street from Comerica Park, home of baseball's Detroit Tigers. For most fans, there is one side from which to exit the building. At the end of the game, 65,000 ticket holders would flood out of the main doors, hang an immediate left, and head for Gratiot Avenue, where more than 100 buses waited to return about 5,000 fans to their downtown hotels. That was the plan, anyway.

"It's the fourth quarter and there's four minutes left on the game clock," Dan began. "The score is 28–7. A fatal shooting has been reported on Brush Street, the main pedestrian access, just beyond the security gate, short of Gratiot Avenue. The police don't know who he was, why he was there, what happened to him, or where the assailant has gone. They have cordoned off access from the area to preserve the crime scene and protect the public from further danger."

Given the scenario and lopsided score, fans may have already been heading for the doors to beat the end-of-game rush. Commanders of the Detroit Police Department (DPD), who participated in our tabletop exercise, informed us that they were sealing off the security perimeter and closing the gates. Matters of public safety are always the jurisdiction of law enforcement. The Super Bowl security team, informed by DPD of the closure, began deploying guards to the stadium doors to keep fans from exiting the building. In the meantime, we wrote a scripted message for the public address announcer to inform the fans that they should remain in the stadium, and ideally in their seats, at the end of the game due to "a police investigation outside the stadium." The announcement would be made at the first whistle stoppage in play. It was likely to create tremendous concern in the audience, but it was better to keep as many fans as possible in their seats than to have tens of thousands of them in the concourse trying to get out. It would be much easier to keep them informed while they were inside the seating areas. The tense fans would need to be kept informed during the closing minutes of the game to avoid the panic that might ensue in a vacuum of information.

Although Blackberry texting devices had already been in use by 2006, Twitter would not roll out until a month after the game, Facebook was just a baby, and iPhones had not yet been introduced. We were prepared for this tectonic shift in news gathering and dissemination by the time the lights went out in the New Orleans Superdome in 2013 at Super Bowl XLVII. If we had done the same exercise today, the complexities of managing messages and combating rumors swirling on social media would have been an important part of our contingency planning.

Because the announcement would likely rattle the teams and the players, the football operations group would pick up the phones on the sidelines to let the coaches know that the game should continue and that we would keep them informed as well. After the game was over, they would be told to stay in their locker rooms.

The broadcasting network, as well as other television stations, would likely start covering the incident as a news event, so the media relations department would keep the 3,000 media inside informed and connected with the police department, who would be tasked with providing authoritative facts. Our operations team discussed how we would approach the postgame period. We would repeat the message to the fans at least twice more before the end of the game and provide verified information periodically. The championship team would receive their trophy while the losing team would go to their locker room. But their buses could not leave until they were cleared by the police.

"There's now a minute remaining on the clock," Dan interjected. "The police have determined that the victim had actually been a criminal that threatened passersby with a knife and was "neutralized" by law enforcement. The police have determined there is no danger to letting fans leave the stadium, but that the route to the buses is sealed off as a crime scene." The scenario had changed. We could now announce that fans would be able to safely leave the stadium, but how were we now going to keep 5,000 people who were looking for their buses from walking into the crime scene barricades like the parade band marching into the blind alley in *Animal House*? We determined there was no good way to get people to the buses, and we had no contingency for a back-up bus pick-up area if the primary location was inaccessible. It would be a good idea to have one. Good work, Dan.

In a later year's exercise, Dan posed this scenario: "It is less than an hour before the game. Most of the fans have passed through security and are watching player warm-ups or enjoying refreshments at one of the stadium clubs. A tanker truck on the adjacent highway jackknifes and its cargo of ammonia appears to be leaking. The toxic gas may be drifting toward the stadium." Before we set our sights on how we would react, I asked our security-and-law enforcement team whether there was a HAZMAT ban on the closest highways on

Super Bowl Sunday. There was not then, but by game time there was. The exercise strengthened our plan by greatly reducing the probability of that issue.

Dan and I felt that one really important part of the plan had to involve an interruption of the "chain of command." That is, what if one or more of the key decision makers tasked with managing the response was suddenly inaccessible or unable to perform. So, for one exercise, he took me out of the equation. I honestly don't remember the scenario that needed solving, except that while setting up the details, Dan added that I had slumped to the floor unresponsive. The team worked together to identify the problem, isolate the issue, and set in motion a rational, actionable response. I was proud of them, but disappointed that no one thought to call an EMT to try to revive me. I hope that was unintentional.

Notwithstanding their intrusion into our business or school days, no one questions the importance of a fire drill, a rehearsal of an essential emergency response plan. A tabletop exercise simulating the rollout of your product launch, opening day, rebranding, or crisis plan is nothing less than a rehearsal of your operational response to potential threats. It is challenging to solve tough problems in a simulated environment, but I assure you it is much easier to do that than to try to solve them in a real-life, heat-of-the-moment atmosphere, when time is your enemy and every moment is precious. A tabletop exercise can acid test your plan, expose gaps, and if you act on the results, reduce the probability of things going wrong when it counts most. Over the course of nine years, we incorporated many tabletop learnings into our contingency-planning strategies. As important, it helped to guide better decision making when things really did go off the rails in the real world.

PREPARING FOR ANYTHING, NOT EVERYTHING

We didn't know it when we first started this annual practice, but we discovered that our tabletop exercise helped us do far more than just explore how we would deal with specific issues. It established a team-oriented, problem-solving culture in which the collective group thought through solutions collaboratively in a time-constrained environment. Because the Super Bowl moved to a different city and stadium each year, there were always important new teammates joining the decision making structure, including the stadium's management, local law enforcement, and recent hires. Conducting a dry run to give everyone an opportunity to become more familiar with those they would be working beside on a very busy, very long game day was an enormously valuable benefit. Every member of the group came away with a better understanding of who would assume responsibility over which elements of the response to something going wrong.

When you feel swamped with contingency scenarios, remember that you simply can't anticipate every potential problem. You should plan for the most likely and predictable, but some things are neither likely nor predictable. So, your plan and decision making structure must ensure that you are ready not for *everything*, but for *anything*.

In the nine years that we staged these tabletop exercises, we never responded to a scenario involving a power failure. But, when the power did fail at the New Orleans Superdome, our senior team quickly swung into action as though we were faced with another tabletop exercise. Many who were at NFL Control that night agree that the tabletop simulation contributed significantly to our calm, collaborative, and systematic approach to managing that crisis.

When have you finished contingency planning? Never. It's a continuous, iterative process. After you've identified potential threats and problems, develop a strategy to avoid them or mitigate their effects, and plan how you will implement those strategies. You will constantly refine the plan based on new information, new realities, and new insights (like the results of tabletop exercises). You may need to circulate your contingency plans to others for review or elevate them for approval. And while you do that, without question, you will discover additional threats and problems that need an entirely new set of contingency plans. But "planning for anything" can help you respond to something going wrong—after you have run out of time or resources—in order to develop more contingencies and a variety of strategies that can provide applicable options for responding to the unexpected.

COMMUNICATE OR DIE

The first *NHL All-Star Faceoff*, a celebrity ice hockey match held before the 1996 NHL All-Star Game in Boston, was taped for an MTV special. Television personalities of the time like Matthew Perry, Michael J. Fox, Jason Priestley, Dave Coulier, Richard Dean Anderson, Jerry Houser, and Alan Thicke jumped at the chance to rub shoulders with NHL stars beneath the stands and take to the same ice. We believed that anything that exposed the sport to young American entertainment seekers could help to generate a new crop of fans for the "Great Frozen Game." Whether we actually achieved that, I can't say, but we felt that positioning popular stars as fans of the game was a strategy worth pursuing to promote the sport.

Both MTV and the NHL gave it another try the following year, 1997, in San Jose, California. The celebrity team would play two abbreviated periods with MTV's cameras rolling. The game proceeded as planned, with camera crews capturing as much spontaneous verbal sparring from the team benches as play on the ice. As the exhibition neared its end, two Zamboni ice resurfacing machines waited in the tunnel for the players to finish so we could quickly prepare a fresh sheet for the NHL stars to take their warmup skate. Everything was designed to precisely fit the available time before the puck dropped on Fox's coverage of the NHL All-Star Game. All we needed to make it work was perfection.

Perfection eluded us very early. The celebrities didn't skate to their locker room when the game ended. MTV's host kept some of the most popular stars on the ice to capture interviews and inaneness.

While time slipped away, I realized I had no way to communicate in real time with the MTV camera crew and no way to communicate with anyone who could communicate with them.

The Zambonis moved onto the ice and idled in the far corners for seven interminable minutes until the crew and players finally moved off, finally enabling the machines to begin smoothing the ice. We struggled to make up the time, canceling video features and other pregame entertainment. I turned to Todd, the TV commercial coordinator standing beside me at the timekeeper's bench sandwiched between the penalty boxes and warned him:

> *"We are going to be late."*
> *"How late?"*
> *"I don't know yet. Right now, it's seven minutes, but I'm working on getting it down to about three or four by the time we start the game."*

About 45 minutes later, when the cameras started broadcasting live, we were less than two minutes behind schedule, which admittedly isn't a long time unless, of course, all 120 seconds go horribly wrong. Which they did. Instead of the host's "Welcome to the 47th NHL All-Star Game coming live from San Jose Arena," the TV audience joined the show during a patriotic non sequitur starting with the last half of *The Star-Spangled Banner*. Because the TV commercial coordinator beside me failed to let the producer in the TV truck know about the delay, the Fox production team was as surprised as the viewers. Rather than disrespectfully talking over the national anthem, they were forced to just let it play, starting the show without a welcome or an explanation from the middle of the song.

● ● ●

The root cause when something goes wrong can be a flawed plan or an entirely unforeseen phenomenon, but very often incrementally more damage can result from a lack of communication or miscommunication. In our case, poor communication was the root cause of both the problem and our inability to manage it to a better result.

First, we had no way to communicate with the MTV camera crew. Second, we had no staff member responsible for supervising their time on the ice, and no one who could skate out to interrupt them. We chose not to force them off the ice, which we could have done by signaling the Zamboni drivers to start their resurfacing laps. Flattened celebrity hockey players might have been an even worse outcome.

A FAILURE TO COMMUNICATE

We learned the hard way that things *are* most likely to go wrong when we do not or cannot communicate effectively. When events are in progress, our team typically communicates with walkie-talkie radios, various types of intercom systems, and, when all else fails, with phones and texts. We neglected to consider how we would communicate with a third party, MTV, upon whom we were dependent to stay on time. Had we been able to reach the camera crew directly or through an intermediary, the original seven-minute delay would have been far shorter, we would likely have been able to get back on schedule, and the broadcaster would have avoided airing half of the national anthem.

A focus on establishing a comprehensive, unhindered, and free-flowing system of communication before, during, and after a project is key to managing problems, regardless of the industry, company, or organization. Having quick access to the important internal and external stakeholders, problem solvers, and decision makers is essential. When time is of the essence, you can't waste any of it not instantly knowing how to get to the people most qualified to help fix a problem, provide guidance, authorize direction, or respond to the aftermath.

KNOWING WITH WHOM TO COMMUNICATE

The most basic tool to encourage and accelerate the movement of information is a contact list that provides the phone numbers and e-mail addresses of everyone working on the project. Do you think that's obvious? You would be surprised how many projects I encounter that don't publish one. You may be less surprised to find out that we had a contact list for the NHL All-Star Game, but that no one from MTV was on it. MTV people should have been on the contact list, but they were overlooked because they were a third party. That turned out to be a disastrous omission. It doesn't matter whose business card one carries. If they have a role on the project, include them, even if they are an outside resource.

An alphabetical directory of names may be convenient for smaller projects or for teams in which everyone knows one another. For larger projects and teams, however, a simple roster may not be enough. Although we as project leaders should know everyone's roles and responsibilities, many of our teammates may not be as intimately familiar or knowledgeable. If that's the case, consider adding job functions for each participant on the list, organizing the directory by department or responsibility, or adding a "who to call" for various kinds of help or to share important information.

The Super Bowl contact list, containing hundreds of names, was so complex that we circulated a booklet that included an alphabetical listing and a list by function to make it as user-friendly as possible. In later years, we also added a hotline with a knowledgeable "dispatcher," someone who could receive information from anyone and then immediately disseminate it to the most appropriate members of the team. We published the pocket-sized booklet in printed form so teammates could keep a copy with them at all times, and also because sending it as an e-mail would be of little use if, say, the reason they had to contact someone was because their computer or smartphone was not working properly or our servers were down.

KNOWING HOW WE WILL COMMUNICATE

As important as it is to make it fast and easy to identify and reach the right person with whom to share information, it is equally essential to have a system in place to reach an entire group of people who may need to receive the information. Our primary pathway to communicate might be our mobile phones, texts, e-mails, or walkie-talkies. However, it is also essential to develop a backup plan in the event real-time communication is interrupted. As illustrated at the beginning of this chapter, a failure to communicate to those who may be affected by something that has gone wrong can cause more, and more serious, failures to follow.

My projects are often staged in stadiums or arenas in which people who are accessing the Wi-Fi system are relatively densely packed together, which can impact connectivity and slows down the transfer of data for customers and people behind the scenes alike. For those who require constant access to the Internet, we install Ethernet cables for uninterrupted connectivity. Sometimes, mobile phone service is challenged for the same reason. We add landlines for teammates who are stationary, or walkie-talkies as backups for those who are on the go.

Your business or project may not operate in a stadium, but connectivity issues that can interfere with communication between teammates and with our customers are still something to think about during contingency planning. Computer servers can fail under normal circumstances and may have even more devastating effects during more stressful project periods. Which teammates do you need to have on speed dial to restore the system? Is your project protected with a backup server? If there is a power failure, which of your communications systems will be functional, and for how long? Be sure your team knows how to communicate or receive information when their primary pathways are interrupted, and if all efforts to remain connected with the team fail, what you expect them to do.

At events, I make sure that my production team has our *run of show* document, the minute-to-minute description of what is supposed to happen and when. If the only thing that goes wrong is me being cut off from being able to communicate during an event, the team can use that document to make sure that the event unfolds as it was supposed to. Prepare and circulate the documents that tell your project team *what* needs to happen, and *when*, if appropriate, even if you are not able to guide them.

THE DANGERS OF HOARDED INFORMATION

Our national-anthem-related foul-up at the 1997 NHL All-Star Game in San Jose started with no pathway for communication at all, and was made immeasurably worse by the human factor: the TV broadcast coordinator's failure to use the equipment he did have to communicate with the TV truck. Although talking to the coordinator was the customary way to keep the TV broadcaster apprised, it was my error to assume that he was doing that. It was my responsibility to confirm that he was with a simple direct query like "are you keeping the truck informed?" That night, we discovered that a failure, at any critical link, to pass along information can be just as damaging as no communication at all.

The TV producer, who was tucked away in a windowless mobile broadcast studio under the stands, was not aware that we were running behind schedule—or by how much. So our failure became his failure—an even greater, more nationally noticeable moment gone wrong. It also resulted in an ugly, well-deserved visit to the Commissioner's Office when we got back to New York. He was an exceptional communicator and very clearly shared his extreme displeasure with the both of us.

Not wanting to ever repeat the experience in San Jose, we learned the value of having *methods and processes* for constant communication and confirmation during events along the *entire* chain of responsibility. We also learned that the more complex and departmentally siloed an organization, the more vulnerable that chain is to having information fail to flow the way it should.

I have never kept statistics on how often something goes wrong, or something goes from bad to worse, because someone simply didn't think it was important enough—or not his or her job—to share the information he or she possessed. It's most often not malicious. It's just that people do not appreciate that the information they have is important to others on whom they rely to deliver a particular outcome. Changes to our plans, no matter how seemingly inconsequential and innocuous, can lead to unexpectedly poor results.

During the week leading up to Super Bowl XLIII at Raymond James Stadium in Tampa, Florida, in 2009, we received a call from the loading dock. Approximately 70,000 "fun-size" Snickers bars were being off-loaded for free distribution to fans as they entered on game day. We knew about the promotion and had expected the shipment to arrive late on the day before the game, the ideal time to accept a delivery of delicious chocolate confections in the most likely climactic conditions of Tampa—sunny, hot, and humid. Instead, the truck arrived unexpectedly several days early, dropped the pallets of candy bars, and departed.

According to one chocolatier, it is ideal to store chocolates in a cool, dry place at a consistent temperature between 65 and 68 degrees, at a humidity of less than 55 percent. Tampa that week, however, was a sticky 80 degrees with 80 percent humidity. We had requested a last-minute delivery because every available cool space was stocked to capacity with consumables for game-day concessions and catering, so it was very likely that tens of thousands of units of the fan-favorite candy bar were going to be in suboptimal, perhaps soupy conditions after a few days on the loading dock. We called the NFL's sponsorship group to find out what had gone wrong. Apparently, our colleagues knew that the truck was going to arrive days earlier than scheduled and had not thought it was important to let us know. After all, they thought, an early delivery is better than a late one, right? It was now our problem and we had no good place to store tens of thousands of candy bars. So, as the temperature and humidity continued to provide conditions inhospitable to Snickers bars, I sadly imagined them slowly softening to an unintended redefinition of smooth, creamy chocolate, nougat, and caramel snuggling roasted peanuts.

Just a few days before the premature delivery of the Snickers bars, the *New York Times* reported on "one of the largest food contamination scares in the nation's history," a story that was growing in prominence and ubiquity. Recalls had already been announced for more than 400 products containing peanuts "after eight people died and more than 500 people in 43 states, half of them children, were sickened by salmonella poisoning." In fact, the recall was expanding daily, and although there were no indications that Snickers bars were ever going to be affected, M&M Mars decided to quietly abandon the Super Bowl fan giveaway and sent a truck back to pick up the shipment. As a result, no one opened a single gooey package of chocolaty, peanutty goodness on game day. Sometimes things go wrong and few people notice. Usually, I'm not that lucky.

SHARE CHANGE

Plans change all the time. It's a natural outcome of the emergence of new information, continuing refinement, and the actions of outside forces during the planning process. As details change, there is almost always a need to share those shifts with project teammates and stakeholders. Without that flow of information, unnecessary work, anxiety, and confusion can reign, and desired outcomes can be subverted.

Dispatching an early delivery of Snickers bars is a seemingly innocent occurrence, but it precipitated wasted effort during the very busiest of times. Had our coordinator let the TV producer know that we were running late back in San Jose, we would have avoided breaking into the broadcast halfway through *The Star-Spangled Banner*. Failure to communicate provides proof positive of the truth of *Murphy's First Corollary*: "Left to themselves, things tend to go from bad to worse."

When overseeing a project team, it is essential to establish an environment in which sharing information is a mandatory expectation. That is why the "mantra" for my second year at the NFL shifted from "Assume Nothing, Double Check Everything" to "Communicate or Die." A project as complex and visible as the Super Bowl had to be managed in a culture of personal responsibility for sharing information and an intolerance for carelessly failing to pass along important details as plans and schedules changed. When we need to make even a minor alteration in the scope of our projects, we must consider who needs to know so that they can fulfill their jobs effectively.

Minor changes may affect only a small number of teammates, but more impactful changes to the plan may require wholesale communication to the entire team. Ready-made distribution lists for the dissemination of certain types of information can often be helpful, reducing the potential error of omitting someone who should have been informed.

SURPRISES SUCK!

Taking responsibility as a project leader to share pertinent changes with teammates does more than buy back valuable time and productivity. It models the behaviors you wish to promote: an environment of swift and open notification in both directions that will avoid unnecessary, unproductive, and unwelcome surprises. Effective leadership is all about modeling desired behaviors. If we keep our teams informed and express the expectation that they will do the same for us, the likelihood of a surprise development that someone else in the organization anticipated, but didn't share, can be greatly reduced. For our Super Bowl team, this mandate was expressed with another wry "mantra" one year—"Surprises Suck!" No one wanted to have to say it, but just as important, no one wanted to have to hear me say it because they withheld information.

At what point does information flow become a case of over-communication? In my opinion, there is no such thing. It is up to us as project leaders to evaluate the importance of all information we receive and act on information that we believe is of the highest priority. That said, I would rather be over-informed than over-surprised.

Cultivating a culture and expectation to communicate changes and threats on a timely basis can help lessen the likelihood of something going wrong or can reduce the severity of the impact if it does go wrong anyway. There are other important components to communications planning that will prove essential when the very worst impacts are unavoidable:

- Define how we will make critical decisions.
- Define how we will manage critical communications with the outside world after something goes horribly wrong.

COMMAND AND COLLABORATE

t seemed like much more was going wrong than right. Snow and ice had been cascading off the roof since Friday, flattening the massive clear-span tents that were installed to serve as sheltered extensions to the stadium that contained additional rest rooms, concession counters, and merchandise kiosks. Instead, they had become a hazardous no-man's-land, filled with mangled, misshapen steel beams, acres of tattered nylon, and scattered debris of destroyed furniture, fixtures, and equipment. None of the entrances to the stadium behind the wreckage were usable, and the area was still too dangerous to clear any of the damage before the fans were scheduled to arrive. Temporary grandstands inside the stadium were still being installed and the push to complete them before admitting the public necessitated a delay in opening the gates.

This description is of the North Texas Super Bowl XLV in 2011, discussed earlier, during which thousands of fans were stranded in massive queues on the wrong side of the building, and it seemed as though one intractable problem piled up on the last one all day long. Our operations team huddled early at NFL Control. Reminiscent of NASA's Mission Control Center, team members responsible for every facet of the operation sat at long rows of tables, chairs, and equipment, looking through enormous glass windows at the field instead of video feeds from outer space.

It seemed very natural to have everyone at NFL Control facing the field, since the seats in the stadium generally faced in the same direction. As more and more things went wrong that day, however, it proved to be an extremely inefficient configuration for working as a team to respond to problems. Strategically sandwiched between the lead teammates responsible for security and broadcasting operations, I sat in the front row of NFL Control monitoring multiple radio channels. But I was largely unable to communicate with others in the command center without radioing, phoning, or texting them. That day, a great deal of coordinated effort was required to manage all that failed, and many of us spent hours standing, turning, and shouting across the stair-stepped rows stretching the width of the room. It was apparent very quickly that this was a great arrangement for everyone to be able to see the game while things were going well, but far from the best configuration for a command center requiring collaborative problem solving when things were not going well.

Just a few years before, I visited the Pagoda Tower at the Indianapolis Motor Speedway (IMS) to see how they managed race day at the Indy 500. Given the vast footprint of the 2½-mile oval track, there is no spot where anyone could see everything, and the command center was no exception. From Race Control, all team members who had a need to see the action were seated at the windows overlooking the "Yard of Bricks," the 36-inch strip that comprises the start and finish line, dating to when the entire Speedway track was paved with bricks in 1909. Stretching out in front of the team members was a bank of TV monitors displaying images covering every square foot of the oval track. Each teammate was on the lookout for crashes, car parts, and dangerous debris in their assigned section of the track. The race director stood at the corner windows watching the front stretch; beside him was a large TV screen displaying a swirling cascade of Global Positioning System (GPS) coordinates, representing each car on the track.

As cool as the technology was, what impressed me the most was on the other side of the elevator bank: the large rectangular conference table located with no view of the race at all, which was decidedly low-tech. Seated around the table were the IMS team members with responsibilities that did not require a view of the track—security, transportation, facility operations, and more. As the Speedway filled with fans, this group worked swiftly and efficiently together to manage operations, share updates with one another, and solve problems collaboratively, all because they were seated around a rectangular conference table looking and talking with each other, rather than facing forward in a classroom-style configuration.

It took the woefully inefficient and frustratingly ineffective experience of trying to manage multiple problems at Super Bowl XLV, in 2011, for us to consider redesigning NFL Control. For Super Bowl XLVI, held in Indianapolis in 2012, we applied the intelligence gathered during our visit to the Indy 500's Race Control facility. We positioned the people who needed to see the field to best do their job—officiating, football operations, broadcasting, and media relations—facing the window. Right behind them, we installed a large rectangular conference table, where representatives of each area not directly related to the activities on the field—stadium operations, transportation, medical services, and social media monitors—could keep each other updated and work collaboratively to solve problems. For several of us facing the field—including myself, the head of security, and public safety officials—we could easily swivel our chairs around to face the conference table should our input be required. Although we installed additional TV monitors, game clocks, and time-of-day clocks for those seated at the conference table to keep tabs on the game, I'm sure it was a highly unpopular decision to take people away from their view of the field. But, we all understood that we were there to do our jobs to deliver the best outcome, and without question, this proved to be a better way to do it.

YOUR COMMAND CENTER

Setting up a single location where key constituents and stakeholders can gather and work together as a project rolls out—your own "NFL Control"—is a smart move and one that can significantly improve timely, informed decision making when something goes wrong. You don't have to be managing a major event for this to make sense. You may be preparing for a potential threat, such as a negative news story, a court decision, or a labor dispute.

We set up such a workspace as a deadline approached threatening the NHL with its first strike in 1992. Our "crisis communications center" was filled with banks of phones and TV monitors, enabling representatives of all league business units to stay consistently on-message and equipped with the most up-to-the-minute information. With details rapidly unfolding, information could be quickly, accurately, and simultaneously disseminated across the business. So, too, we could collect and compare market sentiment from our most important customers, clients, and the press, and then elevate consistent themes to the highest levels of management.

We called it the "crisis communications center" because we were truly facing significant brand and economic risk. But you don't need to be facing an existential crisis to establish a central location from which to monitor and manage a new project. A temporary installation—where the project leader and representatives from all relevant support areas are housed—is as good an idea for gathering results and reactions from the marketplace as it is for the quickest coordinated response to when things go wrong. It is also the singular place where senior management can get a comprehensive real-time snapshot of a project's performance.

Forces operating outside of our organizations can often impact results and cause us to make midcourse corrections to our plans. In addition to installing televisions showing broadcast coverage of the Super Bowl, NFL Control monitored news feeds so we could be instantly apprised of any news or business developments that might require us to make adjustments or last-minute decisions. Do the same in your project office, keeping a close watch on news and other feeds most relevant to your company or industry. Our digital media team combed through social media platforms to inform us of conversation trends, observations, and complaints so we could respond to emerging issues. Your project control center might also benefit from dashboards displaying essential real-time performance metrics such as orders, sales, social media sentiment, stock prices, and news streams.

Every company or project office can have a designated location—a room equipped with phones, teleconferencing equipment, computers, and other communications gear, white boards, and office supplies—where problem solvers know to get together when a crisis or challenge unfolds. Identifying a command center can be as simple as designating a company conference room that can be quickly activated when something unexpectedly goes wrong. There should also be a predesignated rallying alert to send word out that an emergency meeting or a coordinated response is needed. With just a little advance planning and at a manageable cost, getting the word out quickly to gather is easy.

We subscribed to an emergency texting system with which we could manage an infinitely subdividable database of text numbers and e-mail addresses. If something that went wrong required instant communication with everyone, say a last-minute cancellation or an evacuation, we could instantly and simultaneously reach out to our full database of teammates working with us at the Super Bowl. We also divided the database into functional subgroups to whom we could communicate messages tailored for more specific audiences—the executive management team, department heads, the operations team, the security department, the event operations group, and many others.

The database management-and-communications system was used to keep specific segments of the staff informed with the latest operational information, such as travel times and waiting times at gates. Thankfully, we rarely had to issue a communication to the widest, all-points audience, but if our off-site staff parking or check-in facilities were inaccessible due to, say, a fire in the area or a road closure, we would have been able to reach thousands of team members with a single text message command. This system would have given us the ability to instantly contact and quickly gather the most appropriate group decision makers for coordinated responses to critical problems.

Having a method to rapidly communicate with your entire team, or with selective subgroups of key department, project, and contractor staff, can save valuable time mobilizing responses. Many organizations use e-mail distribution lists for this purpose, but I've found that brief texts tend to cut through the clutter and are reviewed by recipients with more urgency. It just takes a little advance planning and thoughtfulness to set up the most likely subgroups you or your organization will need to contact in a hurry. Having a predetermined place where project leaders can collect senior decision makers and gather additional teammates for assistance can also greatly reduce response time when minutes count.

On Super Bowl Sunday, the place to gather was NFL Control. But, because fans and the media could look in through the big windows facing the field just as easily as we could look out, we designated a smaller, secondary room nearby with no windows, just in case an issue was so serious or sensitive that it required the Commissioner or other publicly recognizable figures to meet with us to be briefed, provide direction, or issue decisions in the midst of a crisis. Bud Selig, apparently, did not have easy access to such a place in 2002 when his 11th-inning All-Star Game briefing was conducted in front of millions of TV viewers.

THE WEB OF COMMAND

On July 21, 1944, American forces stormed the island of Guam in the western Pacific, launching a costly, weeks-long struggle to retake territory captured 2½ years earlier by the Japanese Imperial Army. As the heated battle raged, communications between the Japanese troops and their commanders were cut off. During the ensuing confusion, surviving members of Shōichi Yokoi's platoon evaded capture by escaping deep into the tropical jungle. In the absence of orders from their superiors, as many as 1,000 troops hid in caves and dense vegetation, succumbing over time to starvation, capture, and suicide. Yokoi, the last known survivor of the battle, was discovered by two American hunters setting fish traps in 1972, 27 years after the end of World War II. Malnourished but still under standing orders to resist capture, Yokoi attempted to disarm one of the hunters before being overcome and marched to the local police station. Yokoi was returned to Japan a few weeks later to a hero's welcome and to a world he could not have imagined. He died in 1997 after having spent two years less time in postwar Japan than he did waiting for a new set of orders from inside a cave in Guam.

Few of us are as resolute, persevering, or as unquestioningly loyal as Shōichi Yokoi. In his story, the chain of command was irretrievably broken, and as a result, his orders stood immutably frozen for 27 years. Your team may not be able to wait even 27 minutes for direction; nor should they, when something goes wrong. Many times, things go from bad to worse precisely because of inordinate delays while the team awaits answers to questions that have made their way up the chain of command. Decentralizing how decisions get made and delegating levels of authority to members of the team along the chain of command is one of the best ways for leaders to head off emerging issues and avoid having small problems becoming bigger ones. Often, there is not just one chain of command operating at once in an organization, but many. If all those chains are elevating a combination of routine and urgent messages all at once, it is more likely the decision maker(s) at the top will be overwhelmed and timely responses to the most important issues may be delayed.

Managing my first Super Bowls, it seemed like almost every problem was elevated to someone sitting at NFL Control. I know that's an exaggeration, and that many decisions were being made out in the field. The high volume of radio and phone traffic, however, resulted in a queue of issues waiting either for me or someone in the command center to respond to in some order or priority.

One of the areas of most frustration for our supervisors and teammates in the field, we learned, was "waiting for answers from NFL Control." From my perspective, it felt as though an enormous number of requests for noncritical decisions from nearly every area of the business were thrown into a funnel; the funnel narrowed down to a constant, high-pressure stream to be handled by a very small number of people. So, when falling snow and ice, unfinished construction, overwhelmed gates, and long delays occupied all of our attention in the command center, we were unable or unavailable to provide direction for many routine decisions that were normally elevated to NFL Control. More decisions HAD to be made at different levels along the chain of command or in the field and on-the-spot.

There was not one decision-making chain, but multiple chains, all operating at the same time and terminating in the same place. Some were directly involved in managing the many difficult challenges that day. A great many more were not affected, but they were still sending information and requests for action on other issues to their "prime decision maker" at NFL Control.

In the aftermath, and following lengthy and exhaustive consideration, we determined that it was essential to push more authority for decision making down each chain, *away from* NFL Control. The command center would continue to be the location where issues of the greatest implications for the game, event, and organization were evaluated and managed, or where responses requiring the greatest degree of coordination were directed.

We delegated decision-making authority for managing many smaller, localized matters to supervisors and teammates on the ground. Along with that authority, we assigned responsibility for developing collaborative, coordinated solutions to localized problems directly between the chains of command most affected by the issue and in the best position to solve them. This interconnectivity between chains of command formed more of a web of decision making. (See Figure 10.1.)

Providing quick, relatively low-cost solutions to lesser experiential problems were similarly delegated. Any teammate could take the name and e-mail address of a fan whose clothes were torn by a sharp edge on a barricade or stained by a dirty seat and agree on the spot that we would pay for repair, replacement, or dry cleaning without getting clearance from NFL Control. (What's a $15 cleaning bill on an $800 ticket?) A gate supervisor was assigned to every security checkpoint who could make decisions on better organizing queues, call directly for maintenance or repairs, or communicate with other gates to divert excess traffic to less-crowded locations. In addition to streamlining decision making and enabling NFL Control to better focus on handling bigger, more impactful, and more encompassing problems, this new redistribution of authority also resulted in the entire team taking a greater ownership over their personal contribution to the fan experience at the Super Bowl.

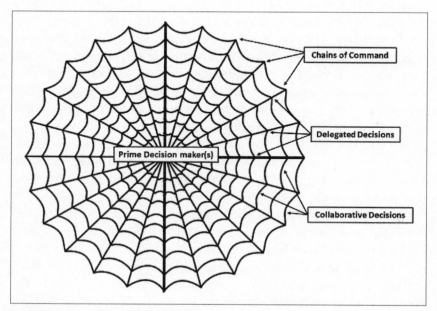

FIGURE 10.1. Web of Command

To be entirely accurate, the ultimate decision maker at the NFL on any given day is, of course, the commissioner and above him, the owners of the 32 football clubs. On Super Bowl Sundays, the authority to make operational decisions had been delegated to those of us at NFL Control, and we only occasionally had the need to elevate problems up to those highest of levels.

Think about how the chains of command for your business, department, or project are structured. When the most senior levels of management are absorbed with so much routine decision making that teammates regularly spend an inordinate amount of time waiting for answers, the organization is not well positioned to respond to an unfolding problem or crisis. In such an environment, important deadlines can be threatened, small problems can fester into big ones, and things that could have been made to go right go wrong. Define what kinds of challenges, questions, or problems need to be elevated to the highest levels, and what can be handled on the supervisory or field level. Identify the limits on financial impacts of decision making. That is, determine the cost, if any, that you will allow each level in the web of command to commit to in solving localized problems.

When something does go so awfully wrong that senior management is entirely absorbed defusing an existential problem, we cannot allow a rigid decision-making structure to cause every decision to stall, or operations to grind to a halt. Shōichi Yokoi spent 27 of his prime years hiding in the jungle waiting for orders that would never come because he and the rest of his unit were given no authority to make decisions if the chain of command was interrupted. Before being faced with a crisis, identify and communicate how you expect each level along the web of command to operate when the focus of senior management is diverted to solving more major problems. Identify one or more interim decision makers who senior management can rely upon to manage routine operations; pass along to senior management only information that is relevant to solving a bigger problem.

Streamlining and decentralizing decision making may require a decided culture shift in your organization. Developing a team-oriented culture focused on collaborative problem solving is the next step in preparing to handle the things that may go wrong.

BUILDING A SUPER TEAM

Successfully managing a problem when something does go wrong starts long before any challenge even has a chance to present itself. It begins with finding, enlisting, training, and managing the staff, colleagues, contractors, and vendors who you will trust not only to do their jobs to make things go right, but also to help avert disaster when things don't.

If you build a team and can't trust them to do their job and do it well, you have one of two significant issues: (1) you either have the wrong team; or (2) you are the wrong leader. The first is avoidable, the second is fixable.

THE RAW MATERIALS OF A SUPER TEAM

Many project teams are composed of more than just our day-to-day teammates. We may require the help of outside resources such as temporary staff, third-party agencies, vendors, and independent contractors. How do our customers and business partners tell the difference between a full-time permanent staff member, a temporary employee, a contractor, or a vendor? They can't, and we shouldn't expect them to.

Every participant on the team represents our brand, whether he or she carries a company business card, is a vendor employee providing specialized expertise, or is a short-term, part-time laborer. In the eyes of our customers, they are all part of the brand experience and there is absolutely no difference from whence they draw their paycheck.

Our permanent event staff at the NFL was a group of 28 event planners. On Draft Day, our team numbered in the hundreds; on Super Bowl Sunday that number increased into the thousands. If any one of them did their job poorly or contributed to a bad customer experience, it didn't matter whose employee they were. It would be our failure as far as our fans were concerned. We and our teams need to recognize and embrace this fact as soon as we can.

A *team* is a blended family comprising everyone who contributes to the product, service, and brand experience they provide. Since every contributor is viewed as a member of the team by the outside world, they must communicate the same messages and expectations, be adequately trained to be ambassadors of our brand, and be managed similarly, as well. In short, we must make our nonstaff team members our teammates.

Importing Teammates

It is common to bring on outside resources when we require expertise that is not resident within our company. Importing temporary talent enables us to accommodate inconsistent workloads, such as projects and seasonal spikes in business activity, without having to hire permanent staff for the busiest times and have them be idle the rest of the year.

When we bring new, transient teammates on board, the probability of something going wrong can increase if we do not imbue them with the same sense of belonging and responsibility as though they were permanent employees. That's why I believe that we should take as much time and care to qualify temporary employees, contractors, and vendors as we do for full-time staff.

Our onboarding and training regimen for a temporary workforce includes: how to dress and behave in the workplace, how to invoice or report work hours, how to fill out expense reports, and how to report an illness. These and other processes are all very important operational necessities, but are simply procedural instructions. So, too, are most job descriptions (or for vendors, scopes of work), which are often just lists of what each teammate's specific responsibilities will entail. None of these truly inspires, motivates, or creates a teammate out of anyone.

We can add great value to our orientation strategy by adding an hour or two to share not only "what and how we do things" but "why we are doing them." This provides temporary teammates and vendors, along with permanent staff, with a greater sense of our collective purpose. What can be even more transformational is an overt admission that our success is in their hands. By sharing how and why we will rely on them, individually and together, we begin to instill a sense of shared ownership in the end result. Teammates begin to appreciate how their individual jobs matter, and how they fit into the bigger picture.

I like to communicate these perspectives in person, in sessions that blend permanent, temporary, and vendor staff. When we do this, we further break down the walls otherwise defined by who people work for; this is a vivid demonstration that we are all part of the same team. It is one thing to require permanent and temporary staff to attend a team-building orientation. But, is it realistic to expect key vendor staff to participate as well? You bet it is. In fact, make it mandatory if you can. If they are reluctant, they may not be the right partner for you. Wouldn't you like to know that they might not work as part of a collaborative team before something goes really wrong?

Specifications versus Expectations

When we first compose our team, we start filling our roster with the most important position players, the people with the skill sets that our business or project requires—designers and engineers, accountants and analysts, planners and marketers, operating staff and subject specialists. Perhaps we already have a core team in place or must manage a project team stocked with "volunteers" from our company's internal departments. Often, corporate titles and job descriptions, and if we're lucky, actual skills, will define the individuals best applied to the effort. If nothing else, they already know the processes, procedures, and politics of the corporate environment.

If you can be selective for any of the essential functions, it is relatively easy to identify candidates with the technical or operational expertise you require. With a minimal investment in time and training to indoctrinate them with knowledge of the nuances, idiosyncrasies, and processes of your project, you will soon be able to trust these people to get the job done to your *specifications*. But, more importantly, will you also be able to trust them to deliver to your *expectations*?

What's the difference between the two? Anyone who has managed people knows that having a team of good, hardworking people who faithfully and meticulously follow specific instructions and processes is the hallmark of an efficient, productive organization. These tireless, often selfless workers can methodically apply proven procedures, meticulously adhere to exacting schedules, complete complex checklists with precision, and contribute to guiding the process from Point A to Point Z. You can trust these dedicated, talented teammates to routinely make things go right way more often than they might otherwise.

Expectations, however, can and should go well beyond simply meeting specifications. To contribute to success in a more impactful way, removing threats and dealing with their consequences, our teammates need to be able to think three steps ahead, to imagine and plan, and to respond to things that go wrong with creative and effective solutions that are not necessarily written in an operating manual. Our expectations should also include teammates proactively collaborating with their colleagues across the organization to identify and manage weaknesses, threats, and areas of concern. If they do, we have a much easier time trusting them to do what is required without constant direction and that they will contribute to getting things back to right when things go wrong.

Trust: The Common Denominator

By now, I'm sure you've grasped the common denominator in delegating responsibility and authority—*trust*. This is very easy to say and extremely hard to live by. After all, it challenges the pervasive ideology that the careers of staff members are solely in the hands of their superiors. The truth is a leader's career is just as much in the hands of the team. Successful recovery when things go wrong will be just as reliant on the skillful contributions of individual team members as on the deft management of their leaders.

As leaders, we must communicate our expectations in clear, understandable terms, whether we are managing a wholly new team, an inherited staff, or a work group composed of colleagues drafted from other business units around the organization. Selecting and applying competent individuals with the necessary skill sets to tackle the right job is the most basic requirement to keep things going right. Molding individuals into an invested, collaborative team that we can trust to proactively evaluate threats and work together to correct the damage when it matures into a problem is a great deal more difficult. So, how do we look beyond work histories, titles, and job descriptions when we select our team members and search for character traits that are not often evident on a resume?

JP Morgan Chase alumna and veteran talent development expert Nancy Gill views the process of building a collaborative team as a two-sided coin, and the responsibility for both sides is entirely on us. Our first task is to assess how prospective teammates will work cooperatively with their colleagues under pressure, and cope with the stress that will inevitably be generated when things do not go as planned. Clearly, there is no way to be completely assured that a candidate will contribute positively, collaboratively, and confidently when problems arise simply by looking at a resume.

Recognizing that the best predictor of future behavior is past behavior, Gill recommends paying careful attention to a prospective teammate's responses to strategic screening questions that probe for desired "behavioral competencies":

- "Give me an example of a situation where you understood ahead of others what was called for."
- "Tell me about a time when you had to make a quick decision in a difficult situation and your judgment turned out to be right."
- "Give me an example of where your self-confidence permitted you to take an action you would have otherwise avoided."
- "Tell me about a time when you brought up or said something that others were avoiding."

Answers to these open-ended questions, and others you may add that are specific to your industry or project, can reveal a great deal not only about how the candidate team members have approached problems, but also some key behavioral indicators. Aside from demonstrating good problem-solving skills:

- Do the answers indicate a tendency toward collaboration and a shared responsibility for the outcome, or a fondness for recognition, credit, and self-promotion?
- Do the responses show initiative and leadership, or instead assign blame or focus on the shortcomings of others?
- Are the answers delivered with confidence and candor, or is the prospect nervous and uncomfortable sharing information?

Look for responses that indicate a behavioral competency for a calmness under pressure and an ability to think quickly. But also take note of how the candidate team members tell their story, and whether they portray themselves as a single character, or one in an all-star cast of problem solvers.

After interviews have narrowed the field to those being seriously considered, Nancy Gill is also a strong advocate for the use of assessment tools, which are available through many talent development and coaching companies. These tools objectively gauge responses to carefully crafted questions designed to tease out attitudes, inclinations, and tendencies as indicators of likely behaviors in the workplace. Gill made certain to have a test like this administered to me when she was the senior vice president of human resources for the National Football League. The more essential the position and the more likelihood that the individual being evaluated will be responsible for leading the response to a crisis, the more essential an assessment tool may be to a successful response and recovery when things do go wrong.

For all companies, especially those that have neither the time nor the resources to avail themselves of a third-party assessment tool, Gill recommends benefiting from the richness of intelligence that can be amassed through *a hiring panel*, a series of interviews hosted by other teammates and project stakeholders, rather than only by a single individual. "A greater diversity of subjects, perspectives, and questions from different points of view make it harder for the candidate to prepare for the different areas that they will be probed on. It is also more interesting and engaging for the candidates," she adds. The more engaged the candidate feels, the more information and intelligence will naturally emerge from the interview.

In some cases, we will not be hiring an entirely new set of teammates to undertake a project. We may, instead, be drafting colleagues from other areas of the company who possess experience and expertise that will contribute to the success of our project. Often, we may have no voice in the matter and will not be drafting them at all. Rather, we may be working on a project with colleagues who are assigned to the effort by their respective leaders, and hopefully have the expertise that is required. In this frequently encountered circumstance, there is no way to ensure our colleagues possess the behavioral competencies that will embrace the cohesive, team-oriented environment so critical to the outcome whether things go right, or horribly wrong.

"In my humble opinion," says Nancy, "the single most important contributing factor to a team's ability to succeed in the face of a big problem is the leadership that built the team and the collaborative culture they inspire." That's the other side of the coin, whether we are leading a team of colleagues, an entirely new one, or a hybrid of the two. Expectation, collaboration, and trust have to go both ways, not just from the bottom up, but also from the top down. The culture we as leaders establish and maintain is as important to our success when responding to challenges as the expertise and attitudes of the team with whom we have surrounded ourselves.

LEADING AND LETTING YOUR TEAM DO THEIR JOBS

Leading is indeed a big job, but it is not the same as doing everyone else's job. Leaders set the vision, expectations, and culture for a business or project. They guide, motivate, and coach their teams, hopefully to a successful outcome. Leaders, when all appears to be going well, let their teammates do the jobs they were hired to do to contribute to that success. Leaders share credit when things go right and take responsibility when they don't. When things go wrong, leaders manage the response and provide decisive and timely direction, while also inspiring confidence from and in their team.

Between the light of success and the darkness of failure is the looming specter of the threat not yet realized. These are the situations that can put our leadership skills to the ultimate test.

On one hand, we recognize that there is nothing as dispiriting as second-guessing our team and jumping in to "rescue" what they were already in the process of solving. On the other, we would be derelict if we allowed them to fail because we didn't act or help. Where's the balance when something starts going wrong? When do we step in? That's the million-dollar question. It depends on your nerves, your degree of trust and confidence in your team, and the scope and scale of the problem. We trust our team to do the job when things are running perfectly. In many cases, they are still the right people to trust when things start going wrong. (Admittedly, I'm still a work in progress.)

It's our job as leaders to ensure that the people best suited to manage a particular problem are aware of our concerns when we perceive an emerging threat. Many times, the "best-suited people" may, in fact, be us. More often, our teammates are the right people because of their skill set, their proximity to the problem, or because we have other pressing concurrent priorities. Let them know that you know there's a problem. Ask them if they are prepared to handle it, and how you can be helpful. Make them responsible to let you know if they need you to step in. Then, let them solve the problem and keep you informed of their progress. When they are forced to manage us, they are diverting some of their focus and attention away from whatever went wrong and often at the worst possible time.

Here's an example. Removing the Super Bowl halftime show from the field was one of the most stress-filled moments of the day. We only had eight minutes to get hundreds of people and tons of staging off the field. Every year, the halftime team executed this flawlessly. One year, though, it seemed like that was never going to happen. As the clock ticked down, big pieces of the stage got snagged in the access ramps, blocking anything else from leaving. Our stage manager and his team worked through the solutions and were able to remove the very last bit of the show just as the clock hit zero and the broadcast resumed. If, however, I had diverted their attention from finding ways to accelerate the stage removal to fielding less-informed (and less-valuable) suggestions from me, I would only have wasted more of their time. I won't tell you it was easy. I desperately wanted to contribute to the solution, but this problem needed their expertise far more than they needed my input. I let them know that I trusted them to do what they needed do and they delivered. Could I have similarly trusted a team that was composed of contractors and vendors? Absolutely. None of the halftime crew worked for the NFL.

When problems strike that rely more on your team's prowess than your own, let your teammates know what the non-negotiables are (in this case, being late was not acceptable) and let them work out the problem, especially when time is of the essence. If you select your people and partners well, clearly communicate your expectations, and give them the responsibility—and the authority—to get their job done, your crisis will never be one of confidence.

STEP THREE
EXECUTE

MANAGING THE
INVERTED PYRAMID

A starched white shirt with an anachronistic paper collar, a pair of crisply pressed navy-blue pants with a pencil-thin line of piping, a tight-fitting double-breasted jacket trimmed above the hips, and a pair of thick white cotton gloves. That was our uniform at Radio City Music Hall.

At that time, Radio City Music Hall was the largest theater in the world, just shy of 6,000 seats. It was as much an architectural wonder during the 1970s and '80s as it was when it opened its polished brass doors in 1932. We ushers had a language all our own, which included hand signals that were visible over long distances, despite the theatrical darkness thanks to our white gloves. With a series of hand gestures, an usher standing in Aisle A on the 50th Street side of the building could communicate with the usher captain, standing way over in Aisle H (a city block away), that there were 150 available seats in Aisle C.

Saturdays and Sundays were the theater's busiest days by far, and no one ever had those days off. It was mandatory for Radio City Music Hall ushers to go to "Sunday School" about a half-hour before the theater opened for the matinee. The entire crew gathered in a large circle around Bill Davis, the senior theater manager, dwarfed in the magnificence of the 60-foot high Grand Foyer. Mr. Davis imperiously reviewed the schedule for the day, delivered news about upcoming shows, rattled off important announcements on a variety of subjects, and drilled us mercilessly about everything he just said, or had said at previous "Sunday School" sessions. If we were asked a question and didn't know the answer, there was a reasonably good chance we would be verbally humiliated, and an outstanding possibility of being sent home without pay. The "service staff," doormen who were a minimum of six feet tall, and the more altitudinally challenged ushers, hailed from a diversity of backgrounds, neighborhoods, and cultures. Notwithstanding what made us different, we had two things in common. We were incredibly proud to be working at "the showplace of the nation" (and we hated the guy).

Occasionally, Mr. Davis sermonized about the significance of working in such a remarkable place. Radio City Music Hall meant something to people, he said, and we meant something to the delivery of an experience in front of the curtain that complemented the quality of the experience presented from the stage. If we had thought about it, we would have recognized that Mr. Davis's weekly "Sunday School" sermon, his deadly question-and-answer session, and his incessant, uncompromising insistence on excellence in every detail communicated that we were part of the guest experience, part of the show, and as such, essential to the business. If only he had outright said that.

When the patrons arrived, the first representative they met was not a highly-paid C-level executive from the suite of offices hidden above the arched ceiling of the auditorium. It was the doorman managing the queue. The patrons purchased their tickets not on the stage from the producer of the show, but at one of the tiny box office windows from another barely compensated employee. They presented their tickets at the door not to the lead singer, but to an usher. And, none of the people they would interact with between the lobby and their seats were members of the Rockettes. The people were ushers and concessions workers. The fact is, in most businesses in today's experience economy, the people you count on the most to deliver your company's brand message are often the least paid and/or least appreciated—the customer service representatives, online chat agents, salespeople, clerks, cashiers, security guards, and, yes, even ushers. They may actually be the ONLY people your customers will ever meet in person, online, or over the phone.

Frequently, the only training customer-facing staff members receive is procedural in nature. They are instructed how to clock-in and clock-out when they report to work, log into their computer, operate the cash register, write up an order, fill out an expense report, allow only properly credentialed people past a certain point, or direct a ticket holder to the correct seat. Ensuring that the staff can do their core jobs accurately is essential to a high-functioning organization, but it is only half the job. We have all encountered people working for a wide range of companies and government agencies who may be efficiently and precisely accurate but deliver a memorably miserable experience.

Enlightened leaders understand the importance of developing an environment where every representative of the brand—whether they are the lowest paid or are more competitively paid employees, contracted staff, or vendors—care as much about each other and the customer as do their better compensated, behind-the-scenes colleagues. It is paramount to engage the customer-facing staff to represent themselves as an essential delivery system for your brand's experience. We have to transform them from a roster of employees into a team, and from a collection of colleagues into teammates. Our teammates must fully grasp the importance of their role, and how dependent the company, brand, and/or project are on them. To realize this, it is incumbent upon managers and leaders to reinforce that message directly with words, actions, and behaviors.

TURNING THE PYRAMID UPSIDE DOWN

The ancient Egyptians built the earliest pyramids more than 4,600 years ago, and they remained stable and durable by planting the biggest flat surface firmly on the ground. Although the ancients have long departed, the pyramids stand in silent testimony to the Egyptians' ingenious feats of engineering and construction. No one has had to make any sort of adjustments to keep the pyramids right where they are, in the very same location and oriented in the very same position.

Most organization charts organize and manage workforces in the shape of a pyramid. The large base at the bottom is typically composed of positions considered the least essential, empowered, and compensated. These individuals are directed by a series of managers in levels of diminishing size and increasing responsibility as one ascends through the structure, finally reaching the senior leadership—the smallest number of individuals in the positions of ultimate authority—at the very apex of the pyramid.

I believe organizational pyramids should be precariously poised on the tip of an inverted pyramid. (See Figure 12.1.) Because so much is riding on direct or indirect human interactions with the customer, I put the most populous group at the top to symbolize their importance, rather than at the bottom. I call this front-line staff *the service team* because that's what they are there to provide—outstanding service—whether in the form of a simple greeting; assistance; conflict resolution; a sale; or a safe, clean, and smoothly operating environment. If any of these touchpoints go wrong, more problems can follow.

The next most important group is *the product team*. This is the group critical to delivering on the customer's expectations of the brand. Sometimes they are very visible and synonymous with the product or service itself (singers, dancers, athletes, designers, physicians, and nurses) and sometimes they are entirely unseen but nonetheless essential to the delivery of a flawless experience (mechanics and engineers, chemists and researchers, assembly line workers, stage hands, project planners, programmers, and technicians). Membership in the service and product teams is not mutually exclusive.

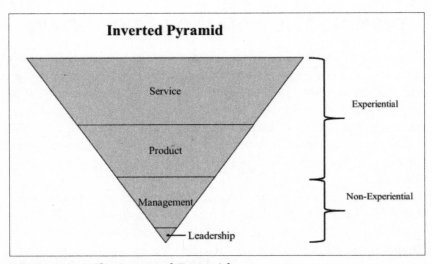

FIGURE 12.1. The Inverted Pyramid

It is possible to be simultaneously part of both. We depend upon physicians and nurses for their professional skills, but no matter how stellar they are at delivering medical care, the experience is better when they have good bedside manner. We may have been greeted at the departure gate by the most ebullient attendant and thanked at the end of the flight by the most gracious and skilled pilots, but if the baggage handlers don't care about where your luggage goes or how it looks when it gets there, the customer's overall experience and relationship with the brand can be significantly endangered.

The next team in descending order of size is *the management team*, a group that is almost always invisible to the customer, but upon whom members of the product and service teams rely for guidance and support. This is the level of teammates that may not directly deliver the customer experience, but can significantly impact the effectiveness, efficiency, and attitudes of those who do. It is populated by managers and supervisors across the entire business, and teams of professionals representing marketing, financial services, human resources, and other essential functions, They, too, have a part to play in ensuring that things don't go wrong within their area of responsibility, from overseeing informed budget planning and accurate forecasting to compliance with government regulations and the development of effective promotional campaigns.

Finally, the smallest group upon which the entire pyramid balances is *the senior leadership*. This is the level that implements policies, establishes culture, and sets the direction of the company. The fact that they are on the bottom of the inverted pyramid does not belie their importance. The entire organization balances on the extremely fine and precarious point the senior leadership represents. The decisions they make, the direction they provide, and the environment they promote among their teams on every level can keep the pyramid upright or cause it to teeter and topple. In this model, the responsibility to keep the pyramid upright belongs to *everyone* on every level. If something goes wrong on the service or product levels, senior leadership has the responsibility to make decisions that can readjust the balance. Think of the United Airlines conflict from Chapter 1. An exceptionally poor experience was delivered to the passenger, but decisions by senior leadership may well have made the effect on the brand worse, more far-reaching, and more long-lasting.

ORGANIZATION CULTURE CAN MAKE THINGS GO RIGHT

Without question, establishing and nurturing a collaborative corporate culture that recognizes the essential contribution that every individual can make at every level will help make things go right more often. Kevin Catlin, managing partner at Insight Strategies, Inc. in Los Angeles, California, likes to share the story with his clients of a practicing surgeon who was being interviewed by a news crew as he walked through the halls of the hospital he also managed. The doctor interrupted the interview briefly to chat with a janitor working in the hallway. After a few moments, the two chuckled and shook hands. The interview resumed as the janitor returned to cleaning a windowsill. A junior reporter asked the janitor what he and the surgeon had discussed and was startled by his response:

"Saving lives." What possible role can a janitor in a hospital play in fulfilling its mission to save lives?

"This hospital is teeming with germs," he explained. "Every time a child touches this windowsill as she walks past, puts her hand to her own mouth as children often do, then kisses Grandma in her sick bed, she can literally kill her with a kiss. That is not happening on my floor."

The surgeon in this story is a rare individual who simultaneously inhabits all levels of the inverted pyramid. He was the senior leader of the company who, in fact, had had a long history of successfully turning around struggling hospitals. He was a practicing surgeon who was both part of the product patients came to the hospital to receive and he had a clear and personal focus on the service side of the equation. His chief contribution, as illustrated in this story, however, was establishing a culture that embraced a clarity of purpose.

The mission of the hospital was to save lives. Everyone in the organization understood their contribution to achieving it. This is not about getting employees to care about their job. Caring only about the job is simply an act of self-preservation. We must imbue teammates with a genuine understanding and appreciation of the contribution they make. When they do, they care about doing things right, and keeping things from going wrong, just like our valued friend at the windowsill.

In a 2013 Forbes.com article, Kevin Kruse, founder and CEO of LEADx, offered one of the finest definitions of leadership: "Leadership is a process of social influence which maximizes efforts of others towards achievement of a goal." Kruse explains that his definition is not limited by authority or power, and that the people being influenced don't need to be "direct reports." It has no requirement of title or personality traits, and acknowledges that "there are many styles, many paths, to effective leadership." It is further defined by "a goal, not influence with no intended outcome."

Let's face it. You are just one person and if you are leading a company, business unit, or project team, there is a lot on your shoulders, for example: the profit-and-loss (P&L) performance; the launch of new brands or products; and the management of a myriad of operational details. Leading is not the same as directing every activity or fixing everything that goes wrong. I learned this the hard way because I'm a perfectionist. I want everything to be flawless and I sometimes did things that I could have had other people do because, well, since I know how I wanted it to turn out, wasn't it just easier to do it myself?

Kruse suggests that leading is not telling people what to do or how to do it. He says that leadership is *influencing* and *motivating* those around you to get the best results possible. The team we need to assemble is composed of people who WANT that, too. There is nothing so demoralizing as people who worked hard but didn't accomplish what was expected of them. Many times, it was because no one told them what was *actually* expected of them or what goal they were working toward. You can be an expert archer and shoot arrows with exceptional precision. But, if you shoot an apple cleanly off someone's head, it doesn't count if you were supposed to be aiming at a nylon target safely attached to a bale of hay.

You might think that excitement and the desire to do a great job was preprogrammed into everyone working on the Super Bowl. After all, you're working at the *Super Bowl*. But, checking credentials at a gate for eight hours, with only the distant, muffled roar of the crowd to connect you to the excitement, you might not feel all that invested in providing a wonderful fan experience. Perhaps you are in a location where you don't see fans at all.

In an average year, there were 18,000 people who wore Super Bowl credentials. Fewer than 1,000 people worked for the League Office. The rest were stadium staff, concessions and catering workers, temporary staff, contracted security, production staff, drivers, host committee volunteers, and many others. They worked for a patchwork quilt of different companies, contractors, and agencies. But, to our customer, the fan, they ALL worked for the NFL on game day. Every one of them was an ambassador of the brand. Given their diverse responsibilities, pay scales, and employers, how was it possible to get everyone on the same page? By making sure they were reading the same book, one that clearly communicated the mission, the purpose, and the values shared by everyone working on Super Bowl Sunday.

DEFINING THE TEAM'S MISSION

The project team's mission is often related to, but not the same as, the company's business objectives. The metrics used to measure their respective success can be quite different. Business objectives may include: achieving certain financial goals, increasing the company's share of market, enhancing customer perceptions of the brand, or boosting awareness of a new product. But, an effective mission for the broader team is frequently expressed in relatable terms that every teammate can share and embrace. By making the mission common to everyone, regardless of their role, team members can contribute significantly to the company meeting its objectives, whether directly or indirectly.

A *mission statement* should consist of a single sentence that is easy to understand, personalize, and express. For example, an airline might establish this shared mission: "We ensure that when passengers deplane, they are already looking forward to traveling with the company again." Nearly everyone who works for the airline can understand how their jobs can impact that mission, not only customer-facing gate staff, flight attendants, and pilots, but also baggage handlers (luggage should arrive the quickest and safest), custodial staff (our cabins should be the cleanest), and the Information Technology (IT) department (our website should make finding, booking, and paying for a flight the easiest). The mission given above will beat "we have to increase revenues by 25 percent" every time. It's relatable, personal, applicable, and easy to sustain.

Think of your own company, department, or project, and you will discover that anyone and everyone can have an impact your customers' experience, either directly by delivering a positive interaction or by contributing to an environment that ensures they occur. At a sports stadium—which includes food preparers, escalator mechanics, groundskeepers, parking lot attendants, IT technicians, bus drivers, and electricians— there is no role that cannot contribute to, or potentially detract from, creating lasting memories. If everyone understood their integral, incremental contribution to our purpose, like the janitor in the hospital or the guard at the gate, things would go right more often. Conversely, things go wrong more often when teammates are ambivalent, unappreciated, and do not understand the importance of their role and how much we count on them. So, as leaders, we have to tell them. Often.

THE EARLY WARNING SYSTEM

Every leadership group, regardless of industry, can take maximum advantage of the early warning system built into their organization to reduce the number of things that could go wrong or contain the severity of their effects when they do. At the Super Bowl, our early warning system was composed of 18,000 credentialed staff and contractors. As leaders, our responsibility did not end with defining and sharing the mission and how each teammate fulfilled our shared purpose. We also recognized that the flow of communication could be even more powerful and effective if we encouraged it to move more freely in *both* directions. Leveraging the real-time observations of all 18,000 teammates, and communicating our encouragement that they should share them, provided us with indispensable diagnostics on how we were performing. The team in the trenches—invested in the mission and clear on their purpose—have more eyes, ears, and brains in the field, and can help us make midcourse corrections in real time to avoid having small problems become larger ones. We shared the notion that it is everybody's job, and it is part of everyone's purpose, to be on the lookout for something that didn't look right. It is not, by any means, an understanding that is implied. We, as leaders, must make that expectation explicit.

During the weeks leading up to the Super Bowl, we hung banners from hundreds of light posts, across roadways, and on hotels and office buildings. On a windy day, a banner might pull loose from the hardware that kept it in place. It was not just the banner-hanging company responsible for refastening the banner to the building. It was not solely the NFL event department staff member who contracted the banner company who had to tell them it was flapping about in the wind. It was the job of any one of the 18,000 teammates who passed by that banner to let us know it was loose. By doing so, we greatly increased the likelihood that it would be repaired before it could pull away from the building entirely and cause injury or damage to property.

We all know this as the "see something, say something" philosophy promoted by the law enforcement and security communities. It applies just as much to our businesses and projects. In the United States, reporting problems is easy. If we see a suspicious package, what we believe to be a crime being committed, or a situation that requires help, we call "9-1-1." We need to make it just as easy for our team to surface issues, as well. For members of the Super Bowl team, we printed a hotline number on the back of every credential, along with the expectation that they would use it to communicate a problem. Any problem.

Collectively, businesses wisely invest billions of dollars on security equipment and personnel each year to prevent physical and financial loss. Empowering every teammate to identify emerging or existing problems, and giving them an easy way to inform management, can significantly add to our preparedness without significant cost. It is essential to communicate our belief that it's everybody's job to be part of the early-warning system, and that time is of the essence when something looks like it's going wrong or has gone wrong.

Keep in mind that the larger and more dispersed the workforce, the more important it is for us to provide a simple way to elevate their observations and concerns. Certainly, informing a supervisor is the usual, most timely, and most appropriate first step. But if a supervisor is not reachable or the nature of the problem is not directly related to the teammate's core responsibilities, a central reporting system can be very powerful. That's why I like the *hotline approach*—a common and easy-to-access text or phone number any teammate can use to elevate literally anything that might be going wrong. On the receiving side of the hotline, assign an individual or team to monitor incoming reports of threats and problems, and to route information quickly and efficiently to the teammates who are best qualified to solve or manage them. Be sure that teammates who use the hotline receive a confirmation that their report has been received and that it is appreciated.

● ● ●

A useful way to communicate our reliance on every teammate's vigilance is to distribute laminated wallet cards that display both our common mission on one side and the hotline information on the other. Putting both messages in the same convenient and accessible place can reinforce our expectations and our dependence on our team. Getting them to use it, however, requires building a culture of empowerment.

BUILDING AN
EMPOWERMENT
CULTURE

t was approaching 11:00 p.m. and I hadn't eaten much of anything since noon. I absently scooped out a small handful of crumbs from the deep bowl of tortilla chips that had been sitting for hours on the credenza in our 2001 NHL All-Star Weekend production office. We had been buried deep within the windowless bowels of the Pepsi Center in Denver since early morning; our only glimpse of the outside world peeking in was from the television permanently tuned to ESPN. It was a typically long day of rehearsals for the next night's on-ice pregame show.

Our talented and exhausted associate producer Tanya had left the office about a half-hour before to get a little rest. Musing that I really didn't relish another midnight run for sliders, I turned to a fellow teammate who was furiously clicking away at his keyboard. "With Tanya gone for the day, you know what would go really well right now?" I reflected as one of the arena's catering staff cleared away the dirty bowls. "A peanut butter sandwich and a tall glass of milk." Tanya was allergic to peanuts and we were painstakingly careful that our provisions never included any trace of the magical bean. In other circumstances, I could, and often did, eat peanut butter for dessert.

I ventured out into the darkness of the empty arena to watch our lighting director programming effects for the player introductions from his massive console. No more than 20 minutes later, I returned to the office and there, sitting on gleaming white china beside my computer was a freshly prepared peanut butter-and-jelly sandwich on hand-cut whole wheat bread accompanied by, yes, a tall, ice-cold glass of milk. I was pretty sure there weren't many catering staff working near midnight on a rehearsal day, so it is entirely possible that the same person who quietly gathered up the dirty bowls took it upon himself to make a snack for a hungry client. It was a gesture of care and kindness that continues to impress me about the Levy Restaurants brand more than 15 years later, as much today for how an empowered staff member late one night built a lifelong relationship on behalf of their company as for the most appreciated peanut butter sandwich I have ever consumed.

THE POWER OF EMPOWERMENT

Companies routinely budget many thousands of dollars to host focus groups, develop customer surveys, and analyze social media to gauge customer sentiment about their brand. All these instruments have been proven to be effective as barometers of engagement with the customer, but none have much of an effect on that interaction while it is actually taking place. If something has gone awry, these tools can provide us with valuable intelligence, but sadly, only *after* the fact.

Empowered front-line teammates can, however, impact the quality of the experience, and facilitate the recovery from a poor experience while the interaction is taking place in person, on the phone, or online. Properly trained, informed, and engaged, empowered teammates can help a company build stronger, more positive, and more personal customer relationships when things are going right, like my peanut butter–providing friend. These teammates can also identify new challenges and shortcomings, keep problems from "going bad to worse," and keep management apprised of potential failures on the horizon.

Instituting and nurturing a culture of empowerment imbues and inspires our teammates with tangible, palpable manifestations of management's trust. In turn, it confers to them the responsibility to act more independently, applying good judgment to making informed decisions that deal on-the-spot with things starting to turn wrong. Empowerment is a powerful motivator, one that instills a strong personal relationship between our teammates and company, brand, or project leadership. According to a 2017 study by the Society for Human Resource Management (SHRM), 61 percent of U.S. employees surveyed ranked "trust between employees and senior management" as "very important" to overall job satisfaction; this was mentioned as often as "overall compensation." Sadly, however, only 33 percent of those surveyed reported being "satisfied" with the level of trust they experience.

As discussed in Chapter 4, *time* is our most limited and precious nonrenewable resource. We can employ more teammates, but no matter how many we hire, we can't gain more time. Senior management, however, can borrow time from empowered teammates to assume responsibility for a greater share of the routine decision making. Writing in the *Houston Chronicle*, freelance small business columnist and adjunct instructor at Central Maine Community College Kristen Hamlin explains: "When employees don't have to wait for approval from a manager or supervisor, workflow doesn't slow down or stop. Employees solve their own problems and move on to the next task." This frees us up to do other things and solve bigger problems when they present themselves. "Empowered employees feel as if their contributions matter," Hamlin continues. "When the company trusts them to make decisions, morale increases, and as a result, so does productivity. Empowered employees often feel as if they have a stake in the organization and their work and strive to consistently produce quality results."

Teammates that feel a sense of ownership, "a stake in the organization," will make better decisions on behalf of the company. Although we may have key directives for them to follow, they begin to understand that they are not there simply to follow directions. When we give them the opportunity to identify problems, errors, and other situations requiring attention, they are more likely to make the effort to either correct the problem themselves or elevate their concerns. Because they feel trusted, and trust that their leaders will make the best use of the information they provide, they will also feel the satisfaction of having contributed to the solution.

INVESTING IN EMPOWERMENT

I recognize that empowering your team takes an enormous leap of faith. That's what makes it so profoundly impactful when you do. Empowering is similar to delegating, but it is not entirely the same. You can delegate without empowering, but you can't empower without delegating. Delegating shifts the responsibility for completing a task from one person to another person further away from the center of the web of command. By itself, it adds useful time for the person doing the delegating at the expense of time invested by the person to whom the task is given. It may, but does not have to require, any level of creativity, problem-solving skills, or judgment. Delegating confers responsibility, but not necessarily authority.

The teammates who are empowered, on the other hand, are given not only the responsibility to complete a task, but also the authority to apply the best of themselves to make decisions that ensure the best outcome. They should also have the authority, within the limits we as leaders define, to participate directly as problem solvers. This may include making decisions that are in the best general interest of the company, brand, project, or customer, even if they are not directly related to the teammates' core responsibilities. Those decisions may result in our teammates *personally* acting to correct the effects of something that went wrong, referring problems to other teammates who are better qualified or more authorized to take remedial action, or simply conveying information through the web of command.

ESTABLISHING THE GUARDRAILS

Empowerment does *not* confer limitless authority. Defining and communicating clear boundaries and understandable guidelines for each teammate's individual and shared responsibilities, as well as limits to the teammate's authority, helps empower all teammates to better understand what is expected of them and what is their accountability to the company. Communicate what teammates can do to help solve problems and encourage them to reach out when it's time to inform management of something that needs to be addressed.

At a minimum, all Super Bowl teammates were empowered and expected to relay to their supervisor or to the hotline anything they witnessed going wrong (a leak, flood, dangerous crowding, a security breach, an injury, etc.). It was everybody's job, at the very least, to identify problems and quickly communicate issues that were beyond the limits of their authority or their ability to solve them directly.

Establish guardrails that define clear boundaries of teammate empowerment and share expectations during formal orientations, job training sessions, and in documentation that the teammates can reference. Key messages may include:

- Your assigned job is integral to our overall success. If you are not confident that you fully understand your job, please ask your supervisor for a thorough explanation.
- If you cannot fulfill your mission for any reason, or something interferes with your ability to get your job done, you must let your supervisor know as soon as possible.
- We are all members of a team that shares this purpose— _____. If you see something that will keep our team from fulfilling this important purpose, and you can correct it easily and quickly without endangering your mission, please do so. If you cannot correct it, you must let your supervisor know as soon as possible. If you cannot immediately reach your supervisor, use our hotline and we will send help.
- It is important to communicate the most accurate information available to our customers. If you do not have the answer to a question, please ask a teammate or your supervisor for help, or direct the customer to someone who can better help her.
- It is all of our jobs to respond when things go wrong or look like they may go wrong. If you see something, say something immediately. Provide your supervisor only with information you know is correct and do not embellish the details.
- You should never take any action that is illegal or dishonest.
- You should always contact your supervisor before:
  - Taking any action that you know violates company policy.
  - Taking any action that involves spending money or committing company funds.
  - Taking any action that interferes with the mission of a fellow teammate.
  - Taking any action that detracts from the enjoyment of others.

- It is everyone's job to ensure we are providing a safe environment for our customers. Never do anything that endangers your safety or the safety of others.
- We are not authorized to speak to members of the media, even "off the record." If you are approached by reporters or camerapersons, please refer them to our media relations department.
- Treat every customer as though they are a VVIP (Very, Very Important Person). And treat your fellow teammates the same way!

This illustration is most applicable as a guide to customer-facing teammates, but most of these points are just as appropriate for sharing more broadly with all other levels of supervision and management. Our expectations of everyone on our team is that they all participate as active members of the same early-warning system and they go out of their way to help solve problems and complaints, regardless of their job.

WHERE ANGELS DARE TO TREAD

It is often easier for us to trust the teammates over whom we have some level of management supervision, whether directly or through a third party that we have contracted. The strength and continuance of our business relationship requires them to be wholly accountable and cognizant that they will be judged on how they perform. How much do we trust our own colleagues within the organization—the teammates who we rely on, but over whom we have no direct supervisory relationship? Let's be totally honest. We know from past experiences where the potential weak links walk about in our own hallways— the colleagues on the same or higher levels who we count on and we attempt to collaborate with, but who are difficult to manage or hold accountable. They may plan inadequately, miss important meetings, be imperfectly informed, communicate poorly, or simply not care as much as we do about the mission at hand. A failure by anyone on the team is a shared failure across the organization, and responsibility for that failure will land at the feet of whoever is at the lead.

If we perceive a vulnerability due to a colleague's lack of engagement—either owing to similar past experiences or acutely from the red flags of unfulfilled deadlines, a lack of responsiveness, or general disinterest—we are still responsible to ensure they deliver what is required for our collective success. Here are some practices we can employ to manage reluctant colleagues:

- **Overcommunicate.** It is a good idea to distribute written minutes of important meetings to everyone, but don't expect they will read them carefully. Schedule a briefing session on the phone or in person with colleagues who have missed an important meeting to relay essential information, updates, and revisions to the plan.
- **Check In Often.** Arrange a quick meeting, stop by, or call to ask, "How is everything going?" Doing so can be very effective and communicates your reliance on your colleagues' contributions. Ask them where their greatest areas of concern lie, and how they might handle them if things go wrong.
- **Offer Help.** Ask how you and other members of the team can be helpful to their efforts. Get one or more secondary contacts for when a colleague is unavailable. Include the secondary contacts in meeting notices and on written communications.
- **Keep Calm and Remain Vigilant.** Although I am a great believer in letting experts do their jobs without interference, pay particularly close attention if you think a job isn't being done. Check in more often as deadlines approach. Have your own Plan B on how you will handle problems stemming from any area where you perceive vulnerabilities.

There is one last point to make before we conclude the conversation about building an environment of empowerment and investing trust as leaders in our colleagues and teammates. It is exceedingly easy to undermine empowerment and obliterate trust. For me, all it takes is a lie. Just one. Personally, I cannot invest trust in anyone—colleague, superior, contractor, vendor, stakeholder, or customer-facing teammate—who proves to be untruthful or deceitful. When something goes wrong, we must be 100 percent sure that our decisions are based on complete and reliable information. Fixing a problem is far more important that assigning blame, and we cannot effectively manage or respond to a problem if the information we have is based on a lie.

I hold myself to the same standard. I will not lie to you when something goes wrong, or at any other time. That is how I will earn your trust. Lie to me and you're dead. Simple.

EARNED TRUST

Investing trust in our teammates is only one-half of the equation. It is equally important to nurture the trust of the teammates we work with in us, starting with the most immediate level of our direct reports, and through them, to the rest of the organization. We must earn that trust from the first day we engage with our teammates, and on every day thereafter. We don't earn that trust by proving how smart, capable, and talented we are. In part, we earn it by communicating our expectations, motivating teammates to meet or exceed them, and investing our trust in them. We also earn their trust by consistently, conscientiously, and honestly following through with our statements—doing what we say we will do.

By instituting and maintaining an environment of empowerment, we can transform a group of managers, supervisors, line staff, and contractors into a team focused on achieving individual and shared goals. As leaders, it is incumbent upon us to demonstrate *daily* our belief in the importance of every individual's contribution as a member of our community of problem solvers who are on the lookout to keep things going right. One of the most effective ways to achieve this is by leveling the playing field by modeling the standards and behaviors we want our teammates *across* the organization to emulate.

LEADING A COMMUNITY OF PROBLEM SOLVERS

t was the day of our first "Fans First" rally, an orientation, training, and rah-rah session for 7,000 of our front-line security, customer service, and volunteer hosts from the community. Under the leadership of sports event veteran Allison Melangton, and Mark Miles, former CEO of the Association of Tennis Professionals (ATP), the Indianapolis Super Bowl Host Committee had already established an inspiring volunteer program, which was representative of the warmth of "Hoosier hospitality." But it was anything but warm that day. It was well below freezing, with a steady breeze dropping wind chills to uncomfortably numbing levels. Nevertheless, our event operations team agreed that it was important for us to brave the cold outside Lucas Oil Stadium, to greet our arriving staff members in exactly the fashion we wanted them to present to our fans on event day. We wanted them to experience for themselves how a sincere-and-friendly greeting in the Midwest cold could add a touch of warmth to someone's day.

Most seemed to be excited as they arrived for the rally at the stadium. This was the day they would become Super Bowl "teammates." With their heads turtled into their coats and scarfs, some were more focused on seeking relief inside from the cold. One woman, as I greeted her, speed-walked past, uttering a mild oath, and added: "It is *not* a good morning. I had to park five blocks away, and I am freezing to death." I did feel bad for her. It was bitter cold outside and she appeared not to be dressed for the walk. "I'm sorry about that, ma'am. Run on in. It is definitely warmer inside," I said as she shuffled past without a pause.

About two hours later, we were wrapping up the rally after a medley of entertainment, speeches by Indianapolis Colts owner Jim Irsay and several players, and a customer-service presentation delivered by experts from The Disney Institute. My own on-stage contribution included an orientation to the 10-day schedule of events and a peek at how the downtown area around the stadium would be impacted leading up to the game. Our event management team that had surrounded the perimeter of the stadium were now positioned at the exits to distribute a special commemorative "Super Bowl Teammate" pin. The only way you could earn one was to have attended and stayed to the end of the voluntary rally. Everyone who earned one wore it throughout the Super Bowl, and those who didn't attend the rally wish they had shown up just to get one. A woman sought me out as I handed out pins to our exiting teammates.

> VOLUNTEER: *"It figures. I would have been the biggest jerk to the guy in charge of the whole thing. I'm really very sorry."*
> FRANK: *"That's okay. Remember, you never know who you are talking to. I might have been somebody important, or I might have been nobody at all. But we have to treat everyone as though they were a VIP."*

She accepted the pin with a handshake and a smile. That was the message we tried to impart to everyone. Treat everyone the same because they are all fans and we should assume they are all VIPs. We couldn't have communicated that lesson as effectively had we not vividly modeled the behavior that we desired our teammates would emulate.

MODELING BEHAVIORS

Influencing the actions of others by modeling behaviors is apparent to anyone who has ever watched the long-running children's program in

TV history. *Sesame Street* teaches youngsters the values of friendship, kindness, honesty, and learning, among other values, by modeling socially desired behaviors observed in adorable, childlike puppet characters. No one on my team, including me, was as warm, fuzzy, or charming as a Muppet, but I believe that modeling the behaviors we wanted our teammates to present to our customers, our fans, contributed significantly to better service and a stronger, empowered team concentrated on keeping things going right. To ensure that our team focused on the experience of our fans, our leaders, managers, and supervisors needed to be attentive to the experience of our teammates. How we treated them, we believed, would have a direct bearing on how they treated our guests. It would also have a direct impact on engaging them enough to share our interest in running a smooth event, especially when they saw something going wrong.

The large "Fans First" rallies were the last in a series of training sessions designed to transform our philosophy into a more engaged, problem-solving culture. We first staged a more immersive and interactive training session for our core leadership team of approximately 50 key event operations staff and contractors. Their feedback and buy-in helped to inform the content for the next gathering held one month later, where they were joined by the 300 additional teammates that they managed directly. By the time of the final "Fans First" rally for 7,000 teammates, the leadership and management groups who had been empowered to help develop the rally were already engaged and invested, and modeling what we were trying to establish—a working environment in which everyone was focused on shared success and on guard against contributing factors to failure.

We wanted to model a collaborative, communicative, and accountable culture. One way we conveyed this was with the use of first-name-and-hometown name tags. I'll be honest. The original reason we included the teammate's choice of hometown was to avoid having visiting fans ask someone from New York for restaurant recommendations in Indianapolis. What it did, however, was break the ice between teammates who first met in a restaurant, hotel elevator, at the stadium, or on the street. Once someone noticed a fellow teammate's hometown and shared that she "had an aunt in San Antonio," what usually followed was "what job do you have at the Super Bowl?" Thus, an usher could initiate a conversation with a television producer, and a team services liaison became the acquaintance of a greeter. Our name tags leveled the playing field, freely opening communication and reinforcing the concept of a team of collegial equals. Everyone, after all, no matter their position, had a first name and a town they call home.

CREATING A COMMUNITY OF TEAMMATES

Introducing universally accessible pathways of communication helped everyone to feel informed, and as a result, be more engaged. Now that all teammates could report problems, it was more likely they would feel empowered and encouraged to do so. But while we had taken steps toward creating a team, we had not yet developed a community. That's where a platform called "Yammer.com" came in. Yammer was a private social media platform that had a universally familiar and easy-to-navigate feel like Facebook, but it was only available to a closed loop of participants invited by the Super Bowl management team.

Every teammate with a Super Bowl working credential received an invitation—from top-level NFL executives to contracted security guards. Once registered, teammates would be kept updated on the latest Super Bowl news, behind-the-scenes fun facts, traffic information, and last-minute changes. Teammates, for their part, could ask questions and post requests for guidance. "I am working for security but haven't received any information on when my first shift starts," notified one user. We were on the lookout for these posts around the clock and would either answer their questions directly or contact the teammates' supervisor to respond. We made sure that the supervisors responded.

Our ability to communicate with the entire database of teammates to inform and engage them more deeply was enormously powerful. Our continuous monitoring of the site enabled us to respond rapidly to posted questions and expressed uncertainties, avoiding problems rooted in a lapse in communication or miscommunication. The Yammer.com app was the perfect place to focus teammates and respond to requests for help. Our posts of exclusive, behind-the-scenes insights made everyone feel like insiders. But what really created a vibrant, active, and engaged community was the app's user-friendly functionality, which encouraged teammates to tell their stories and post photos of the venues, events, players, and celebrities they encountered when they were off-duty. It built a palpable groundswell of contagious excitement. Like many social media platforms, strangers became acquaintances and acquaintances became friends. In New Orleans, teammates even shared gumbo recipes, a thread that one senior NFL executive in New York signaled a failure of the initiative because it had nothing to do with the league or the event. True, but it had everything to do with community, one that felt engaged enough to transform their membership in our team into a social and cultural experience and establish "personal" relationships across the project. Through that membership, we created a team committed to making things go right and poised to respond to things that could go wrong.

CULTURE CHANGE STARTS WITH THE COACHES

As mentioned, our leadership and management teams participated in an interactive "Fans First" working session during which we collected invaluable input that fine-tuned how we would train the entire team. This conferred much of the ownership of the content to managers and supervisors, ensuring that they would embrace the program, reinforce its values, and feel more accountable for the results. It also had a remarkable, and unexpected, effect on how our senior team of planners, area specialists, and designers approached their own jobs. By putting the fan experience at the forefront of how they managed others, it also refocused their attention on how they designed and planned to deliver the best one possible.

Several years before we introduced the "Fans First" program, our parking-and-transportation director hosted a meeting with our leadership team to brief us on game day plans in his areas of responsibility before Super Bowl XLIII in Tampa. He and his team had struggled to identify real estate to cover the reduction in spaces at the stadium parking lots. Security checkpoints, media compounds, the NFL pregame Tailgate Party, and more had been built on space usually devoted to parking cars for Tampa Bay Buccaneers games. Mike Witte, a transportation expert from SP Plus Corporation, with the help of the local host committee, successfully secured spaces at the adjacent New York Yankees training center and in a wide range of unimproved property around the stadium.

MIKE: *"We are contracting with a large lot northeast of the stadium that should accommodate the rest of our needs and is just 0.7 miles from the north gates.*

FRANK: *"That's great, Mike. But just so I'm clear, is it the closest parking space, or the farthest space that is 0.7 miles away?"*

It was the closest point that was 0.7 miles away from the stadium. The walk from a car parked the farthest away would be well in excess of a mile. Not knowing the physical health, age, or mobility of the fans who would park there, we recognized that we should consider a golf cart or mini-bus to shuttle fans unable to make the walk between the lot and the stadium. We were starting to put the fan experience first even before institutionalizing the "Fans First" philosophy, and in so doing, potentially averted inconvenience and, more importantly, something going wrong, like a fan illness from overexertion. Mike became among the greatest proponents of "Fans First" when it was formally introduced and one of the most fan-considerate thinkers in his planning of parking and transportation once it was. He was far from alone.

A plan that put fans first became a common criterion for decision-making by our event management team, and empowered teammates to think the same way across the web of command. Not infrequently, "that's not very *fans first*," was a common reflection during planning meetings and was directed my way more than once. Improving the customer experience always reduces the probability of something going wrong.

EMPOWERED COACHES, INCENTIVIZED TEAMMATES

"Fans First" was a phrase that our customer-facing teammates heard often from the event management team, in training and while on the job. To further empower managers and supervisors, and to incentivize our teammates, we introduced a *recognition program* that was based on doing the job not only to specification, but exceeding expectations. Each member of the event management team—from leadership to management to supervisors—was given a liberal supply of recognition cards. On each card was a blank space for the manager to write their name and a discrete alphanumeric code to ensure its authenticity. Teammates who were observed doing a great job serving the fans or handling problems were given a card that congratulated them for putting "fans first." The card further provided instructions to the teammates to visit our website, enter their code, and tell their own story on why they were recognized. But doing so, they were automatically entered into a drawing for prizes like autographed memorabilia and merchandise. We also captured firsthand accounts of service success stories and situations that required intervention. It was just a card, with no intrinsic value of its own, but when we handed them to the teammates, it visibly brightened their day and created a contagion of courtesy and vigilance across the entire team.

Then, there was an exceptional incentive—a rare, specially minted coin that would be awarded to those teammates who had gone beyond all expectations. Each senior manager received only five coins to distribute. The rarity of the coins and the limited number of people who could award them made them highly prized and sought after. I'm pretty sure the coins were even 20 percent rarer than we planned because most managers kept one as a keepsake for themselves, leaving only four to distribute. I know I did.

Many companies don't have the ability to mint limited edition coins and it may not be practical or on-brand to give away autographed footballs and jerseys in a random drawing. Perhaps company T-shirts and caps would have the same effect on your customer-facing teammates, but you should resist awarding something off the shelf. Don't underestimate the effect of a company-branded item that is exclusive only to teammates who exceed expectations. And don't be surprised if your team raises the level of their engagement in competition so they can be recognized.

SAVE 100-DECIBEL MANAGEMENT FOR 100-DECIBEL PROBLEMS

The time, money, and effort implementing communications platforms that empower teammates across the organization can pay enormous dividends in engagement, enthusiasm, and efficiency. Trusting teammates to make more decisions in the field can yield impactful results without clogging the arteries of communication. Yet, something often goes wrong that cannot be addressed without the assistance of senior management. How we respond as leaders to these situations can inspire continued vigilance on every level or can entirely discourage future engagement.

If a teammate perceives something is amiss, and they act to (1) try to prevent it from happening, (2) keep it from developing into a more serious problem, and/or (3) reach out for assistance the moment it is required, there should be no repercussions if it goes wrong anyway. I tend to hold colleagues more responsible for ignoring conditions that later led to problems, not acting to correct them, or failing to elevate the issue to a higher level when appropriate.

Sometimes, of course, something goes wrong—or goes from bad to worse—because of negligence, carelessness, inattentiveness, ambivalence, or an outright dereliction of responsibility. That's when it's important not only to hold our teammates and colleagues accountable, but to do so definitively and without any shadow of a doubt. If we react with the same level of force and volume to problems large and small, we begin to manage in an environment of fear and tend to blunt the efforts to empower our team. That said, some situations require a response that is strong, unmistakable, and consequential. The trick is to scale our reactions to the scale of the problem.

The people I work with—and for—know me as a pretty relaxed guy, at least on the outside; I'm someone who gets headaches rather than gives them. I don't generally yell or stomp off into the distance when I'm pissed off. There's often a better way to get the message across without turning the volume up to 11. When there isn't, or I've simply had enough, my evil twin, "Skippy," emerges. He doesn't appear very often, but when he does, he is a very important member of the team. He doesn't offer a pat on the back or answer every e-mail promptly. Skippy, quite plainly, can be a jerk.

Skippy doesn't often appear during a true crisis. He is the first to run for the emergency exit. But, when something goes wrong because a teammate, contractor, or other project stakeholder lied, withheld critical information, or was just egregiously careless, Skippy takes command. My assistants at the NFL, Joan Ryan-Canu and Sherri Caraccia, would let anyone in the immediate vicinity know when Frank had left the building and Skippy was in charge.

Skippy showed up uninvited at a staff dinner in 2002, before the 52nd NHL All-Star Weekend in Los Angeles, California. The schedule of events had been designed to better familiarize a nontraditional hockey market to a sport that was more a part of the culture in Canada and the northern United States than sunny southern California. The weekend before the game started on January 29, 2002, with a massive indoor fan festival called "NHL FANtasy" at the Los Angeles Convention Center. Because this was only the first of many events staged before the NHL All-Star game, held on February 2, 2002, our staff had been working around the clock for weeks. A let-your-hair-down team dinner, free of work obligations, I felt was just the thing to keep us energized. Our permanent staff of 15 had swelled modestly with the addition of another dozen or so interns and contractors. Everyone looked forward to an evening of breathing calmly, laughing generously, eating heartily, and making a respectable dent in a keg or two of good Canadian beer.

It is not a given that bringing up work in a social setting will turn things sour, but this time, it certainly did. Jerry (not his real name) had created a marketing program for "NHL FANtasy" targeted to sports entertainment seekers in downtown Los Angeles. Thousands of "table tents"—those self-standing display cards in restaurants that we usually ignore near the salt, pepper, and ketchup—were printed with a ticket discount code and a series of five or six engaging hockey trivia questions. The table tents had been distributed that afternoon to participating restaurants, including the one where we were about to have dinner. As we ordered our first round, Jerry drew our attention to the table tents atop every table. I picked one up and tried my hand at the questions.

I don't recollect many of the questions and answers, except to say that the level of difficulty must have been developed for recent arrivals to North America. Even Americans from the hockey-deficient markets of Appalachia would have been able to conjure up the single answer that I do still remember.

I read the question aloud to my teammates at the dinner: "He was the holder of the NHL record for most goals (894), assists (1,963) and points (2,857)." The answer was also the owner of a trophy case overflowing with Stanley Cups, Harts (regular season MVP), Conn Smythes (playoff MVP), Art Rosses (goal scoring), and Lady Byngs (gentlemanly play), among others. A player so idolized that his trade from Edmonton, Alberta, enraged a nation and simultaneously established a cult of frozen celebrity in Southern California. A player so dominant over 20 seasons that his "99" jersey was retired leaguewide soon after hanging up his skates.

I looked down to the bottom of the table tent to discover that the answer was not who I thought it was. The answer was apparently "Wanye" Gretzky.

I read the answer out loud. "Wan-ye Gretzky . . ." I adjusted my glasses and took a closer look. All the letters remained right where I left them. "Wan-YEE," I wondered even louder to those at the table. At that moment, Skippy, who wasn't originally invited to the dinner, made an unexpected guest appearance as quickly as I had departed. Jerry, his immediate supervisor, and several of his colleagues also departed to collect and destroy every box of tent cards, and to inspect every table in every participating restaurant to ensure they were all recovered on the very first night of the promotion.

Jerry knew he had messed up. He may have even known how badly he messed up, but I wasn't sure just how messed up Jerry had messed up. I was hoping that it was not so much that I would read about it in the Los Angeles sports columns the next morning. Jerry's decision to show me the table tent that evening, and the quick dissolution of our team dinner contributed, at least in part, to containing the brand damage. Thankfully, it never made the papers.

I didn't relish the situation, but Skippy made sure that Jerry got a sense of where he fell short, and it was a learning moment for our entire team. It wasn't because he made a mistake. We all make mistakes. It was because of carelessness and the real danger to which he exposed the brand. A few moments invested in proofreading would not only have inoculated us against that risk, but also would have helped Jerry to launch what I am confident would have been a successful promotion.

As you may have gleaned, it is not my style to scare people or make them feel bad. I like making people feel good, valued, and essential to the success of whatever we are working on together. Sometimes I succeed, and sometimes I don't. Skippy, notwithstanding his gruff exterior and unfiltered bluster, is a helpful partner because his authentic candor makes Frank more genuine and believable most of the time. Skippy didn't show up when I was just disappointed or frustrated, like when people showed up late to meetings. It took more than that, but when he did appear, our team understood that something unusually egregious, disappointing, and frustrating had happened.

I believe that a good leader scales their response to situations when things go wrong. Skippy usually wasn't in the room when there was a crisis-level issue that needed to be solved and time was of the essence. He wasn't invited when problems were beyond our team's control, or "stuff just happened." But, he wasn't shy when stupid or deceitful things happened. That's my threshold for bringing Skippy into the room, but I recognize that everyone has a different definition and tolerance of when to release their inner Skippy. I have found it the most useful, effective, and productive when that tolerance is not only understood by my team, but also when it is scarce. If it's not a rare occurrence, you either have the wrong team, or you may have the right one but have to work on your anger management skills.

Steven Spielberg knows a thing or two about the dramatic effect of infrequency. In his landmark 1975 film *Jaws,* a murderously famished 25-foot great white shark terrorizes a small New England beach community. The first time the audience sees the shark is almost 77 minutes into the 124-minute film. Until then, the tremendous tension in the film was generated by the audience's knowledge that the malevolent shark might be out there prepared to strike unsuspecting victims, the scenes of the destruction he wrought, and only the scarcest visual hints of the shark's physical presence. In fact, the great white shark only appears for a total of four minutes over the entirety of the film.

None of this is to suggest that building tension and drama into your daily interactions with your team is an effective way to manage, although I'm sure we've both encountered managers who thought so. What I am suggesting is that, like Bruce, Skippy was effective because he appeared so seldom. When he did appear, it was a learning moment for the victim, as well as for the rest of the audience.

I'm not suggesting you adopt my personality or management style, but what I am suggesting is that sometimes you need to find ways to cut through the noise and get people's attention, whether it's in a group, one-on-one, on the phone, or in writing. Differentiating your responses to challenges will help your team perform better, navigate solutions, and prioritize when things go wrong. Pick the strategy and the tipping point that is most authentic to you.

EVERYTHING AFFECTS EVERYTHING ELSE

I can imagine Yogi Berra saying that nobody drives in my hometown because the traffic is so bad. We New Yorkers understand, of course, that if no one drove, there would be no traffic, but because it can take us 90 minutes to go 10 miles, we consider driving here to be an act of pure masochism better left to others. We jam onto the subway instead, which is too crowded. As uncomfortable as moving around is, New Yorkers don't stand still. We deal with it, and that's why most people know exactly where they are, where they want to go, and how they plan to get there.

MetLife Stadium in East Rutherford, New Jersey, is less than 10 miles from Times Square in Manhattan, but on Sundays, it can take an eternity to get there. You can ride Amtrak to see the Giants play a road game in Philadelphia in less time than it takes to get from Long Island to the stadium in the Meadowlands. Since Super Bowl XLVIII between the Denver Broncos and the Seattle Seahawks was to be played at MetLife Stadium on February 2, 2014, we focused on the experience that fans unfamiliar to the area would face traveling from their hotels in Manhattan to the stadium across the Hudson. If fans drove, as they did to most Super Bowls, they would have to travel over some of the most congested roads in America into a stadium that didn't have enough parking for everyone. Located in a swamp connected to the rest of civilization only by a highway interchange, there was nowhere else to park and walk to the stadium.

New Jersey Transit (NJT) had developed a rail spur that operated on event days as a convenient and inexpensive alternative to traveling to the new stadium by car. On a normal game day, as many as 12,000 Jets or Giants fans take the train to the game. The Super Bowl, though, is not normal. Most people coming to the game were neither Jets nor Giants fans, and therefore, had no concept of how attractive the railroad option could be—or how horrific the traffic and expensive the parking they would encounter.

We, therefore, went on the offensive and publicized to all incoming fans that using the train was by far the *best* way to get to the stadium. We understood that using mass transportation is not as common in many cities as it is in New York, and if fans of the two competing teams came from cities where mass transit was totally foreign to the local culture, it could have some really bad consequences. So, we and the New York/New Jersey Super Bowl Host Committee redoubled our efforts to stress the benefits of taking the train.

Our contingency plan, in case no one listened to our entreaties, involved renting offsite parking and shuttle buses. We, along with our friends at NJT, also had a plan if more people than normal opted for the rails. NJT replaced its single-level passenger cars with double-deckers from other routes, increasing capacity by 40 percent, and added two more cars to each train. So, we were 100 percent prepared if 50 percent more people used the train than the savvy, well-informed locals. We were ready for 18,000 people, more than had ever ridden the trains before.

THE LAW OF UNINTENDED CONSEQUENCES

On game day, we painfully learned about the "Law of Unintended Consequences" because we solved the parking problem too well. An estimated 28,000 passengers attempted to arrive by train, and after the game more than 32,000 tried riding back. The result was waits of two hours just to get onto the platform. The satellite parking lots? Deserted.

Is it possible to feel both really smart and really stupid at the same time? Yes, and "The Law of Unintended Consequences" will prove that to you. My old boss, NHL Commissioner Gary Bettman, used to love to talk about it, and I'm sure he still does. The words he used were: *"Everything depends on everything else."* While I know Gary didn't invent this concept—that distinction belongs to sociologist Robert Merton, who also coined the terms "role model" and "self-fulfilling prophecy"—I'll give Gary all the credit in the world. You see, when your boss imparts something that is so profound, so true, and yet so simple in just one five-word sentence, it's worth remembering. One season, I even co-opted it as that year's Super Bowl mantra.

What Gary was really saying was this: "If you think you planned well enough for things to go flawlessly, you probably haven't thought of everything that could still go wrong." If you believe you are home-free after thinking through every possibility, you're deluding yourself. This is especially true during the planning process, the time when we are all trying to grapple with the universe of things that can go wrong. That's the reason that Gary gave us a year to think through all of the potential pitfalls of the crazy idea of playing a regular season NHL game in an outdoor stadium, an audacious notion brought to us by the Edmonton Oilers.

The success of this risky venture depended on making clear-and-objective decisions about whether NHL players could perform safely and at their very best outside in potentially subzero temperatures, and whether it would provide a great live and TV experience. We covered all those bases, and some years later, the highly successful NHL Winter Classic (first held on January 1, 2008, at Ralph Wilson Stadium in Orchard Park, NY) and the NHL Stadium Series (first held on January 25, 2014, at Dodger Stadium) was born.

But we also had to consider what we would do if it was 70 degrees in mid-November in Edmonton, as unlikely as that might have been. What would happen to the ice if it rained or sleeted? What if a blizzard raged at game time? As we have seen, having a plan for those things is something we could think about well in advance because it's possible all along the probability curve. But the flip side of "everything depends on everything else" is when, despite all the meticulous planning, something bordering on the unlikely and improbable goes wrong, all of a sudden, and you are charged with fixing the problem quickly and definitively. Solving problems in real time is particularly perilous because you don't get a year to figure it out. You may get a few minutes, or just seconds, to think through all the ramifications of your decisions. That's when "The Law of Unintended Consequences" is most likely to kick-in full force.

Robert Merton, a Columbia University professor, explained how, in a complex system, a seemingly simple action could result in side effects that the original actors never, in their wildest dreams, considered. Even a sound strategy can create unexpected challenges.

Here's a story that illustrates that concept at work. It's a truly chilling tale of what might have been, and it honestly still haunts me. But for one small decision—made by someone who wasn't me—it's a story that would have been on the national news for a week. It's about a guy named Kurt William Havelock and what he did—or didn't do—just before Super Bowl XLII in Glendale, Arizona.

Havelock was 35 years old, had a girlfriend, a couple of kids, a dog, and an apartment. He had never been in trouble with the law. He had a regular guy's dream: to open a bar in Tempe, a suburb of Phoenix. His marketing idea was to make it a horror-themed destination, "The Haunted Castle." The neighbors on the street became concerned when they heard rumors that it might be called "Drunkensteins."

He needed a liquor license. While Havelock went through that process, some of the neighboring businesses quietly expressed their concern about his plans to city officials, and his dream to open a bar was stopped dead in its tracks.

This is where the story turns chilling. Havelock went out and purchased an AR-15 rifle for $800, totally legally. He went to the local shooting range to learn how to better use the weapon. He bought a sizeable amount of ammunition—250 rounds—but nothing that would arouse suspicion. Again, legally. The day before Super Bowl XLII, Havelock wrote a "manifesto" of sorts, containing a series of terrifying threats. He sent the letters by Priority Mail to a list of news outlets, including the Associated Press and *Los Angeles Times*, planning that they'd be read the day after the Super Bowl.

> "No one destroys my dream . . . I will not be bullied by the financial institutions and their puppet politicians . . . All this boils down to an econopolitical confrontation. I cannot outvote, outspend, outtax, or outincarcerate (sic) my enemies . . . but for a brief moment, I can outgun them . . . The Patriots versus the Giants . . . do you see an ironic parallel? How many dollars will

you lose? And all because you took my right to work, to own a business, from me . . ."

Havelock figured out something that the NFL Security Director, the FBI, and the Secret Service had known, but that I had not fully appreciated, and since has become all too apparent at venues and events around the world. The Super Bowl is a National Security Special Event, on the same level as the State of the Union address or the presidential inauguration. The reason for that is simple. More people—lots more people—watch the Super Bowl than watch the State of the Union or a presidential inauguration. That is what makes the game, and the stadium where it's played, what security experts call a target-rich environment.

With that in mind, we took security very seriously. We were concerned about someone bringing a weapon and explosive, or something equally dangerous, inside the building, and to prevent that, we installed airport-style security checkpoints all around the stadium. The Super Bowl had required more meticulous security since 2002, and all NFL stadiums use walk-through magnetometers (mags) today. Everyone walked through one.

Havelock, however, recognized that you don't have to get through the security checkpoints to wreak havoc. By encouraging crowds to queue *outside* the security checkpoints prior to screening, we had inadvertently created a target-rich environment. It would take a very resourceful evil doer to breech these measures and enter the stadium with a weapon, but because we had inadvertently created a crowd-concentrated environment outside the checkpoint, Havelock put himself in a position to hurt a great many innocent people without having to get through a single security check. A suicide bomber at the exit from a pop concert in Manchester, England, in 2017, sadly, employed the same strategy.

On Super Bowl Sunday, an hour before game time, Havelock parked his car in a nearby lot, grabbed a duffle bag, and made his way toward the University of Phoenix Stadium in Glendale. He walked up a little hill, which gave him a perfect view of several security checkpoints and the people funneling toward them. He had a loaded rifle, hundreds of rounds of ammunition, and a clear vantage point outside the most widely watched single-day sporting event in the world.

Our nightmare was unfolding, even though we didn't know it was happening, but on that day, we got lucky. Instead of picking up his gun, Havelock picked up his cell phone and called his girlfriend. She convinced him to return home. His family ultimately talked him into turning himself in at the local police station.

Ironically, the local police couldn't find anything to charge Havelock with, given that he had bought his gun and ammunition legally and he didn't actually fire the weapon. He was convicted on six counts of mailing threatening letters and sentenced to a year and a day in prison. After Havelock served his sentence, the U.S. Circuit Court of Appeals ruled 9–2 to overturn his convictions. The judges reasoned that Havelock's manifestos weren't mailed to people but to corporations and were delivered *after* the Super Bowl. His menacing language didn't constitute a threat, in their opinion, but were planned as posthumous explanations of actions he never took.

Since Havelock wasn't detected or intercepted on the day of the event, I didn't even hear about the incident until the following day. It's no secret that among the many security measures on game day, teams of concealed snipers are positioned at key points around the stadium. I never before wanted the details and never asked, but I knew that they were there. The next day, I quizzed Bob Hast, a former FBI agent who was then our director of event security about what would have happened if Havelock picked up the gun and started firing.

He would have been dealt with, Bob assured me matter-of-factly. "But not before he took out about 30 people." That would have been 30 people approaching a security checkpoint that we had installed the week before to protect them. The unintended consequence of installing necessary security checkpoints is the concentration of crowds waiting to be screened. The act of making the stadium more secure simply moved the area most vulnerable further away. To make that area more safe, other measures are required, like more robust surveillance.

ANTICIPATE THE RIPPLES

The good news is that most of the time, our decisions don't have life or death implications and you won't have to rely on a madman's pang of conscience or an anxious girlfriend's appeals to avert a disaster. But there are practical lessons from this chilling tale. Don't get so focused on solving the problem right in front of you that you lose sight of how potential solutions can affect the big picture. We all love it when we can solve a problem cleanly and completely. Unfortunately, that doesn't happen as often as we hope.

Over the last 30 years of managing big events, I've seen that when you think you're solving a problem you're often just moving the problem elsewhere. It might be, as in the Havelock case, shifting the problem from one place to another. At other times, it might be shifting it in time—kicking "the proverbial can" down the road. Does your proposed solution shift the responsibility from one person to another? That doesn't really make the problem go away and probably won't even take the problem off your shoulders entirely.

Your solution might seem relatively simple, but it could well affect a complex system. Anticipate the ripple effects. Doing that literally saved the Super Bowl during its darkest moment. Before the Baltimore Ravens and the San Francisco 49ers ever knew they would be playing against each other at Super Bowl XLVII at the New Orleans Superdome, the local energy utility recognized that power service into the stadium was less reliable than it had been 11 years before. It was the first Super Bowl in the city since Hurricane Katrina, and nothing stresses a power supply more than a Super Bowl. With that in mind, the energy utility upgraded the two main power cables serving the Superdome, ensuring that any degradation sustained during the hurricane would be thoroughly addressed. In the process of doing so, the energy utility also installed state-of-the-art relays. It was one of these relays, sensing a power surge after the half-time show, which acted like a giant circuit breaker and triggered a blackout. To the computer brain of these relays, the unusual pattern of power demands of the Super Bowl seemed like a malfunction.

As a later investigation determined, the relays were adjustable. Like many devices you might buy for yourself or your home, they were delivered and installed with the default factory setting. For the two months prior to Super Bowl XLVII, they worked perfectly and kept the lights on. On Super Bowl Sunday, as we will explore in more detail later, they also worked perfectly, shutting off the lights and almost ending the game.

The best time to think through whether decisions you make will generate unintended consequences, of course, is during the planning stage. If you have the time and resources to test new systems and processes early on, that's when to do it.

The Olympics, for example, conducts full-on test events to make sure every venue, every piece of equipment, every traffic and crowd flow strategy, is sound and all systems perform well. It gives the organizers the chance to make the adjustments in order to mitigate any nasty side effects that may present themselves before the main events take place. It's the event world's answer to beta testing a product.

If we had done that for the new power infrastructure at the New Orleans Superdome before the Super Bowl, we would have had a better chance of finishing the game 34 minutes earlier. Less than a year later, we did just that. We put the electrical system at the entire Meadowlands Sports Complex through exhaustive and expensive testing simulations for Super Bowl XLVIII in East Rutherford, New Jersey.

New Jersey, however, was the place where things went wrong in real-time because of our insistence on pushing fans to use the train. Notwithstanding the changes made to the rail service on Super Bowl Sunday, we couldn't test for the possibility that way more people would heed our advice than we thought. However, we could have planned for the possibility. Instead, we had considered only the opposite—that fewer people than normal would take the train. That we had a plan for.

How could we have prevented the crowding and delays? We could have explored whether tickets to the game day train could be sold in advance. That might have helped educate us on what to expect ahead of time. We might have had a contingency to send trains to the stadium earlier, when passengers first started arriving. At the end of the game, we could have had buses waiting in the MetLife Stadium parking lot as an alternative to relieve pressure on the train. (Ultimately, buses were moved to the stadium to help ease the crowds, but that was only *after* the crowds had collected and the problem was already in full bloom.) We assumed that our challenge was getting fans to take the train. We were so preoccupied with solving that problem that we didn't adequately consider the other: the unintended consequence of an informational campaign that worked too well.

Unintended consequences are not necessarily a result of poor planning or insufficient information. Often, they arise as a product of good ideas and sound decision making. It is better, of course, to more fully consider the possible outcomes during the planning stage. But when something does go wrong in real time, try to resist the temptation to act too quickly, without regard to how your response may affect the outcome in other areas. That doesn't mean don't act fast. Just act fast enough to keep things from getting worse, but not so fast you end up making things worse. If you have to respond, remember to anticipate the interconnected consequences that can arise every time you make a decision. Do that consistently and you'll make Gary Bettman proud. Or, at least impress your own boss.

REAL-TIME MANAGEMENT

"Make the plan. Execute the plan." I heard and repeated that expression quite a lot after I joined the special events department at Radio City Music Hall. It sounds obvious and straightforward, but we didn't really believe it was of any prescriptive value even then. So our team added two more phrases to bring the motto closer to the truth as we experienced it: "Make the plan. Execute the plan. Change the plan. Execute the planner."

There is a time to put the pencil down and get down to the business of executing. We have imagined our ideal outcomes and metrics for success, and all the dastardly things that could get in the way of achieving them. We have merged the processes of imagination and planning to develop contingencies that will prepare us for many of the most probable and damaging things that could go wrong. We have put a team in place that we will lead, manage, and empower. Then, everything runs flawlessly, like clockwork, with smooth precision. Until it doesn't.

Almost every project plan will require midcourse corrections, tweaks, and changes that will yield the results we are striving for. We have a Plan B if we see that something is not working the way we had intended, and Plans C, D, and E for the circumstances we can foresee. Sometimes, a challenge emerges for which we don't have any predeveloped alternatives and must make decisions based on our assessments, experience, and expertise. NFL coaches and quarterbacks refer to this as "calling an audible."

CALLING AUDIBLES

On the football field, *audibles* are not a fix for something that has already gone wrong. The ball hasn't been snapped and nothing bad has happened quite yet. But the quarterback sees the opposing defense set in an unexpected formation, which is a very strong indication that the play that was planned will probably not work or may result in a very negative outcome.

Few players were better at calling audibles than retired quarterback Peyton Manning, who played for the Indianapolis Colts and the Denver Broncos. In the huddle, Manning relayed to his teammates what play they were expected to execute and how they were going to advance the ball. As his offensive squad took their positions, and with the pressure of the play clock ticking down, Manning surveyed the opposing team's defense. If the position of the linebackers suggested a blitz or a formation that was likely to defeat the play he shared in the huddle, he shouted the word "O-MA-HA" to indicate a quick shift to Plan B. The entire process, from the time the previous play ended until the last possible moment the center snapped the ball for the next play, took less than 40 seconds. For the quarterback, that's 40 seconds to dust yourself off, huddle up, communicate the next play, set your formation, read the defense, change the plan, communicate the new play, and snap the ball.

In these cases, the plays that Peyton Manning's coaches planned were not as important as what Manning called at the line of scrimmage. No one cares about the plan if it is no longer appropriate to the circumstances. What we care about are the results. So what you had planned is not as important as what you actually do when it looks like a blitz is coming your way.

SHARE THE PLAN

After the players break from the huddle, everyone knows their role, position, and route, and knows what to do if the quarterback calls an audible. Not every player is expected to run or catch the ball, but every one of them knows what they are expected to do when play begins.

Managing your own team is no different. It is important that all teammates know their role, position, and the route. If you need to call an audible, they will need to know not only the overall game plan, but also your Plan B, what might precipitate a change, and how that change might affect their areas of responsibility. The Super Bowl, as a complex project composed of myriad details, never went strictly to plan. Audibles helped to keep things nudging in the right direction, when required.

INFORMATION IS POWER.
SHARING INFORMATION IS INSURANCE.

In 2017, the Pentagon's Special Inspector General determined that the United States Army wasted as much as $30 million on camouflaged uniforms for Afghan soldiers. The pattern selected by the country's defense minister was a design ideal for concealing soldiers in a wooded environment, but only about 2 percent of the sparsely populated country is forested. Rather than concealing the soldiers, the proprietary motif of dark brown-and-green splotches made them fashionably conspicuous targets.

The reason the Army agreed to pay a premium for a proprietary camouflage pattern was to keep the enemy from copying it and then blending in with the troops which, at face value, does make some sense. I imagine, however, that the Army has camouflage experts who might have flagged that the design was inappropriate for the environment. Yet, somehow this expensively deadly solution was approved, ordered, and . . . yes . . . worn in active service.

To be honest, I'm not sure you have to be an expert to know that a leafy green-and-woody brown concealment pattern does not work very well in a place that does not have a lot of either color. But, for now, let's assume that either the right people with the right skills asking the right questions were *not* part of the decision-making process, that there was little collaboration or communication on how and why that decision was made, or perhaps, worst of all, that no one was paying very close attention.

Anyone who has ever worked in a company with more than one employee knows that these kinds of outcomes are often the result of people working in *silos*. It's natural. People have lots to do within their defined scope of responsibility, and it is often faster and easier to make decisions in a vacuum than to get the insights or opinions of either people who are subject experts, or those who might be affected by the outcome.

The Super Bowl is no different. Try as we might, there is no way to eliminate the tendency for teammates to plan and manage within their own areas of responsibility without collaborating, gathering viewpoints, or sharing information. It is simply quicker not to. In a siloed environment, errors go undetected because information is not shared, and mistakes are made because changes aren't circulated. It is essential that we combat this very human predisposition by establishing a consistent and dependable forum for socializing, adjusting, and changing plans to suit emerging information and new realities. Socializing is an active, iterative, and participatory process; it is not simply a presenter sharing with a listener.

We gathered 300 Super Bowl managers and contractors four times each year for exhaustive briefings on all areas of the execution plan. At the first briefing, held in April, each area presented their preliminary plan for the next event; this provided everyone in attendance with the opportunity to identify flaws and omissions, and correct faulty assumptions. It was everyone's responsibility to use the next 90 days to resolve the conflicts in the plan, correct erroneous information, and revise their strategies.

The group reconvened in June, at which time we repeated the cycle of review and critique. By the time we reached our December "all hands" meeting, we were all acting on the plans that were considered final. Until the plans changed again. The truth is, making changes to the plans never truly stopped, even after that final meeting. During execution, we conscientiously monitored progress—looking for delays, flaws, and mistakes—and informed the team when we needed to call the audibles required to keep us on track.

We, as leaders, must model our expectation that teammates share changes and new information. Get them out of their silos often enough to share their plans, share their problems, and collaborate on solutions. Most importantly, when they or you need to call an audible, the word must get out quickly to every teammate who may be affected, or who can contribute to the solution. O-MA-HA!

THE CALM OUTSIDE. THE STORM WITHIN.

I recognize that everyone has a different management style, and you have probably worked with them all. Some leaders manage with the force of their personality, while others manage through the volume of their voice. Some managers want to be considered the smartest person in the room and some managers truly already are. There are probably as many nuanced management styles as there are managers.

I'm generally thought of as a calm, confident person, someone who keeps Skippy hidden away as deliberately as Norman Bates from the movie *Psycho* hides his mommy issues. To be totally honest, though, I am not that calm on the inside, even when things are going right. No one sees that, either. What has helped me, however, is that I'm not that much different when things are going wrong.

Notwithstanding more than three decades of leading event project teams, I still don't eat much on the days leading up to an event. I used to grade the difficulty of events I worked on by how many pounds I lost during the month before. Relatively simple projects were usually "two-pounders." Tougher projects were "four-pounders" or "five-pounders," and I'm proud to say I survived a couple of "eight-pounders." That said, it is important to state that working on events is not a medically sound or safe weight-loss strategy.

During the planning process, throughout the execution process, and even more so when we have to respond to things that have truly gone wrong, your team will be looking to their leaders and managers for sound direction, clear communication, encouragement, and support. The concept of modeling the behaviors we want in our teammates is never more appropriate than while we are busily executing our own projects, because in the execution of their own jobs, teammates are more likely to behave the way their leaders do. If their leaders are outwardly anxious, nervous, irritable, and loud, teammates will tend to be so also. As for me, I'll let my calm outward demeanor belie any internal turmoil, especially when things are going just fine. You should, too. I have learned that if you are in a position of leadership and you are showing how nervous you are, you must stop it and get over yourself. Because it's not about you.

TAKE CARE OF YOURSELF

"If there is a loss of cabin pressure, an oxygen mask will automatically drop from the compartment over your head. To start the flow of oxygen, pull the mask towards you. Place it firmly over your nose and mouth, pull the elastic bands to tighten, and breathe normally. If you are traveling with a child or someone who requires assistance, secure your own mask first, then assist the other person." Over all the years and all the commercial flights during which this announcement has been made, it's remarkable that it has never sparked outrage from parents who find it morally repulsive to suggest that they should take care of themselves while their helpless progeny negotiate the thinning atmosphere of a leaky, oversized toothpaste tube.

I would say: "Hey, let me try that on and make sure I know how to use it before I actually have need of it. Oh, and by the way, let me try one on my kid, too. Since the bag will also not inflate if oxygen *isn't* flowing, can we test that out? And, let me try on that life jacket to make sure I can put it on securely before water comes through the windows."

I'm an event planner and I'm reticent about doing anything without a rehearsal, but what the airplane safety announcement says is very smart. It may seem counterintuitive, but you are a much better parent if you do put on your oxygen mask first. If you struggle trying to get your child's mask on without having the oxygen flowing for yourself, you might just pass out in the process. Then, you are no good to anyone, and your kid still doesn't have an oxygen mask.

It's our responsibility to get the job done right, and to be able to respond when things go wrong. So, by extension, we have to put on our own oxygen masks and make sure everyone else does, too. How does that work for someone whose nerves are overactive and whose stomach is churning beneath a calm exterior? I keep some trail mix in my desk and throw a selection of nutrition bars into my backpack in case I can't find the time to force myself to eat. During the weeks leading up to the Super Bowl, our medical team kept an eye on us— as well as on the fans and teams—to make sure that we all stayed hydrated and healthy.

Take care of yourself so you can take care of your team and your project. That includes getting enough rest ourselves, both mentally and physically. Our body's requirement for sleep becomes painfully obvious when we spend too many hours sacrificing rest for the sake of answering a few more late-night e-mails from bed.

Less obvious is our need for intermittent breaks during our work days. Psychologists have determined that a step outside for a cup of coffee, a walk around the block, or even just a brief saunter down the hall for a change of environment can provide the quick mental break that can boost our overall productivity, creativity, and stamina. Periodically stepping away from our computers and e-mails improves our ability to focus on problem-solving, and, as counterintuitive as it sounds, enables us to accomplish more overall.

TAKE CARE OF YOUR TEAM

The radio traffic on our walkie-talkies was constant, and it seemed like almost every call for information, assistance, or direction was coming my way. I was Radio City Music Hall's director of talent for the May 1986 finale gala of the Coca-Cola Centennial in Atlanta, an intimate party for 14,000 guests at the Georgia World Congress Center. With 700 musicians performing on a dozen different stages, I had my hands full. It was an extremely long day rehearsing every group, every stage cue, and calling audibles despite the months of planning. In short, it was an "eight-pounder."

Late in the afternoon, as rehearsals began to wind down, my head suddenly felt lighter. It wasn't because I was passing out. My boss, Mike Walker, had lifted the radio headset from my ears.

"Go get something to eat," he said.

"But, we're not done yet," I protested.

"Go across the street, take a break, and get something to eat," he repeated evenly. "They'll figure it out while you're gone," he said.

Mike took the walkie-talkie off my belt. Mike was a pretty calm and very smart person. He must have seen that I was about to hit the wall, and there was a very long night still ahead. "Frank is going off headset for 30 minutes," he announced to everyone and no one in particular.

I have never enjoyed a Chick-fil-A combo meal as much as I did that one. I sat in the food court across the street from the convention center and felt the energy returning that I didn't know had left. Mike sensed that I was running low on fuel and was in danger of running out of gas at a more critical time. Soon, I was ready to get back to work and finish strong. Had he not stepped in when he did, I am not sure that I would have been able to finish at all.

Our teams also need rest, nourishment, and hydration. As leaders, we can try to keep their stress levels as manageable as possible, at least by not adding more. Be watchful and make sure they have quick access to water and food if they are unable to walk away for more than a momentary break at their busiest and most stressful moments. Program breaks and a place to take them into the schedule. An engine out of gas will simply stop running.

BUILD BENCH STRENGTH

"I'm in a really tough spot," he admitted. "We made some investments over the past year and we're out of cash. We don't have the money to fly our team to the planning meeting. I am not even sure we can continue operating."

Here we were, just a few months before the Super Bowl, and the company that we had contracted for our fleet of buses and limousines for years was in such dire straits that they could not even purchase airline tickets. We had to make a change quickly and, at least to our guests, seamlessly. Luckily, one of the companies that had been working as one of their subcontractors was able to pick up more of the responsibilities for transportation and parking. The subcontractor company was able to do this magnificently well because they were already a small part of the team, and they did not have to start from scratch. More importantly, we did not have to waste time vetting an entirely new vendor while the calendar inexorably advanced toward game day.

Sports teams dress more players for every game—pinch hitters, relief pitchers, second and third quarterbacks, and back-up goaltenders—than the coach will need or intends to use. If one of the team's players is sick, injured, or is just not playing up to expectations, the coach takes someone else off the bench to replace him. They don't stop the game and go searching for a player when they first realize they have a problem. They have players who know the playbook and are ready to get into the action. That's *bench strength*, and we had that in our transportation area. From that point, I told our managers, it is important for other key areas to develop bench strength as well. We got lucky the one time that we had it in place when we suddenly needed it. Hoping it wouldn't happen again is not an acceptable strategy.

Building bench strength, that is, having a Plan B and an extra layer of resources at the ready to implement it, is also a good practice when developing your team. Challenge every leader to designate and empower a second-in-command, someone who can step in when or if the leader is unable or unavailable to make decisions, take action, or receive information. Share this expectation early so all direct reports can start grooming a "number two" if they don't already have one.

KEEP IT SIMPLE

There is a reason that telephone numbers in the United States are arranged in groups of three and four digits. That's because most people can easily remember strings of three or four numbers and chunks of three or four things in sequence. If you are among the memory experts who can recite the value of *pi* to thousands of digits, more power to you. As for me, if I have to focus on more than three or four important things, I better have them written down and handy.

Remember that your teammates, as exceptional as they are, have a limit to the messages and details that they can retain. They have their own priorities to keep track of, so reduce complicated information to concise easy-to-digest chunks. That doesn't mean being short on detail. Rather you should articulate the one or two details most essential to retain.

Our final meeting the day before the game focused on only one thing: what to do if something went so catastrophically wrong that the stadium had to be vacated. Evacuating tens of thousands of fans and teammates would not be a simple process. What was important, we told them, was to listen for what they should do if pandemonium ensued. We added just one more important thing to remember: "Where do I go if the worst happens?" Honestly, if you remembered only one thing, wouldn't you want that to be it?

CLARITY AND PRECISION

I met Klaus at the Olympiahalle, an indoor sports venue in Innsbruck, Austria, the day before the NHL's 1998 preseason game between the Buffalo Sabres and the Tampa Bay Lightning. Although the players were from all over Europe and North America, they were used to playing in NHL arenas where English, and often French, were the familiar languages. I, therefore, asked the Austrian promoter to arrange for a bilingual public address announcer who was knowledgeable about the sport. That's how Klaus and I came to work together.

"Announce in English, then in German, so the players understand the announcements first," I said.

"English? No," he protested. "I do German."

I was confused. Klaus was the bilingual announcer I had asked for. He may not have been entirely comfortable with English, but his English was far better than my German, and he clearly understood our conversation.

Klaus, it turns out, was quite familiar with the sport, and indeed, a very competent bilingual announcer. But, in the western state of Tyrol in the Austrian Alps, bilingual announcers speak German and Italian. I debuted the next day as an English-speaking hockey announcer. This responsibility was added to the job I already had managing the overall presentation of the game.

If you think this is an extreme example of being misunderstood because of language differences, you could be right. But, consider how often what we say is innocently misunderstood, misinterpreted, or miscommunicated between teammates and customers who speak the same language. This almost comical situation taught me the importance of being as clear as possible with directions, and more precise with my language. It's a skill I know I will spend a lifetime trying to refine. This experience helped:

- To sensitize me to the importance of being deliberate and thoughtful in communicating
- To make sure I totally understand the information I receive
- To make sure that my teammates fully comprehend plans and instructions that I am trying to articulate. The best way to find out is to ask them if they do.

TWO-MINUTE DRILL

The most intense moments of a football game often unfold during the last two minutes. It is do-or-die time for the team that is behind, as they attempt to move the ball steadily toward the end zone without wasting a single precious second. The *two-minute drill* is a strategic, rapid-fire succession of techniques proven to work best when the pressure is at its highest, like these effective time-preserving execution strategies that I use to keep things going right while managing my projects.

STAY NIMBLE

"What do you actually do on game day?" asked Allen St. John, *The New York Times* best-selling author. I had to think about that, but the question shouldn't have surprised me. He had already spent a year observing and interviewing members of the behind-the-scenes army responsible for overseeing some aspects of the game, broadcast, parties, and stadium for his book, *The Billion Dollar Game: Behind the Scenes of the Greatest Day in American Sport—Super Bowl Sunday.*

"Well," I told St. John, "I start the day pretty early in the morning, checking on final preparations around the stadium, the Fan Plaza, our hospitality venues, and the Tailgate Party." I continued describing my final quality control checks for the biggest event of the year, taking notes, sending texts and e-mails, and asking lots of questions. That's not really doing anything, I thought to myself. It's checking on what everyone else is doing. That must not sound all that important.

"Then," I continued, "I park my Segway and move up to NFL Control, where I can monitor everything that is going on at and around the stadium, downtown, and everywhere in between." I would be continually apprised of security issues, the admission count at the gates, crowd flow, traffic, and a host of other details. But monitoring is listening and not really affecting anything unless something needs to be addressed.

"I keep the staff apprised of the pregame time clock leading up to the most time-critical elements, like when the teams need to come out of the locker rooms, when they need to be lined up at the field tunnel, when the ball needs to be kicked off." I did a lot of the same things for the halftime show and postgame trophy ceremony.

"So, what does the general manager of the Super Bowl actually do?" St. John ultimately wrote. "On game day, at least, as little as possible."

St. John wasn't trying to be clever at my expense. Quite the opposite. What he revealed was the value of "management by doing nothing" in an environment in which dozens of things could be expected to go wrong among the millions of details that might go wrong. I was actually quite busy on every single game day, but I could never say with what ahead of time.

"In general," he quoted me as saying, "my job is to catch the passes as they come toward me. I try not to have a specific function at that point because my hands are tied to whatever the issues are, and my job is to deal with those issues as they come up, and they come up pretty fast."

If you are leading a project and are saddled with a great number of operational responsibilities, your ability to evaluate or detect developing challenges, make informed and timely decisions, and communicate desired actions can be significantly impacted. The play clock will always be ticking. Trying to balance too many critical operational priorities can seriously delay your response or force decisions without sufficient focus or time to think through the options or consider "the law of unintended consequences." On Super Bowl Sunday, I had just two inviolate responsibilities:

1. Ensure the ball was kicked off at 6:28:30 p.m.
2. Avoid any halftime show-generated delay to the second half.

Besides those two important mandates, I was open and prepared to handle any of those passes when I saw them coming toward me.

PRACTICE PRIORITIZED DECISIVENESS

Often, there wasn't just one pass in the air. There were many of them coming all at once; this was another reason why it was so important to be relatively free of having too many direct operational responsibilities. This was true not only on game day, but every day for weeks leading up to the event. Although it was important to make decisions quickly to ensure issues did not pile up to an unmanageable number, it was also essential to make decisions that were both informed and definitive. That meant differentiating between the relative importance of making the fastest decision versus making the best decision.

Super Bowl XLI, on February 4, 2007, between the Indianapolis Colts and the Chicago Bears, was the soggiest Super Bowl Sunday on record. A call came in to NFL Control that we had a problem at one of the gates at Dolphin Stadium in Miami. The tickets for a group of 125 very upset foreign fans were rejected by the barcode scanners as having been used earlier that day. According to their English-speaking leader, the group had had their tickets scanned to enter the stadium two hours before, and after deciding not to dine on overpriced hot dogs in the rain, had gotten back on their buses to enjoy a drier lunch in a nearby restaurant. Most of them were not conversant in English, the leader explained, so they did not understand or did not take notice of the large "No Readmission" signs. It was still more than an hour before kickoff, but members of the group were confused about being delayed, the rain from their clothes puddling on the checkpoint floor.

"Let them in?" asked the gate supervisor, who wisely elevated the issue to NFL Control.

"No," I replied. We can't just let in 125 people. "Have them wait just a bit."

I thought about the problem as I stickhandled through a few more issues, no doubt made more numerous by the lousy weather. Admitting dozens of people on rejected tickets was not something to do, especially at a National Security Special Event, until the story was checked out more thoroughly. I asked the chief of Security to inquire whether anyone on his team had observed what would have been very noticeable—more than a hundred people leaving through an exit at a time when no one should have been leaving. It took perhaps 10 minutes to get answers from all the checkpoints. No, no one had seen a large group depart the premises. I then asked the transportation director to find out if any buses had exited the bus parking lot over the past few hours. There would have been three or four of them. An answer came back a few minutes later. No buses had been seen leaving the bus lot. Bus parking permits were expensive, so it's possible that the bus dropped them off somewhere else, like at the shopping plaza a few blocks away, and then returned to pick them up for their unscheduled lunchtime road trip.

Problem solving is usually not *linear*, that is, managing one problem at a time before moving on to the next problem. A few other items of interest rose up to NFL Control as I wondered how we could verify whether the people had been dropped off at another location. In the meantime, another call came in from the gate. It had been 15 minutes since the group had been stopped, and they were reportedly getting testy. The gate supervisor was almost as exasperated. "These people are standing in the rain. Why aren't we helping them out?"

Pissing off fans who could have traveled a great distance to experience one of the world's great sporting events was abhorrent to me. But, I also recognized the profound security implications of making a quick decision just to put it behind us. We needed to be completely sure that their story checked out before waving them through. Deciding to let the group in would have been final. Finding them again in a crowd of 74,000 might prove impossible if we later determined we had made a mistake.

"Apologize again for the inconvenience," I told the gate supervisor. "Gather up five random tickets from the group and bring them up to NFL Control." We needed to make sure the tickets, printed with both obvious and undisclosed anti-counterfeit features, were authentic. Ten minutes later, it was my turn to call the gate supervisor.

"Waiting on the tickets. Are they on their way up?" I asked.

"No. They all left." The "tourists" had vanished before relinquishing their tickets and did not materialize anywhere else to try to make their way into the stadium. We never saw them again and when the game began, there was no block of 125 empty seats in the stands.

"Was this a remarkably well-planned and well-executed scheme to sneak into the Super Bowl, one that depended on the flurry of game-day activity—as well as the sheer scope and audacity of the plan—to overwhelm the NFL's checks and balances?" St. John wondered in his book, *The Billion Dollar Game*. Probably, but to this day, I don't honestly know for sure. What I do know is that a fast decision could have had a cascading effect on other things that could have gone wrong, possibly very wrong.

"How do you make 125 wet, complaining foreign tourists disappear from the stadium on Super Bowl Sunday?" St. John mused. "You just ask for their tickets," he concluded.

TRUST YOUR GUT

For just a fleeting moment, I thought I had arrived. "Sir Richard Branson is on the phone," said Joan. Talking to the founder of the Virgin Group would be very cool. But I quickly reminded myself that I was not on speed dial for many billionaires beyond those who owned NFL teams.

"Is it Sir Richard Branson or his assistant?"

"It's him."

I got over myself in a hurry. "No. No, it isn't."

I didn't really know for certain, but I picked up the phone and a very polite gentleman with a very proper British accent introduced himself. His girlfriend was in Miami, he told me, and he wanted to purchase four hard-to-come-by Super Bowl tickets for her and three friends. She would be able to stop by our office and pick them up and price was no object. It occurred to me that someone as influential as the world-renowned founder of the Virgin Group would have been able to call the Commissioner or any one of the team owners with whom he might have even dined or golfed. He would certainly have known their names before mine. Nevertheless, I had to be diplomatic, just in case.

"I'm sure you can appreciate that you don't know me, and I don't know you." I asked him if there was a way that he could verify he was who he said he was. Of course, he replied, and he launched into a list of personal achievements, passions, and possessions that would authenticate his identity. He was probably reading from the same website that I had already opened on my laptop.

"Fax me over something on your letterhead," I told him, "with your address and phone number." We still used fax machines back then. He promised me he would, expressed his thanks, and finished the call. You can guess whether I ever received it.

Ten minutes later our director in charge of premium ticket packages burst into the office. "You'll never guess who I just got a phone call from. Sir Richard Branson!"

"No, you didn't," Joan and I said in unison.

Would something have gone horribly wrong if I had sold Super Bowl tickets to faux Branson's girlfriend? Probably not, other than opening myself up for more requests from fake celebrities.

What the story does illustrate, however, is the value of trusting your gut instincts. Call them intuitions, or red flags, alarm bells, or "spider sense," if you'd prefer, but *don't* discount them. Psychologists believe that *gut instincts* are subconscious connections between what we are experiencing now and what we have learned from past, similar encounters. Sometimes, those connections don't surface up to our consciousness right away, which is why we seem to have epiphanies after "sleeping on things" or while in the shower. In the heat of the moment, we don't have time to wait for those memories to reestablish themselves. So when we make decisions based on our gut and things go right because we did, it creates a positive feedback loop that encourages us to trust that feeling more often in the future.

Yes, there really is a scientific reason why we trust our gut instincts more often as we advance in age, expertise, and experience. There was something about faux Branson's call that just didn't seem right, and probably because I had been conned a hundred times before, I could sense the fraudulence as it unfolded. I knew that busy Type A executives don't make calls to people they don't know personally. They let their assistants handle the calls. They don't want to waste time leaving a message or waiting for the other party to come to the phone. Are our gut instincts infallible? No, of course not, and they don't take the place of informed decision making. But, I will trust mine more often that I won't.

STAY AWARE OF THE OUTSIDE WORLD

The rally at the State Capitol was the largest of the week. Union supporters were out in force, protesting the legislature's bill that would make Indiana a "right-to-work" state. There had been rumblings all week of a potential truck blockade of Interstate 70, cutting off vehicular access to Lucas Oil Stadium—where Super Bowl XLVI would be held on February 5, 2012—and the entire downtown area. We were watching the developments all week long from our headquarters hotel just across the street.

On the other side of the hotel, the NFL's annual Super Bowl Kids Day program was getting ready to wrap up at the Indiana Convention Center. NFL Experience, the league's massive interactive football festival, was opened that morning to local students with their classes. At the end of the session, a special guest performer entertained, and speakers including Indianapolis Colts players, the team owner, and the NFL Commissioner shared inspirational remarks before sending the kids home with a bag of goodies and lifetime memories.

Indianapolis had dramatically changed how cities supported the Super Bowl. The host committee's "Super Bowl Village" filled the downtown streets with football-themed activities that guided multitudes of fans into the NFL Experience, welcomed hundreds of the reporters at the adjoining Super Bowl Media Center, and treated everyone to free nightly concerts and fireworks after the NFL events had ended for the day. The toughest ticket in town was the Super Bowl Village zip line that allowed fans to glide high above the excited crowds and right past the entrance to the NFL Experience.

I had passed along the committee's invitation to the commissioner to experience and be photographed on the zip line, and we had agreed on having him soar over the crowd at the end of the Kids Day event. In the interim, the protest was heating to a boil. The legislature had approved sending the bill to Governor Mitch Daniels for signature on that very day—and at that exact time. The protestors erupted, loudly chanting "See you at the Super Bowl!" but they didn't wait until Sunday to start mobilizing. The demonstrators began marching from the State Capitol to Super Bowl Village, just a few short blocks away. My phone rang as soon as the march began, and not long after, I chatted with the commissioner. We agreed that it was not a propitious time to be seen zip lining over a crowd filled with protestors. The march reached Super Bowl Village as Kids Day wrapped up just inside, and the protestors peacefully exercised their first amendment rights before dispersing into the crowd.

Passage of state legislation is generally not an NFL, football, or sports issue. It was, however, a development that required some sensitivity on our part as well as some quick, responsive contingency planning for the truck blockade that, gratefully, never materialized. It is very easy to get so caught up in the intense details of our own urgent, time-sensitive projects that it completely consumes our attention around the clock. It is essential, however, to keep our antennae up for outside factors that can rapidly impact our plans—such as breaking news, political developments, and natural disasters, to name a few. Any one of these can instigate shifts in public sentiment and receptivity, swamp the environment with noise that can overtake our messages, or change a carefully crafted, cutting-edge campaign into an exercise in questionable taste and appropriateness.

STAY FOCUSED

Staying focused and on-task is not easy, not for us as leaders, and not for our teammates in the field. There are many reasons we get distracted, ranging from boredom and exhaustion to excitement and overstimulation. Dr. David Rock, Director of the NeuroLeadership Institute in New York City, explored the metabolic and mental processes behind distraction in a *Psychology Today* article discussing his fascinating book *Your Brain at Work*.

Dr. Rock cited that: "Employees spend an average of 11 minutes on a project before being distracted. After an interruption it takes them 25 minutes to return to the original task, if they do at all. People switch activities every three minutes, either making a call, speaking with someone in their cubicle, or working on a document." It seems that being distracted is more "normal" than staying focused.

Our mobile devices—the essential tools of communication and miracles of technology as they may be—can divert our attention in ways previously unimagined. We can be reached instantly by anyone just about anywhere, make contact with anyone else just as easily, and be tempted to post our latest experiences, opinions, whims, and wonders to our ravenous followers on Twitter, Instagram, Facebook, and Snapchat. I've been known to tweet before and after an event, but after an infamous string of tweets posted between 8:53 p.m. and 9:04 p.m. Pacific Time on February 26, 2017, I'm less likely to post anything during an event ever again. That's when a PriceWaterhouse-Coopers accountant apparently uploaded photos of Emma Stone, congratulating her for winning an Oscar as the year's Best Actress. During the same time frame, he handed Warren Beatty and Faye Dunaway the wrong envelope for Best Picture.

Maintaining our focus for more than 11 minutes is a difficult proposition. When possible, give yourself and others "brain breaks" to defer distractions and refreshment breaks to maintain your blood-sugar levels. Set and communicate clear ground rules on mobile device usage for non-mission-critical activities. It's natural to be distracted, but it's not okay when intense focus is required. That's when things go wrong the most.

YOUR MIC IS ALWAYS ON

"Kids eat free on Tuesdays at Ruby Tuesday." Nobody said anything afterwards, but I know everybody heard it. Maybe fans thought it was an advertisement and took little notice, but the real reason it echoed through the cavernous expanse of Radio City Music Hall during the NFL Draft was because the public address announcer had not shut off his microphone after revealing a late-round pick. Staying focused for 14 hours of the NFL Draft is a nearly impossible task, and we clearly didn't accomplish that. We were bored and distracted by the endless hours of not much happening between the NFL Draft selections. So we passed some of that time talking about subjects of no particular importance, like where we took our kids to eat.

Someone else's microphone captured 2012 presidential candidate Mitt Romney sharing a political perspective that might have ultimately cost him an election proving that nowadays, we don't have to have a real microphone in front of us to be captured saying or doing something we would rather not have shared. There are enough mobile devices in enough hands to do that for us. An inadvisable text or e-mail sent in frustration with a single, unassuming "forward" click to just one person can inadvertently undo months of planning, team-building, and brand cultivation.

If you don't want to read what you said or wrote in the media someday, remember that your "mic" is always on, especially when something goes wrong. And, assume you are sending that e-mail directly to the *New York Times*.

ASSUME NOTHING, DOUBLE CHECK EVERYTHING

One last tip on managing project execution. Don't let something go wrong because you've assumed that everyone and everything is ready to go just because you are ready. We may have provided precise instructions, clearly communicated expectations, and distributed the documentation that everyone needs to get their jobs done. As launch time approaches, you too should assume nothing and double check everything.

Thanks to many painful experiences, I walk through every space to make sure it is staffed and ready to receive guests long before we open. I contact every direct report before we begin to ensure they can hear me and that I can hear them. I confirm with our talent team that every featured cast member has arrived well before their performance time approaches. I make certain that every stage manager is in their proper place. Having a preparatory double check checklist before pressing the start button on any project is a smart move to avoid making assumptions that everything is ready, and then find out that not everything is.

My projects usually require time-sensitive actions and responses. Broadcast and live event producers use "standby cues" to ensure their team is ready when something important is about to happen. Those standby cues warn our team members 30 to 60 seconds ahead of time to remain alert for the next instruction. We then count down from 10 seconds to the precise moment we will have them execute their task. Your project may not need such a high degree of time precision, and important cues may unfold over days instead of minutes. But, don't let something go wrong because you didn't ask, "Are you ready?"

Your project is now underway, and everything is going spectacularly well. Then, suddenly, it isn't. You will have to respond quickly, decisively, and effectively now that something has gone wrong. Are you ready?

STEP FOUR
RESPOND

CONFRONTING THE "OOPS–DAMN" MOMENTS

I f you were enjoying a peaceful amble along the Waikiki shoreline at 8:07 a.m., on Saturday, January 13, 2018, you might have noticed fellow strollers suddenly bolt off the beach to join a stream of frenzied pedestrians running anxiously along Kalakaua Avenue. Had you not left your mobile phone in your room, you would have received the emergency alert that shattered the calm stillness of that Hawaiian morning:

"BALLISTIC MISSILE THREAT INBOUND TO HAWAII. SEEK IMMEDIATE SHELTER. THIS IS NOT A DRILL."

Damn, you would have thought, what do I do now? Anyone who asked Siri to find the "location of the public missile shelter closest to me," would have found her answer disquieting: "I didn't find any matching places."

Hawaii's Emergency Management Authority estimates the time between an alert and an actual nuclear missile strike from North Korea to be between 12 and 15 minutes, not a lot of margin for error to find the best hiding spot. For future reference, take note of the nearest concrete building with a basement and make sure it has good phone service, because after 38 minutes of public pandemonium, a correction was finally sent:

"THERE IS NO MISSILE THREAT OR DANGER TO THE STATE OF HAWAII. REPEAT. FALSE ALARM."

"Oops," you would have thought, someone really messed up. A routine drill was, in fact, planned as an internal rehearsal for the Hawaii emergency operations center.

What exactly went wrong? According to the investigative report submitted by the state's director of Emergency Management, quite a number of things went wrong. But the factor that first started toppling the dominoes of disaster was *human error*. All missile drills, including this one, were preceded by a loudspeaker announcement in the emergency operations center: "Exercise! Exercise! Exercise!" Yet, for some inexplicable reason, one employee thought an actual missile attack was in progress and activated a "real-world alert." The investigative report later stated that the system in place made it exceedingly easy for one confused or careless individual to activate the statewide alert because the software's *drop-down menu* reportedly offered only two choices:

- Test missile alert
- Missile alert

If you're like me, a keyboard speedster who occasionally sends e-mails referencing something without including an important attachment, or you've ever hit "reply to all" to a companywide e-mail, you can understand how just one or two swift mouse clicks can cause just a little bit of trouble. That is not what happened, but you can understand how it also could have gone down that way.

When everybody's phones in the Emergency Operations Center (EOC) received the warning text, they knew immediately that something had gone very, very wrong. The morning quickly transitioned from drill to damage control. Within the same minute, the EOC immediately began notifying an alphabet soup of government agencies of the error. Within three minutes, the Honolulu Police Department was informed. Soon after, the warning text was canceled, but that only deactivated the alert for cell phones that were not yet powered on. It did not send "all clear" messages to phones that had already received the warning.

At 8:19 a.m., approximately 12 minutes after the erroneous alert, local news outlets and social media feeds began spreading the word that the alert was a mistake. This would have been about the moment that missiles, had they been launched, would have begun pulverizing paradise. In the intense flurry of activity in the EOC, it wasn't until 8:45 a.m., 26 minutes later, that the correction was sent to the cell phones of terrified tourists and residents.

THAT "DAMN" MOMENT

When we are confronted by something going wrong, it is generally of two varieties, and sometimes both simultaneously. There is the "damn" variety, which is something that impacts us from a source beyond our control, such as "Mother Nature," a system failure, or a human action unrelated to anything we did or were doing. The possibilities are endless in their range and scale: receiving a civil defense alert, interference from a right-to-work protest, searching for a missing anthem singer, falling victim to a cyberattack, structural failure, or a contractual "force majeure" clause. These are the literal embodiment of the term "stuff happens."

The recently reseeded turf was still struggling to take root. The wispy, light green blades of grass were still hopeful of standing up to the first onslaught of well-fed, sharp-cleated linemen and backs. Almost 1,400 members of the Super Bowl XXII halftime cast arrived at a damp Jack Murphy Stadium in their full-show costumes for the dress rehearsal. George Toma, the NFL's legendary "god of sod" and the man in charge of the field for every one of at least the first 50 Super Bowls, watched the long trail of 88 grand pianos arriving outside the field door on a soggy Friday evening, pulled in long trains by John Deere tractors. To preserve the still-immature grass, Toma made the only decision he could. He ordered that the rehearsal could only be set up once, on featureless black tarps, and the cast permitted on the field wearing only their socks. Suddenly, the concrete floor beneath the stands began accumulating mountains of identical, brand new, white Adidas sneakers. After a successful rehearsal, the entire flock of wet-footed cast members returned to scavenge through the randomly scattered piles of shoes for more than a half hour to find left and right sneakers in their sizes, amid excited shouts of "Anybody see a left men's nine-and-a-half?"

Most "damn" moments are not nearly that funny or as easily sorted out, for example, a blackout in New Orleans or a bogus missile alert. Although we may have had nothing to do with the root cause of the problem, it is still our responsibility to deal with it and our responsibility to manage, respond, and recover. If we had imagined scenarios with any similarity, we might have been able to activate a planned contingency. If we had not, we must still take control over the consequences by calling an audible, that is, adapt and set a new course of action.

THE "OOPS" MOMENT

Then, of course, there are the "oops" moments. Something goes wrong due to our own actions or because we failed to act when we should have. We, our teammates, or our company made an error, an omission, or failed to have a workable plan for something that we should have anticipated. Most careers are littered with "oops" moments that extend the term "stuff happens" to "stuff happens because we let it." The chief characteristic of an "oops" moment is that it could have, and probably should have, been avoided.

One such avoidable "oops" moment unfolded at the Closing Ceremonies of the U.S. Olympic Festival at the University of Oklahoma in July 1989. We had planned to salute more than 7,000 local volunteers who had contributed to the success of the competitions, marching them in as the evening's honored guests into the stadium to the sounds of tumultuous cheers. All volunteers—resplendent in their uniforms and meticulously organized into a long queue snaking across the adjoining soccer field—had some of their excitement dampened when the automatic timers on the lawn sprinklers suddenly activated, irrigating the turf and everyone standing on it. Had we visited the soccer pitch at the exact same time at any point during the previous weeks, we might have noticed that the field was watered at the same time every sweltering Oklahoma afternoon. That "oops" moment was definitely on me. This was an example of an "oops" moment for which there was a swift and simple solution: get away from the sprinklers.

Most "oops" moments don't escape notice as easily or innocuously. The Hawaii Emergency Management Authority's most infamous example started with an erroneously activated missile alert. Although the EMA team acted quickly to inform state and local agencies and media outlets that the alert was a mistake, direct communication with the public to correct the civil defense text notification seemed to take an inordinately long period of time. One contributing factor to the long delay was the agency's apparent ignorance that they were both capable and authorized to issue an all-clear alert right away. Instead, under the mistaken impression that only FEMA, the Federal Emergency Management Agency, could send the official notification, time was wasted waiting to get unnecessary clearance to correct the public misinformation. In the intervening 38 minutes, confusion continued to reign.

THE "OOPS–DAMN" DYNAMIC

Whenever a human contributes to something going wrong, there is an "oops-damn" dynamic, that is, a little bit of both at play simultaneously and not always in equal portions. The Hawaii EMA had precipitated the error and was in control of every step of the response ("oops"). For those outside the command center, the most important thing was to find shelter in response to an imaginary threat over which they had no control at all ("damn").

Our response to any incident should strive to avoid generating additional "oops" or "damn" moments that echo from our original actions. The Montreal ice storm, which struck on February 6, 1993, and held the Stanley Cup captive in a taxi cab before the NHL All-Star Game, was a "damn" shame over which we had no control. But the fact that we didn't plan to move the Stanley Cup to the arena earlier was clearly an "oops" moment. That we didn't change the plan once we knew about the ice storm was a bigger "oops" moment and ultimately, the Stanley Cup's late arrival and subsequent surrender to the gravitational pull of the Earth was the biggest "oops" moment of all. Although we couldn't prevent the ice storm or defy gravity, we could have prevented absolutely everything in between.

REDUCING AFTERSHOCKS

The term *aftershock* is most often associated with earthquakes. They are the subsequent tremors that are experienced after, and as a result of, the initial, larger quake. The characteristics of seismic aftershocks are strikingly similar to those encountered when something goes wrong and the response is either insufficiently or poorly managed. According to the U.S. Geological Survey, aftershocks can continue for weeks, months, or even years. So, too, can the ramifications of mismanaging an incident or crisis affect your company, brand, or project for an extended period. It is also not uncommon for an after-shock tremor to be stronger and more damaging than the first quake. A bungled response can magnify the effects of the original mistake and transform the incident into an even bigger disaster. In Hawaii, sending the erroneous alert was a terrifyingly bad mistake. What launched an investigation of even greater scrutiny was the 38-minute lapse in time between the initial alert and the all-clear alert.

The best way to reduce aftershocks, if not eliminate them com-pletely, is to activate a plan that is already in place to confront the first "oops" or "damn" moment. Following a decade as the CEO of "Just Say No" International, widely recognized for launching Amer-ica's youth empowerment and drug abuse prevention movement, Ivy Cohen launched Ivy Cohen Corporate Communications, a New York-based agency advising large and growing companies on reputa-tion management and crisis communications. Cohen notes that few crises are "textbook cases," and that most are characterized by a host of unknowns and unexpected elements.

Cohen would be the first to agree that time is never your friend when something goes wrong, and she advocates having a *crisis com-munications strategy* in place well before the first "oops" or "damn" moment to help reduce the time between the perception of a problem and the implementation of a well-fashioned response. She recom-mends these important initial steps when designing your plan:

"First, assess your existing resources. Take into account your nor-mal operational needs, and then consider the additional resources you may have to mobilize in order to support the range of responses you might have to quickly undertake," she suggests. Are they sufficient to allow other parts of the business to continue to operate without being entirely consumed when something goes wrong? Fill in the gaps where you believe your organization might be the most vulnerable when time and attention is being diverted to solving a problem.

"Next," Cohen advises, "formally identify which individuals will be responsible for communicating to the various audiences who will be affected." There will often be a division of responsibility between communications professionals and media-trained senior leaders who will be tasked to speak with the media, and those who are best applied to communicating with internal stakeholders, outside agencies, business partners, and customers.

The crisis communications plan is more than just a pipeline for framing messages and disseminating information. Your communications team can also be incredibly helpful in the overall response if they are leveraged as active and valued participants in the overall decision-making process.

Consider the impact of the original incident in April 2017 involving United Airlines and Dr. David Dao, as compared to the incremental damage from aftershocks stemming from blaming the victim. The company's response, both internally and externally, transformed the unnecessarily rough removal of a passenger from an overbooked flight from an extremely regrettable, but isolated, mistake into a brand statement that instead suggested an insensitivity to the welfare of the flying public. The immediate effect on United Airlines stock was a precipitous drop of 6.3 percent in premarket trading, a loss of $1.4 billion in market value. Although the stock recovered most of its value the following day, the reputational damage echoed beyond the expected lampooning by late-night talk show hosts. The following week, the *New York Times* reported on a survey that public perception of the United Airlines brand had been seriously affected. When respondents were asked to select from two flights to Chicago that were identical in price and schedule, only 21 percent selected United Airlines over American Airlines from among those who *had* heard about the incident involving Dr. Dao, versus nearly half, 49 percent, of those who *had not*.

PREPARING YOUR COMMS
BEFORE THE STORM

Developing your crisis communications strategies should be as integral a part of the project-planning process as the operational contingencies you put in place. Just as decision making will be immeasurably easier if you have a plan on what to *DO* when confronted with the most probable challenges, so too can the aftershocks be less damaging by focusing on what to *SAY*. For this reason, Ivy Cohen recommends that senior communications executives participate as active partners and advisors on any response team. She strongly suggests adding legal representation to provide a liability perspective to the communications team. Also, she recommends involving the human resources department to give guidance on sharing essential information with the teammates who are not directly participating in the response. We will return to these important notions in Chapter 22—Managing the Message.

The crisis communications plan should also focus on *HOW* to best deliver messages—through direct contact by phone, e-mail, text, releases, press conferences, interviews, social media platforms, on websites, or using other platforms. For the Super Bowl, we could communicate with fans already in the stadium through our public address announcer, but to be able to reach the fans before they even entered the building, we printed a text registration option on the face of the game ticket that read: "For exclusive information, text [number] or follow us at @[Twitter handle]."

We introduced this feature specifically to facilitate communication of important information in real time for the fans who opted in, such as schedule changes and delays, gate waiting times, traffic tie-ups, and parking space availability. It was also a great backup option for delivering messages in the stadium should there be an emergency, such as a power failure. But we were extremely judicious in using the database for promotional messages because we recognized that fans would quickly opt-out if they were bothered by a lot of extraneous marketing information.

Preparing the *HOW* for communicating during a crisis is absolutely essential for situations that are probable, developing, or particularly time-sensitive. "Communications—both media relations and public outreach—take on an entirely different level of urgency when you are dealing with emergency situations," says Cohen. "In fact, how you relay information to the media and the public may literally be a matter of life and death."

Cohen goes on to recall how in 2017, "Florida utilities preparing for Hurricane Irma used multiple channels, from social media to mobile phone alerts, to customer e-mails and radio advertising, to keep the public informed. By using predrafted messages for landfall predictions, they could swiftly relay information on power restoration efforts and safety tips to the public throughout all stages of the storm. The companies offered automated messages for those who had signed up for this service that advised customers to prepare to be without power, and what they needed to do to safeguard their family and property."

Knowing in advance how you will deliver communications related to severe weather and other emergencies is essential not only for utilities. Virtually every business and project can be seriously affected by any powerfully adverse condition. You may need to communicate with your team if the workplace sustains damage or if it is inadvisable to make the journey to the office. You will want to advise customers of potential or actual interruptions in service, availability, and operating hours, and inform business partners of changes that can, in turn, affect their businesses.

Establish the databases of opt-in communities that are most relevant to your business or project, and ensure that the platforms of communication that you intend to use are crisis-proof. "Secure backup generators or an independent power source to ensure your website will be operational during the emergency," says Cohen, "and take full advantage of social media to communicate with your various audiences."

ORGANIZING IN ADVANCE OF THE STORM

There are, of course, many time-sensitive situations, problems, and crises your business may face that have nothing at all to do with severe weather, but are also predictable or probable, and for which having a crisis communications plan in place is highly advisable. A labor dispute, accident, data breach, or infrastructure failure—any of these and more can have profound consequences on normal business operations. They can also have serious impacts on public perception of the company. Every message or utterance is subject to examination and reexamination by the public and the media and is open to later legal scrutiny and challenge. These are the most pertinent reasons to add communications and legal professionals to the core group tasked with guiding your company or project through stormy waters of threatening issues and emerging controversies.

The greater the severity of the challenge, the greater the need for a clear strategy that ensures not only a steady flow of information to the media and the marketplace, but also identifies *WHO* will deliver the messages to which audiences. "When I ask companies for their crisis communications plan, what they often hand me is their organization chart," says Cohen. Their assumption is that everyone is expected to perform the roles they fulfill every day when something goes wrong. But, as she points out, crisis communications plans deal with needs that are different from "everyday" operations. Consider your organization's operational needs during a crisis, be ready to reassign staff as required, and ensure you have sufficient trained internal and external resources at the ready to meet the increased levels of activity.

THE COMMS DURING THE STORM

"O.K., we've got to let people know. Do we have PA [public address system]? Do we have access to PA? Let's give people the PA" When the lights went out at Super Bowl XLVII in New Orleans, on February 3, 2013, we had no idea why, and neither did anyone else at the Mercedes-Benz Superdome. We had to ensure that while we sorted out the possible causes and course of action, the fans did not start to panic and flee the building. On one hand, we did not want to tell people to stay if they were in danger, but on the other hand, we did not want them to storm toward the exits if they were not imperiled.

We had to tell them something to keep them calm, and quickly. Without any information, their imaginations could quickly take them to places—mentally, emotionally, and physically—we did not want them to go. Panic is contagious. And, often, patient zero is us.

THE CRISIS WITHIN, THE CRISIS WITHOUT

know how you feel when something first goes wrong. None of us are Superman nor Wonder Woman. We are not indifferent to surprise nor impervious to stress. We may feel a little weak in the knees, we may start to perspire, and our digestive apparatus may feel like its about to release its contents in one direction or another. We may feel nervous, anxious, and maybe even a little panicky. That's all natural. What we are experiencing is imprinted in our *genetic code*. Our body is telling us what to do next, and that's to get out of the jam we're in.

Before I stumbled into a long career in event planning, I was a biology student at Queens College of the City University of New York. What I loved most about the subject, and still do, was exploring how animals behave in their natural environments, a branch of the science called *ethology*. There are physical, chemical, genetic, and learned reasons why crickets chirp at night, rabbits freeze in fear, and some birds sing with an accent. That's right, a Brooklyn house finch sings the same song in a dialect that is distinguishable from a Connecticut house finch. I learned that from Dr. Paul Mundinger during the year I worked as his lab assistant. Dr. Mundinger studied the evolution of bird song and brought recordings back to the lab of birds singing in trees and fields all over the northeast. I'm sure that this mild-mannered, middle-aged professor traipsing around forests, parks, and neighborhoods with a long cardioid microphone aimed toward high branches and rooftops inspired some amount of concern, or maybe even panic, in the humans witnessing his own natural behavior. The birds themselves didn't seem to mind because ethologists know how to move, or more importantly, stand stock still so their presence doesn't influence the natural behavior of their subjects. Unless what they want to do is to provoke a threat response.

In many animals, the continuum of possible responses to danger boils down to "fight or flight." The animal kingdom abounds with behaviors designed to "fight" or vanquish any threat to well-being, a food supply, or a chosen mate. Frilled Agama lizards flash an impressively large ring of throat flaps to make them appear bigger to potential predators. Highly antisocial Betta, also known as Siamese fighting fish, perceive nearly everything as a threat, and flare out their gill flaps when they see another Betta. If neither party backs off, there's a violent fight for dominance, often resulting in the death of one, the other, and sometimes both. You know other threat displays: gorillas beating their chests, moose locked in antler-to-antler combat, and a snake's ominous rattling sound. Lots of animals have innate "fight" responses to threats; some humans are among them.

At the other end of the spectrum is "flight." Dr. Mundinger's finches will take to the air if they sense anything out of the ordinary. Crickets hop about in random patterns when they sense the shadow of an enormous sneaker or rolled-up newspaper. A herd of ibex will suddenly stampede across the savannah when they see a leopard licking her chops. I'd like to tell you that our most common human "fight-or-flight" response is closest to the courageous gorilla, but I think most people's responses are closer to that of sea cucumbers, who literally vomit out their digestive tract, distracting the aggressor and treating them to a little snack while what is left of them squirts away. (They obviously don't eat again for a while, and you may not want to either.)

WHAT HAPPENS IN US WHEN SOMETHING GOES WRONG

When our brain first senses that something has gone wrong, it doesn't waste time evaluating options. It automatically stimulates an immediate release of *epinephrine*, more commonly known as *adrenaline*, from the glands perched atop our kidneys. This hormone, in turn, triggers a suite of involuntary responses across the body, designed to stimulate acts of self-preservation. Our heart rate increases, blood pressure rises, and circulation is diverted from our digestive organs to the muscles in our extremities, anticipating either a running escape or a fight for survival. More blood flows to our heart and the air passages in our lungs expand to accommodate the body's additional oxygen requirements in preparation for an imminent burst in physical activity. Our increased metabolism generates heat and we start to sweat to regulate our body temperature. Our eyelids retract and pupils dilate to increase the amount of light entering our eyes, supporting greater visual sensitivity so that we can clearly see what is coming our way.

All of this starts happening before we have a chance to consciously comprehend what is going on, perhaps in as short as a few milliseconds, and once the adrenaline has been released, it is not possible to jam it back into our adrenal glands. It keeps pumping into the bloodstream until our brain perceives that the threat has passed. Until then, if we haven't engaged in any of the intense physical activity that it was designed to stimulate, the adrenaline already in our system continues stimulating these autonomic responses until it slowly remetabolizes. That is why we may physically shake or fidget for a bit, even after things are back under control. Happily, the release of adrenaline also sharpens mental acuity and problem-solving processes. This helped our prehistoric ancestors evaluate the best options for survival, the best strategy to evade a predator, and the best escape route to safety. In the very short time our primitive forebears had to sort those things out, adrenaline had rapidly prepared their bodies for implementing immediate action.

There is no way we can avoid the initial jolt of adrenaline. The brain's instructions to our adrenal glands is hardwired into us through thousands of years of evolution, or by intelligent design, if you'd prefer. Either way, the system is designed to improve our chances of survival in nearly any situation, so accept it. It's what we decide to do after we process the nature of the challenge that's important. Today, most of us don't have to escape from larger, faster predators who wish to devour us outside of the office, but we still experience echoes of our existential instincts when circumstances threaten our health, jobs, finances, families, self-image, or any number of other concerns that are important to us. So, some amount of *anxiety*, the emotion triggered by these stressful concerns and stimulated by these physical changes, is normal when something goes wrong.

DON'T PANIC

Panic, on the other hand, is a more highly disruptive phenomenon; it is a condition that can trigger extreme, irrational behavior, and magnified physical discomforts from heart palpitations and hyperventilation, to light-headedness and nausea, to sensations approximating a heart attack. In an evolutionary sense, panic is a distinct disadvantage. The mentally and physically debilitating effects of panic would not have helped anyone escaping from dangerous circumstances. Neither do the effects of panic help us evaluate, manage, and respond to an incident or crisis.

In 2013, shortly after Jacoby Jones of the Baltimore Ravens opened the second half of Super Bowl XLVII with a record-breaking 108-yard touchdown, one-half of the Mercedes-Benz Superdome, including our command center, was plunged into darkness. My brain immediately ordered a mandatory injection of adrenaline into my bloodstream a second or two before I stated the obvious to my teammates at NFL Control: "Alright, we lost lights." Then, I turned to the stadium's senior executive in the room and said "Doug, tell me what we do and when we do it."

Though I didn't appreciate it at the time, I'm grateful that Armen Keteyian, his *60 Minutes Sports* producer, and a TV cameraman were actively filming in NFL Control the moment the lights went out, part of a behind-the-scenes feature on the Super Bowl for *Showtime*. They were able to document much of what transpired during the unscheduled 34-minute timeout that I would never have been able to recall as accurately. Before being asked to turn off their cameras, they captured the shadowy footage that aired on the next day's edition of *CBS This Morning*. *Vanity Fair*, referencing the CBS report, posted that the team at NFL Control handled the power outage "without cursing, sweating, or throwing a single walkie-talkie through the glass window of their Superdome box in frustration." They weren't sure whether "the [presence of the] CBS camera crew, preternatural calmness, or anticipatory dosages of Xanax should be credited" with the response at NFL Control. It wasn't any of those things.

That's why I'm so grateful that the footage exists and that most people perceived that we were outwardly calm. I don't remember feeling calm. I remember feeling nervous. I recollect feeling some of the symptoms of anxiety, the rush of adrenaline, and an empty sensation deep in the pit of my stomach. I'm sure I was not alone in feeling any of those things, but the moment Armen Keteyian alerted me to the fact that half the lights were out was the last time I remember anything about him or the TV camera being there at all.

We felt the pressure of urgency and appreciated just how screwed we might be. After our adrenal glands did their job, unbidden milliseconds after electrons stopped flowing along the deactivated feeder cable, each of us at NFL Control began prioritizing our individual and collective responses. That is why my first question to Doug Thornton was, "What do we do and when do we do it?" As the stadium's senior executive, he not only had decades of facility operations experience, but he also had managed the Superdome when the building infamously served as an emergency refuge of last resort during Hurricane Katrina. The Superdome had been heavily damaged during the storm, the roof had been breached, and rising floodwaters had threatened to swamp the stadium's back-up generators, the only source of power available for the sweltering building and for the 15,000–20,000 people who had taken refuge there. Our problem was not nearly as life-threatening as those dreadful days in September 2005, when 1,833 people lost their lives in New Orleans, or as dangerous as the conditions later experienced inside the Superdome. Had the stadium gone completely dark during the Super Bowl, which turned out to be a real probability had Doug and his team not responded as quickly and decisively as they did, a sense of panic could have descended on the fans and the ramifications of that are, thankfully, unknown.

PANIC PARALYZES DECISION MAKING

As for the team at NFL Control, I am often asked how we resisted panic. I truly believe that the annual game day simulations we conducted 10 days before the Super Bowl contributed immeasurably to the entire team's ability to calmly, quickly, and collaboratively shift to a problem-solving mode. (See Chapter 7.) We had previously managed responses to an ammonia spill, a mysterious fatality, and a spray of a powder of uncertain origin on the field, at least as drills. Notwithstanding that adrenaline was flowing liberally through our arteries, we approached the power failure as though it was another drill, though clearly it was anything but.

When something goes wrong, it is the most ancient part of our brain, the *limbic system*, that literally gets things moving. Before we consciously perceive the problem, *the amygdala*, a small almond-shaped structure that processes emotions, tells our bodies that we are in danger. It signals other primitive parts of our brain to get the adrenaline pumping and as a result, we feel stress and anxiety. Like the rest of our bilaterally symmetrical brain, the amygdala is tucked below each half of our *cerebrums*, the larger, evolutionarily newer parts of our brain that facilitate problem-solving. Psychologists have proven that we can consciously fight back against the anxiety generated by our limbic systems by engaging the thinking parts of our brain with tasks involving cognitive and motor activities, that is, by thinking or doing something like solving a problem, incident, or crisis. This conscious refocusing forces our cerebrums to take command over from the unconscious work of the amygdala and other brain structures that give rise to the emotion of anxiety. To put it simply, if we get busy fixing a problem ASAP, we are too busy to panic. That's how people who routinely launch into action in the face of a crisis, like brave first responders, avoid falling victim to panic.

Conversely, if we indulge our anxiety to the tipping point of panic, our conscious mind is focusing on what we are feeling rather than what we need to do to stop feeling that way. We are not problem-solving or sorting out the options. We are not acting correctively or managing the outcome. In essence, unless we consciously focus on switching gears and concentrate on addressing the issue, we will be paralyzed from managing the problem before us.

It is important to note that some people are susceptible to, and suffer from, debilitating anxiety- and panic-inducing disorders that are often initiated and escalated for no direct discernable reason. These are real clinical conditions that require professional and medical guidance, and this chapter is not meant to provide that. What we are talking about, however, are responses to an *identifiable* stimulus, something that has gone wrong in our professional or personal life. The good news is that many of us can choose to override the preprogrammed anxiety produced by a stressful event. We can even better tolerate these stresses if we have, indeed, taken good physical care of ourselves. (See Chapter 15.) Although the bad news is that we can't prevent the primitive parts of our brain from doing what they were designed to do, it was once a very good thing. The limbic system is what kept each of our respective ancestors from being eaten or flattened before they produced the next generation of our predecessors, and why we were eventually born. That's why we get that jolt of adrenaline faster than we can think about it. But remember, it's what you do after that jolt that counts.

We have all heard the expression "take a deep breath" when we react too quickly, too angrily, or yes, too anxiously. That is spectacularly appropriate advice because a common reaction to stress is *hyperventilation*, a greatly increased pattern of breathing that can significantly amplify anxiety and lead to an attack of panic. Hyperventilation literally changes your blood chemistry, increasing the percentage of oxygen in your bloodstream and greatly reducing the level of carbon dioxide. As a result, the affected person can start to feel shortness of breath, sick, and dizzy; these sensations of losing physical control, in turn, can further increase anxiety. The old remedy of breathing into a paper bag works because breathing back in what you just breathed out rebalances the level of carbon dioxide in the bloodstream. So, when you feel that first release of adrenaline, by all means take that deep breath, engage your cerebrum, and get to work solving the problem. That's how you will combat your own panic.

PANIC IS CONTAGIOUS

There is another important reason to take that deep breath and to consciously redirect your anxiety to problem solving. That is because panic is contagious. It is particularly virulent if you are leading the team evaluating and managing the problem. If we exhibit symptoms of panic, one of two things are inevitable. The first is that some members of your team will also tend to panic. They will think: "People around me, including our leader, are losing control, so things must be hopelessly and irretrievably messed up." The second alternative is perhaps a little better. Your team will begin to ignore you and concentrate on what they need to do to avoid panicking themselves. Remember, panic is often characterized by irrational behavior. Who is going to take remedial cues from someone who is not thinking logically or clearly?

It is also difficult for team members to maintain their own composure under stress if another teammate is exhibiting the debilitating symptoms of anxiety or panic. As poorly behaving colleagues can have a deleterious effect on the team's overall response, it is often best to remove those people from the situation until they have recomposed themselves, assuming they can at all. It is not usually effective to simply instruct overreacting participants to calm down, especially when they are in the throes of an extreme case of anxiety and panic. It is better to separate them from the response, and if possible, remove them physically from the scene.

An experience described in the Report of the Director of Hawaii's Emergency Management Authority illustrates this point. (See Chapter 18.) The individual who activated the alarm failed to respond to instructions to send a notification canceling the civil defense message and instead sat inertly and confused at his station. Another team member had to take control of the dazed individual's computer to send the cancellation. According to the report's findings, the unresponsive team member did not contribute in any way to the effort to correct or recover from the incident.

Fortunately, "not panicking" is likewise contagious. A calm-and-focused environment encourages everyone working on a problem to behave similarly. There was certainly a sense of urgency at NFL Control to get power restored as quickly as possible, and there was a significant amount of uncertainty as to what had really happened. There was an enormous amount of stress when the lights first went out and the combined biomass of the room was no doubt thick with adrenaline. But there were no raised voices, no pounding of tables, and no fleeing to the exits. There was only an atmosphere of "What do we do now to get the lights back on and what do I need to do to help with the response . . . just like I did 10 days ago?" Thanks to the drills we had performed, switching from being held hostage by our limbic systems to applying our cerebrums to overcome them was a completely familiar tack.

We did not take flight, physically or emotionally. We stayed to fight through the problem mentally. Immediately after I asked Doug Thornton for his insights into "What do we do and when do we do it?" we recognized that the fans in the stands had even less information than we did. All they knew was that the lights had gone out. Connectivity to the outside world, and within the stadium, was extremely limited. All data access points, telephone antennae, and radio transmitters on our side of the stadium were dead, but the other side of the stadium was still powered, and it was likely that fans were checking their social media feeds and texting their friends and families. We did not know what rumors and misinformation might be circulating and we had to ensure that those rumors, or the absence of information, did not increase anxiety or incite group panic. We didn't have much information yet, but it was essential for us to be the *source* of the most authoritative information as soon as possible, with whatever we had.

With no power to the video screens, we could start texting to the opt-in database of ticket holders, but the only way to get to everyone was with an announcement over the public address system. Most stadium and arena PA systems have backup batteries for just such life-safety purposes. The public address announcer, however, was not at NFL Control. He was in the booth where controls for the video scoreboard and audio systems were located, on another level of the stadium. We hurriedly sketched out a script for him, and one of our teammates sprinted down the darkened staircase to get him the message: "Ladies and gentlemen, we have experienced a partial interruption in electrical service. Please remain in your seat and service will be restored momentarily." Everybody heard the announcement, but many people didn't listen.

Instead, they got out of their seats and went on a search throughout the concourse for beer taps that were still working. They succeeded. The NFL enjoyed the best half-hour of beer sales in the history of the Super Bowl during the partial power failure. And, while fans were breaking beer consumption records instead of breaking through exit doors, NFL Control got very busy.

RIGHT HAS LEFT
THE BUILDING

t only takes an instant for the trajectory of your day to change. We are cruising toward success and, suddenly, we see things turn south before our eyes. Or, perhaps we get the bad news from someone else who is passing it along.

"You've got to get over here right away." Unless you're being invited to your own surprise birthday party, it's never good if those are the *first words* you hear when you answer the phone. My adrenal glands slammed into first gear before the sentence was even completed. "Part of the halftime stage collapsed and some of the crew were pinned underneath." It was the Tuesday night before the game and the halftime team had been practicing the assembly of the stage under a large tent in the Dolphin Stadium parking lot. "Four people have been hurt," the production manager continued, "and two have been airlifted out by helicopter. The media are all over the place." There are no secrets at the Super Bowl, especially not at the stadium. Then, the worst of all possibilities: "There may be two fatalities."

Bill McConnell, our director of event operations, and I had just swallowed the first bite of a long-deferred, late-night bar burger in Fort Lauderdale. "I'll call you from the car. Let me know the minute you hear anything else." We threw cash on the table, abandoned our uneaten meals, and ran several blocks to the hotel to grab my car and race the 20 miles to the stadium. On the way, I called our teammates from the media relations department to meet us for the ride back to the stadium. Then, while still huffing back to the hotel, I called Dr. Ric Martinez and filled him in.

"Call the ER in Miami and find out how many injuries there are and how serious." I told him about the report of fatalities and asked him to speak to no one but the hospital and me. As head of our Super Bowl medical team, Ric had established working contacts with every hospital in the area. While Bill met our media relations team in the hotel lobby, I screeched around to the porte cochère in my SUV. The group of us were on our mobile phones during the entire ride, each communicating with a different set of stakeholders and periodically updating the others as we finished one call and started the next. I had called our legal and finance departments and our insurance agency. Bill was talking to the stadium manager and production director from the halftime crew. Our public relations (PR) pros were briefing their team and monitoring the latest updates from media reports.

From the freeway exit, we could see satellite dishes reaching into the night sky on the tall, spindly masts projecting from the news vans in the parking lot. We drove into the halftime compound, an area that was routinely prohibited to the media to prevent unauthorized photography of rehearsals, and entered the tent to examine the site of the accident and meet with the producer and his team.

Of anything that could possibly go wrong, the specter of a loss of life overshadowed all else. So we all waited eagerly for Ric to verify the early reports. While we did, we redirected our anxiety to exploring our course of action if, in fact, there were fatalities, and the plans to repair the stage if the League determined to go ahead with the show. The stage designer was already working on the latter.

While we checked our phones constantly for missed calls and updated news, we recollected that the NFL had been faced with a tragic incident in New Orleans a decade earlier. One of 16 bungee jumpers rehearsing the halftime show was killed on the Thursday night before the game, striking her head on the floor of the stadium after a 100-foot fall. Appropriately, the league eliminated the bungee stunt from the show and a graphic memorializing her heartbreaking death accompanied the telecast. Tostitos tortilla chips, a sponsor, canceled the airing of a commercial in which comedian Chris Elliott appeared to bungee-jump from a blimp to within arm's reach of a football field to delicately dip his chip into a jar of salsa. A company spokesperson acknowledged that the only respectful thing to do was to air a different ad.

I started when Ric rang us back. He was in touch with the emergency room and reported that all four members of the crew were alive and diagnosed with non-life-threatening injuries. All were conscious and one or two were going to be admitted to the hospital to spend the night under observation. Ric was going to stay in touch with the physicians on the case and alert us immediately if anything changed. We all breathed a collective sigh of relief. Aside from wishing the crew members a speedy recovery, the problem the team would be wrestling with was the repair and reinforcement of a broken section of the stage, not the powerfully devastating circumstances of a fatality on the crew. The show on February 7, 2010, featuring The Who, was staged on game day without further incident as part of Super Bowl XLIV's record-breaking broadcast to 106.5 million American viewers.

DO YOU KNOW IT
OR DO YOU BELIEVE IT?

Under the circumstances, it was entirely appropriate to treat the initial speculation about fatalities from the halftime stage collapse as though it was fact. We began preparing, but not acting on that basis because we had not yet verified the rumor. Yes, there was an accident, and that itself was bad enough. We knew with certainty that there were injuries because the production manager who called us had witnessed the collapse himself and immediately called 9-1-1 for assistance. What we didn't know for sure was how accurate the report of fatalities was until Ric Martinez's call. Meanwhile, as the stage failure was not among the contingencies we had planned for, we collectively began charting our courses of action for two possibilities:

- What we would recommend if the very worst was true
- What we would need to do if the show was to proceed

There was no time to waste waiting for confirmation of either scenario, so we considered them both.

During our years of working together, NFL Commissioner Roger Goodell often pointed to the distinction between "knowing" and "believing" that something is true. For the most part, our conversations related to the other day-to-day responsibilities of my job, but his admonition to distinguish between what we knew and what we believed was even more relevant when confronted with something that has gone horribly wrong. The very first words of the very first conversation, phone call, or text, will activate your body's instinctive trouble response and set the clock in motion toward recovery. In the meantime, the best place to direct the nervous energy in your adrenaline-spiked bloodstream is to engage your cerebrum and begin applying your problem-solving skills. The first step is to make every effort to verify the information you have received. If you have witnessed the problem with your own eyes, then that may be all the verification you need. If you did not, and are hearing about it from someone else, then the second question might be: "Are you there?" "Did you see it?" or, "How do you know?"

Verify the Details

There was no question that a section of the halftime stage had collapsed. The production manager who called me saw it himself and the very first and most appropriate response was to immediately call for emergency medical assistance. The call to me was secondary to getting the injured crew members to the hospital. What was not clear was the extent of their injuries. I don't recollect where he had heard that there were fatal consequences, but that was a "do you know or do you believe" moment, and the reason we called Dr. Ric Martinez right away.

Every time something goes wrong, the areas of priority, focus, and action that emerge will be defined by the details. There would have been an agonizing set of consequences if someone had died, so getting clarity on that detail was exceptionally important. Additionally, a media story of greater tragic significance would have been generated, requiring sensitivity and respect. A candid debate, internally and externally, would have ensued on the advisability of staging the halftime show. An investigation of immense gravity would no doubt have been required. The rest of everything we did that week would have to be evaluated in the context of a regrettable new reality. We began preparing for that possibility the moment we received the first call, but knowing that medical personnel had already been on the scene, we started the process of verifying the details so we could concentrate our responses on what we knew, and prepare possible responses for the things we didn't.

At Super Bowl XL in Detroit, we also knew that an incident involving a star player had unfolded. Though the details were not entirely clear, what I heard was enough to raise the hair on the back of my neck. What fans may best remember about that game were the things that went wrong on the field for the National Football Conference (NFC) champion Seattle Seahawks, and for the NFL's football operations and officiating departments. A series of exceptionally damaging flags thrown by the officials on the field resulted in what NFL Films ranked as "one of the ten most-controversial games in NFL history," and what some sports pundits at the time decried as a rigged result favoring the Pittsburgh Steelers of the American Football Conference (AFC). What I most remember, however, was the phone call I received shortly after Seattle Seahawks quarterback (QB) Matt Hasselbeck's arrival at General Motors World Headquarters earlier that week, and circumstances that would have played very nicely, though falsely, into the hands of the conspiracy theorists.

The building's large public atrium had been converted into the Super Bowl Media Center's "Radio Row," an assembly line of snugly-packed tables where broadcasters from across the country could host their talk shows and sports reports for the week. In car wash fashion, players and coaches, past and present, negotiated through the labyrinth of radio stations, participating in any combination of broadcasts in a very time-efficient manner.

Players and coaches from the competing teams were transported from their hotels or team practice facilities throughout the week in escorted vehicles and driven into the building through a secured underground garage. A guard greeted the two chauffeured cars as they rolled up to the gate, one behind the other. After checking the manifest of expected arrivals against the identities of the passengers in the first car, a guard activated the switch that retracted the heavy steel posts blocking the entrance down into the concrete floor. The system was designed to admit one vehicle at a time, automatically raising the thick, impenetrable posts into position, again obstructing the driveway to repeat the process for the next arriving vehicle. For reasons that are still unclear, the second car in line followed the first through the checkpoint without stopping for the guard as the steel posts ascended, impaling the undercarriage of the vehicle containing, yes, you guessed it, Seattle QB Matt Hasselbeck. At least, "impaled" was the word I distinctly remember hearing when I got the call moments later, and that is why my limbic system began doing its job before I could even imagine a helplessly perforated football star being scooped out of a ruined Cadillac, in whole or in part, by the Jaws of Life.

"What do you mean impaled? Is everybody ok?"

"The bollards came through the floor of the car," was the heart-stopping response. "No one is seriously hurt, but the car is a wreck and we're not sure, but Hasselbeck may have a neck injury."

In football culture, it is common practice for coaches to conceal information from the public and the opposing team to maintain any of the advantage that secrecy and uncertainty can generate. The Super Bowl is an exception only in that there is even more of it. So, after the call on roughing the passer's car, it was not clear whether Hasselbeck's references to neck pain during his visits to the Media Center would eventually impact his appearance in the game. The cone of silence descended over his condition for the rest of the week. We knew the team's medical staff was not going to tell us, or Ric, anything. There was nothing we could do to affect the outcome except manage the media response when there was something to respond to, so we returned to our regularly scheduled program of getting ready for the Super Bowl.

When I first learned about the accident, I didn't think to ask the caller whether he knew that the bollards had pierced the body of the car, or whether he only believed that because someone else had told him, but I should have. Not that it would have changed the outcome, but now, when I hear about a problem, especially a big one, I ask the questions: "Do you know that for sure? Did you see or hear that yourself, or hear it from someone else?" Verifying the accuracy of information is essential to fixing the right problem or managing a response.

Chasing Ghosts

When faced with a challenge, my former colleague Bill McConnell often wondered out loud whether he was "chasing ghosts," that is, acting on something he believed was there, but really wasn't. If you haven't witnessed the problem yourself and you can't immediately verify the details, sometimes you have to err on the side of acting as though the ghosts are real. Our security team, for instance, was regularly confronted with packages or backpacks sitting unattended at one of our event sites, either in plain sight or discovered hiding behind a door or garbage can. Thankfully, in every case of which I am aware, the lone item was an innocent box filled with merchandise, supplies left unintentionally by a careless worker, or a backpack of work materials temporarily stashed in a hiding place to keep it from being stolen.

On April 15, 2013, however, an unattended backpack left near the finish line of the Boston Marathon was anything but innocent or unintentional. Two pressure-cooker bombs exploded, killing three people and injuring hundreds. This occurrence demonstrates the importance of chasing those ghosts every time because there is a possibility that lives, or safety, are at risk. The best outcome is an entirely wasted effort because it turns out to be nothing. The next best outcome would be quickly taking whatever decisive actions are necessary to protect the safety of everyone in the vicinity.

In most non-safety-threatening situations, however, chasing ghosts is unproductive. We may have to do it sometimes because the risks of not acting on some possibilities might be economically or reputationally damaging. For instance, it may be prudent to hold off on launching a new campaign because of unsubstantiated reports that the celebrity hired as a spokesperson was involved in a controversy or a criminal act. The reports may turn out to be based on nothing, but proceeding without cautious investigation would be unnecessarily and dangerously risky.

That's why it is essential to verify as many details as we can in the opening moments of an incident or crisis, helping us identify what problem we are really trying to solve. When 125 people reportedly arrived with tickets that failed to scan at the security checkpoint, we could have been facing a failure of our ticket-scanning equipment, a corruption or loss of connectivity to the database of ticket bar codes, an attempted security breach, or a counterfeit ticket problem. Today, I can't say for sure whether there were 125 people really waiting in the rain because I didn't ask whether the Gate Supervisor had encountered the entire group or had only interacted with the "tour organizer," who may have trotted out the story after his tickets were rejected by the system. Rather than spending time chasing ghosts trying to ascertain whether the scanning system was at fault or defeating the purpose of scanning tickets in the first place by waving through some number of wet and allegedly unhappy people through the gates with our apologies, we tried to catch the ghost by visually authenticating the tickets. In the meantime, as ghosts are wont to do, the problem vanished.

DIAGNOSING SYMPTOM VERSUS CAUSE

After verifying the details, the next component of identifying the problem we are trying to solve is understanding whether we are dealing with the *root cause*, or just a *symptom*. Chris Barbieri was working in the information technology (IT) department of a bank on a Monday afternoon when he and his colleagues became aware that its servers were infected by an insidious software virus. A computer virus can be pretty disruptive for any business, but it can have far-reaching effects on a financial institution that go well beyond simple inconvenience. An inability to access customer data or process transactions can profoundly affect the well-being of not only the bank, but also of the businesses and depositors the bank serves, resulting in significant reputational and financial damage. The problem seemed isolated to just one of the bank's many technology systems and the team moved quickly to restore it to a fully functional condition before the day had ended.

By Tuesday morning, however, it was clear that the virus they thought had been scrubbed from the affected area had been working overnight, infecting virtually every software system in the bank. As more and more symptoms developed, the IT team was under enormous and continuous pressure to keep the bank running without interruption, and with a minimum of inconvenience to its customers. Having acted quickly to knock down one problem, only to have new symptoms develop literally overnight, the IT team understood that the issue they considered conquered was just one symptom of a much larger and more sinister root cause. A virus had been launched to purposefully wreak maximum havoc on their business. Barbieri recollects a frustrating game of whack-a-mole as the team struggled to resolve one symptom, only to have new ones spring up over the course of the week. "What exactly *is* the problem, what and who did it affect, and how do we contain it?" Those were the most important questions Barbieri and the team needed to answer as quickly as possible.

PRIORITIZING RECOVERY

After the fact, Barbieri and his colleagues undertook a *root-cause analysis* to determine how and why the attack happened, and how they would keep it from happening again in the future. (See Chapter 23.) Analyzing precisely why they were vulnerable, however, was secondary in the urgency of time to addressing each of the symptoms as they arose. Since they still had to support the bank's overall business, the team delegated the recovery efforts to the people who could best fix each of the problems as they emerged, and everyone else returned to their day-to-day functions. The business could not suffer from the secondary, unintended effects of all technology resources being focused on the virus attack.

The bank's IT team identified the most important things they had to do:

- Actively engage in recovery efforts for each affected system as they occurred
- Continue the uninterrupted delivery of essential bank services to its customers

The business chose not to allocate all of its specialized resources to solving what had gone wrong, so it could continue to serve the needs of the bank and its customers. Also, it did this to avoid unintended consequences that could arise while everyone else's attention was diverted to the crisis.

Often symptoms must be addressed faster than the root cause. At 5:00 a.m. on Sunday, December 12, 2010—the day of a scheduled game between the Minnesota Vikings and the New York Giants—the snow that had accumulated atop the Minneapolis Metrodome during a powerful blizzard proved to be too much for the air-supported roof to withstand. Crews had been working throughout the storm, using steam and hot water, to clear away as much snow as possible until heavy winds threatened to sweep the crew off the roof. The building's heating system applied warmth from below and more hot air was fed between the two layers of the fabric roof in an effort to melt the snow collecting above. Thanks to the deeply cold temperatures, however, snow continued to pile on top, as deep as two feet in valleys between the roof panels.

Our phones rang a few minutes after the roof failure, alerting us of an imminent all-hands conference call. We weren't jumping on the phone to plan how to fix the Metrodome roof or to investigate why it gave way. We were going to discuss where and when the game scheduled for that afternoon was ultimately going to be played, and to start planning where the final Minnesota Vikings home game would be staged a couple of weeks later.

Similarly, the first and most important thing during the Super Bowl XLVII power outage, on February 2, 2013, was not turning the lights back on. It was to take steps to avoid panic setting in among the fans in the half-dark stadium. That's why one of the first things we did was to ensure that the public address system was activated and that we knew what we were going to say to the crowd.

Transitioning to Recovery

Superdome executive Doug Thornton was fielding reports from his engineering team assessing the cause of the electrical malfunction:

> DOUG: *"Frank, we lost the 'A feed.'"*
> FRANK: *"What does that mean?"*
> DOUG: *"That means we have to do the bus tie."*
> FRANK: *"What does that mean?"*
> DOUG: *"That means about a 20-minute delay."*

Doug and I had discussed the recent upgrade to the electrical system during the planning stage, so I knew what the term "bus tie" meant. The backup cable installed by the power company would have to be connected into the side of the building that was now in darkness. What I really wanted to know was how long it was going to take, and Doug was ready with an answer that proved remarkably accurate. I didn't realize it at the time, but Doug and his operations team had been actively working through the recovery process from the moment the lights went out, and not a moment too soon.

21

MANAGING RECOVERY

I f it was more than a minute-and-a-half that went by, it wasn't by much. The New Orleans Police Department (NOPD) captain at NFL Control stepped in front of me, the tips of his shoes touching mine, and whispered softly. "It's not a terror or cyber-attack." Well, check that one off the list.

While I was talking to Doug Thornton—the Mercedes-Benz Superdome senior executive during the Super Bowl XLVII blackout—and calling for the public address announcement, the NOPD, the NFL's security team, and the full complement of law enforcement agencies working under the Department of Homeland Security (DHS) wasted no time comparing intelligence and assessing the possibility of foul play. There was nothing to suggest it was. Now that we knew for sure that it was safe to tell people to stay in the stadium, one of our teammates ran the hastily scribbled script down to the public address announcer.

We had already determined the power outage was confined to the stadium. No part of the city's electrical grid had failed. NFL Control had no view outside the building and the outage had disrupted the checkerboard of video feeds from the surveillance cameras ringing the outside of the building, but security guards out there confirmed that the lights in the surrounding area were still shining. It was hopeful news that the problem was localized to the stadium and that we were not hostages to a larger and infinitely more complicated problem.

Doug and his team had an existing protocol for full or partial power failures and reported that they were shutting down *all* nonessential equipment on both sides of the building—the side that was still illuminated and the side that was dark. The Superdome had always had a *redundant* power system to start with, even before the backup cable was installed months before. If one feeder failed, the entire building could be powered from the other. This required reducing overall power consumption, and a list of candidate systems to shut down was already in place to accommodate that.

The Super Bowl, however, required a great deal more energy than a normal football game, hence the precautionary decision was made to install the backup cable. If you were at the game and it started to feel just a little bit stuffier, it was because the air conditioning was shut down. Walkway lighting in the unaffected side of the building was reduced. Refrigerators, electric cooktops, sponsor displays, escalators, and other nonessential power drains were in the process of being powered down.

Throughout the 24 minutes it would take for the dark side of the stadium to be completely re-energized and the field to be lit to full brightness, NFL Control was a beehive of activity. We continually asked ourselves and each other:

- "What are we doing?"
- "What still needs to be done?"
- "What should we be doing?"

This time, "What can I do to help?" came from a new voice in the room. It was Eric Grubman, NFL executive vice president of business operations, who was at that time my direct superior at the League. He had run over to NFL Control from one of the League's hospitality suites. Eric had been a U.S. Navy submarine officer and former energy company president, with more than a passing familiarity with electrical systems.

"It's not a safety or security issue," I assured him. "One of the two feeders into the building shut down."

"We're heading down to meet the engineers at the switchgear vault," Doug added. That is where the two feeder cables go before they enter the building. Eric departed with the contingent of people who left to inspect the equipment, and left us to continue managing and monitoring the overall response.

If we had any uncertainties about how the blackout was going to play out, at least we could see what was happening on the field from our vantage point built on the top rows of the upper deck. There was understandably more confusion in the windowless CBS broadcast truck, where producer Lance Barrow and director Mike Arnold were scrambling for information, partially blind and almost totally deaf to what was happening on the field. They could only see patches of the activity on the long bank of monitors lining the long wall of the expanded trailer, most of which had turned gray. We couldn't tell them anything, even if we wanted to, because all connections between NFL Control and the broadcast truck had been cut off. The broadcast was still being fed to the outside world, but CBS could only show images from the 15 of 62 cameras that were still functioning.

Play-by-play announcers Jim Nantz and Phil Simms, from their broadcast booth overlooking the field, could have painted a verbal picture of what they were witnessing, but they were also on the dark side of the stadium and their equipment was dead as well. "The network," as Armen Keteyian told it in his *60 Minutes Sports* report, "was flying blind." Barrow eventually established indirect communication with sideline reporter Steve Tasker through a cameraman who could still hear his instructions. Although neither Tasker nor fellow reporter Solomon Wilcots could hear the CBS team in the truck, their microphones allowed them to report from the field while the network reactivated their pregame set on the sideline.

Social media proved to be the primary source of information (and disinformation) to people in the stadium, viewers watching at home, and to the world-at-large about what was going on at the Superdome. While CBS was reestablishing more meaningful contact with their viewers on television, fans in the stands were communicating with their friends and families on Facebook and Twitter, and they were quick to tweet about the eerie atmosphere in the stadium. Twitter reported an increase from 185,000 tweets per minute when Jacoby Jones scored his 108-yard touchdown to an average of 231,500 during the 34-minute game delay.

The problem for fans was separating facts from the rumors, and news from satire. The volume of the latter was multiplying by the moment. Once it was determined that there was no life-threatening disaster developing in New Orleans, the world could have a laugh at our expense. In two successive tweets, Walgreens Pharmacy posted that they carried candles . . . and lights. Tide detergent bragged that it "couldn't get the blackout, but could get your stains out," Jim Beam Black® promoted itself as the whisky sponsor of the blackout, and PBS encouraged viewers to switch to their concurrent airing of *Downton Abbey*. Nike congratulated Jacoby Jones for his "lights out speed" on the kickoff return, but it was Oreo cookies that was acknowledged as the Super Bowl retweet champion, comforting distressed fans that there was "No problem. You can still dunk in the dark."

While clever brands enjoyed a hearty chuckle and leveraged an unparalleled opportunistic marketing bonanza, the operating team stayed entirely focused on getting the power restored to the stadium and dealing with any issues that flowed from the outage. The electrical engineers were still working on the bus tie. The stadium crew was rescuing people trapped in elevators. And, one shaken Superdome electrician, I was later told, was being strenuously reassured that his work repairing an outlet somewhere in the building was not responsible for the crisis. (To this day, I don't know if that was an apocryphal tale, but it is too delectable not to share.)

IN THE HEAT OF THE MOMENT, BLAME IS NOT IMPORTANT

One of our media relations representatives tapped me on the shoulder to relay that Entergy, the electric utility, had already taken to Twitter to point a definitive finger of blame toward the Superdome. The power they provided to the stadium, they tweeted, had not been interrupted. The problem, they said, was on "the customer's side." The Superdome was reportedly preparing to send out their own dueling Twitter post that squarely placed responsibility for the failure on Entergy's side.

I was asked by our PR team: What did we want to say? "We're just trying to get the plug back in the wall," I answered. "Let the two of them duke it out."

There would be plenty of time afterwards to uncover the root cause and contributing factors, and if the power company was blaming the stadium and the stadium was blaming the power company, let them. No one was blaming us, at least not yet. The conspiracy theories would later mushroom on social media after play resumed, as the San Francisco 49ers threatened to even the lopsided score during the second half. Worrying about where to assign blame was a wasted effort, and the only information coming from us should be: "We're going to get the lights back on, we're going to play the rest of the game, and we'll let you know when we can expect that to happen."

"Stadium authorities are investigating the cause of the power outage," the subsequent NFL statement read. "We will have more information as it becomes available."

"Fried." That's how Grubman described the relay in the switch-gear vault when he returned to NFL Control. He filled me in on the damaged gear and the work underway to complete the manual bus tie. Barring any unforeseen problems, it was appearing increasingly likely that we would be able to restart the game.

I didn't feel any better yet. The blackout itself was an unforeseen occurrence, but frankly, I could very easily foresee another unforeseen shutdown. After all, we might have been fixing only a symptom—one relay shutting down—and not the problem. If the relay was not itself defective, we may not be addressing the root cause that initiated the failure. But there was no time to launch an investigation. If we had any hope of getting the game restarted, we had to restore the power and soon.

RECOVERY REQUIRES A RESPONSE, NOT A REACTION

When something goes wrong, we can choose to either react or respond. A *reaction* is immediate and instinctive. A *response* can take a little bit longer because it results from the processes of judgment, thought, and reason.

When we *react*, we instantly do or say something that we believe is appropriate to address the situation. If we are experienced at what we are doing, we have a reasonable chance that our reaction might be the right resolution to a problem. But then again, we may act so quickly that we haven't had the chance to consider whether it might not be right. How many times have we reacted less than optimally to something someone said or did, and regretted that we didn't stop for a moment, think about what we heard, and process what they meant? How might we have reasoned out a better response? Once we have reacted, it is often difficult to change direction or further refine the message.

When we take even a brief moment to evaluate what is happening around us, we are *responding* rather than reacting. It doesn't have to take a long time because when something goes wrong, we often don't have the luxury of time. But, resisting the impulse to act reflexively when something goes wrong can help us to a better recovery, or at least, not make matters worse.

Chris Barbieri recalls reacting far too quickly at a previous job, when one of the accounting servers at UPS (United Parcel Service) froze, as it was notorious for doing. "The fix then was to hit the 'Big Red Button' as we say," he remembers. "A total reboot. That server happened to be sitting next to another server with the same chassis. The label had fallen off over time and was sitting like a dried leaf underneath. Out of complete normalcy, I just hit the power button and as my finger was feeling the spring-loaded click, I realized that the server I needed to reboot was sitting there fat and happy right next to the one I had just accosted."

Like a modern-day Little Dutch Boy, he kept his finger firmly pressed in place as he stretched across a nearby desk to pull a phone toward him in the other hand. The colleague that responded to his call came in to back up the files on the server that was perilously one-twitch-away from losing essential data by being powered off. During the process, Barbieri absorbed a half hour of lively real-time abuse from his teammates, which resonated for the months that followed.

Back at NFL Control, I noticed from the corner of my eye some dim flickers of life in the dark circles of glass ringing the ceiling perimeter. Today, the Superdome field is illuminated by LED fixtures that achieve their level of full intensity the moment they are turned on. In 2013, however, the gas discharge lamps that were in common stadium use took several minutes to warm up to the full illumination required for an NFL game and an HD broadcast. The lights continued to "restrike," bathing the players stretching and playing toss on the field in increasingly brighter light, but NFL Control remained in the dark because the Superdome operations team was cautiously and systematically restoring one circuit at a time to reduce the risk of another inadvertent shutdown. The lighting on the field finally returned to full strength 24 minutes after half the stadium was plunged into darkness, a delay lasting just 4 minutes more than Doug's original prognostication.

Even before power was restored to NFL Control, the intense pressure that was building to kick off the ball was coming from just about every corner of the Superdome—the teams, the officials, and the broadcasters, to name a few. The lights were coming on, the players were itching to retake the field, and with 30-second commercial spots costing $4 million at the time, no one wanted to dawdle a moment longer. The officials were anxiously waiting for word from NFL Control to tee up the ball and get things started again. We may have had lights in the booth, but I noticed that the TV monitors in the room were still a snowy gray. The security surveillance system was not booted up. It then occurred to me that there may be a great deal more things that might not be ready, and we'd better check everything out. I clapped my hands to get everyone's attention at NFL Control.

"Everybody listen up! This is important. We're not going to start again until I know that everybody's systems are up."

Everything that was needed for the game, and even more importantly, public safety, had to be checked and confirmed as functioning. I turned to Bill McConnell and muttered: "The most important game of the year has been dead in the water for 24 minutes. What's a few more to get this done right?"

After the field lighting, the press box was among the first places where power was restored. CBS coverage moved back to Nantz and Simms in the broadcast booth. At NFL Control, the broadcast feed came back first, then the video screens showing the surveillance camera feeds popped back up, one at a time. Everyone at the Superdome and watching at home was more than ready for the players to line up for the kickoff. CBS just needed a couple of minutes warning before we could start again so they could wrap up whatever they were doing and be sure they were not in a commercial break.

The response took 10 minutes more—a total of 34 minutes since the lights went out—to test all the technology to make sure that we were ready to restart the game. If I had to, I would make that decision all over again. Let's say we reacted and kicked off the ball without testing the game time clock and when the timekeeper pressed the button, it was frozen. The line judge's stopwatch would have kept the official time for the rest of the game. But that is a poor substitute for the large displays in the stadium that the coaches and players depend upon for "clock management," and the fans would not have been able to understand the progress of the game as easily. It might have been tough on the TV viewers, as well, because the little box showing the time remaining in the quarter is tied into the stadium time clock. The score clock checked out.

If there was another score, a coach's challenge, or any number of questionable plays on the field that required a second look, the referee would go under the hood on the sideline to review the instant replay. If the instant replay system didn't work, the story of the game would no longer be, "Why did the lights go out?" Instead it would be, "Why didn't they check the instant replay before starting again?" That would have been the best fodder for feeding the conspiracy theories that would later emerge. Instant replay tested just fine.

The coach-to-quarterback radio system had to work for both teams. If one of them didn't, the team whose system was still functional would have had theirs shut off to maintain fairness. One of them, it turned out, wasn't working. "Let's get it fixed before we start again," I said over the walkie-talkie. "It's the Super Bowl, for God's sake." The contractor in charge of the system worked on that while we continued to check out everything else. The play clocks, the sideline communication carts, the scoreboard control system, the press box Wi-Fi—I knew that all of them, and more that I didn't even know about, had to be checked, and I called out to every teammate at NFL Control, covering every area of operations, one-by-one. When all reported they were ready, we alerted the officiating crew and sidelines. We threw CBS the two-minute warning to get restarted and waited for them to cue the kickoff.

We wouldn't know the root cause for weeks, and I wasn't at all comfortable that we were out of the woods. One side of the building had failed. How did we know that it wouldn't fail again? Or, that the other side wouldn't fail. If that occurred, it was "game over." There were no more backup feeder cables.

> FRANK: *"Doug, please tell me how we make sure that it isn't going to happen again."*
> DOUG: *"I can't."*

It was without a doubt the longest half of football I have ever experienced.

MANAGING THE MESSAGE

J effrey B. Miller, Pennsylvania State Police Commissioner (2003 to 2008), was preparing to take the stage at the University of Maryland to address a law-enforcement luncheon when his phone began to vibrate with a rapid cascade of texts. Miller immediately excused himself, established contact with his team who were in the middle of managing an unfolding crisis at a school back in his home state, and then hitched a ride to the scene on a Maryland State Police chopper.

Miller used every second of his trip to gather reports from the ground, manage the response, and ensure that several important procedures were being implemented. A secure perimeter had been established around the site to protect the public and the scene. Roadblocks were put in place to redirect traffic. The troopers quickly identified a suitable safe location to which to direct reporters and camera crews. The troopers had a process for these things because, unfortunately, tense, terrible things must be managed by the police *all* the time. They knew, from experience, what the media would demand at the scene of an incident—timely and accurate information, an authoritative spokesperson to deliver it, and a view of the scene from a safe distance. These same requirements are essential when the media show up at your place of business or at the location of something gone wrong—most often, on a much different scale, of course.

When Miller arrived, his was not the only helicopter in the vicinity. Choppers hovered above the scene and news vans from local stations had already arrived. Miller's team was ready to manage not only the site, but the media's voracious appetite for up-to-second information, insights, and images. It is after an incident has begun when adequate planning, decisive leadership, empowered teammates, and a conscious understanding of what is happening to your body and mind all come together. The lesson here isn't about how to handle a crime scene. Those of us not in law enforcement will gratefully leave the handling of these matters to skilled and capable police professionals. What we take from this example are the lessons of *how* the Pennsylvania State Police responded *after* the crisis. Their protocols on handling and disseminating information were literally battle-tested because when something happens that requires police response, it is sadly all in a day's work, and will often become a news story of local, regional, or national importance.

We need to have the same expectations of ourselves and of our team. Assuming no one will notice when things go wrong is just hope, pure and simple, and as we know, hope is not a strategy. Perhaps we have, thus far, only been confronted with problems that are internal, addressable, and correctable. But there is a very high probability that our luck will run out eventually. When it does, this is not the right time to start developing our communications strategy.

You don't have to be engaged in combating criminal activity, managing the Super Bowl, or responding to a natural disaster for members of the press to quickly collect outside your door, in your parking lot, or at a location where your company's products or services are sold. The press may be looking for information on a recall, a complaint, a delay, an injury, an illness, or a labor dispute. Even if they don't show up physically, the press—and your customers—can bombard you with calls, texts, e-mails, and social media posts, looking for answers and information. Time is, yet again, of the essence.

Both Police Commissioner Jeff Miller and crisis communications expert Ivy Cohen stress the importance of *getting in front of the situation*; that is, taking ownership of the problem not only to manage and, if possible, solve the problem, but also to be the authoritative source of information about the issue at hand and the subsequent response. Being quick to resolve an incident is not enough. If we don't simultaneously take charge of communicating and managing the message, the message will inevitably end up managing us. Instead of proactively establishing command, clarity, and confidence from the very start, the conversation about the problem will commence in a vacuum. Without having provided *our* information or insights, we will then be forced to confront and correct the misinformation and misperceptions that take root after they are virally dispersed through the press and the public. This is a much more difficult management proposition.

The Pennsylvania State Police identified a location near the scene to distribute information to reporters. They scheduled press briefings for Miller to provide fact-based status reports on the incident, updating the group with new information and fielding questions. Speculation and rumors were identified as such. If a fact was not yet confirmed, or Miller didn't know an answer to a question, he said so, and promised to update the group with additional information at the next briefing. The anticipated times for follow-up briefings were also announced. Miller's protocol is exactly how we should manage and serve the media if we experience a crisis of newsworthy weightiness.

THE BATTLE FOR TRUST

Unfortunately, unlike the police, who are generally perceived as credible authorities when something goes wrong, the organizations we work for are not necessarily as highly regarded or perceived as trustworthy. Edelman, a global communications marketing firm, has been publishing the annual *Edelman Trust Barometer* for nearly two decades. This report annually evaluates public beliefs through a set of statistics referred to as the "Trust Index." This measurement is "an average of public trust, by country, in the institutions of *government, business, media,* and *non-governmental organizations (NGOs).*" According to the *2018 Edelman Trust Barometer,* less than half (48%) of those surveyed across the 28 countries trust the combination of these four institutions. Between 2017 and 2018, trust in these institutions in the United States showed the steepest decline among all nations studied, from 52 percent to 43 percent. Among the general U.S. population, trust in *businesses* declined 10 points from 58 percent to 48 percent;

trust in *government* declined by 14 points, from 47 percent to 33 percent, and trust in *media* declined by 5 points, from 47 percent to 42 percent.

By contrast, the 2017 Gallup poll that tracked American public trust in the police showed an average of 57 percent had "a great deal" or "quite a lot" of confidence in law enforcement, consistent with the overall average over the past 25 years. So, when Police Commissioner Miller stepped to the microphone at Nickel Mines, the public were much more likely to believe and trust his remarks than they were to trust the media outlet that aired the coverage. When your company delivers information about something that went wrong, it is being done in an environment where an average of less than one-half of the American population trusts businesses to do or to say the right things.

Today, the lines of communication with our customers, fans, and partners are wide open and can be activated quickly thanks to the increasing penetration of social media platforms, accessible to both the media and the public. The risk of not getting truthful messages disseminated quickly is vividly illustrated by a 2018 study in the journal *Science*, which found that false information on Twitter "diffused significantly farther, faster, deeper, and more broadly than the truth." How much faster? "It took the truth about six times as long as falsehood to reach 1,500 people," according to the study. The diffusion was not spread by bots, but by actual, verified users because, as Dr. Luba Kessler wrote in *Psychology Today*, "made up stories simply entertain us. Like gossip, they are usually titillating and sensational, and many times they feature a clear villain we can blame."

Being proactive and honest with the media doesn't mean they will tell your story *only* from your point of view. They will often cover the situation from multiple angles. If what went wrong influences the opinions or affects the experiences of your customers, they will almost certainly include these perspectives in their reporting. It is important that your authentic and authoritative version is at least one of the sources on which they base their reporting. They will often ask us tough questions, and it is totally acceptable to not give them access to *every* fact and figure. Let them know that you will investigate, follow up, and update them, and let them know when you expect to do that.

The media are exceptionally good at what they do. Having communications professionals on call who can help you accommodate their needs, manage the volume of calls, e-mails and texts, monitor media reports and perceptions, help draft statements, and answer questions can help you shrink response time and better navigate your response and recovery. This is equally important in managing the message for social media because people start sharing what they believe happened immediately. Although you can't control what people are saying, you must be quick to respond before the facts are distorted and swamped by the vast amount of misinformation that could spread virulently.

Ivy Cohen offers these rules of engagement for responding on social media, though most of these pointers are as valid for traditional media as well:

1. Be the first out with authoritative information if you can. If you can't be first, be quick.
2. Take ownership over the response: "Here's what went wrong, and here's what we are doing about it."
3. Respond factually to reports and posts that are inaccurate. Deliver information you can verify to be true. Don't offer opinions and don't get into arguments.
4. Be sincere, authentic, and candid.
5. Be concise, clear, and helpful.
6. Direct message (DM) people who have a specific complaint or want a specific response. Gather more information from them without bringing that conversation into the greater discourse.
7. Follow through on every promise to provide more or better information, whether as public posts or DMs.
8. Refresh your messages often to make sure you always provide the latest and most accurate information.

LAWYER UP!

There, I said it. When something goes wrong, there are often legal ramifications that may impact what you say and how you say it. When the police respond to questions from the media or the public, they do not want to share information that could taint an investigation or adversely change the outcome. Neither do you. If there is an injury or worse, your organization may be subject to a lawsuit and what you say, in addition to what actions you took or didn't take, could affect future litigation. Liabilities don't require a physical injury. Damages can be pursued by customers or business partners who feel inconvenienced, defrauded, or defamed resulting from a mistake, omission, or statement. Depending on the nature of the incident and the industry in which you work, there may also be inquiries and investigations after the fact from a variety of local, state, or federal agencies.

Have your legal team on speed dial, or better yet, have a legal representative on your project team, so what you say or post online benefits from their guidance. On one hand, you want to be candid and cooperative and do not want to appear as though you are withholding or hiding information. At the same time, you must act in the best interests of all parties—both the public and the company. The intersection of the two requires you to:

- Acknowledge the problem.
- Act authoritatively.
- Speak truthfully.
- Accept responsibility for the response.

Your legal team will be skillful guides to help you navigate the potential risks and manage responses and liabilities stemming from things that go wrong.

Remember that it is impossible to completely walk back something you say or write, and you can never entirely erase the damage of a deleted post. So, do not make snide or sarcastic comments, resist the urge to indulge your ego with self-serving defensive statements, and avoid exaggeration. This is true in e-mails and texts, even ones you send internally. So don't write anything you don't want to read verbatim in *The New York Times*. Keep in mind that your microphone is always on!

DON'T FORGET YOUR PEEPS!

Ivy Cohen schooled me when I asked her about the most common mistakes leaders make when something goes wrong. One of her answers surprised me, and upon reflection, I was more than a bit embarrassed when she said: "allowing employees to be an afterthought." She is 100 percent right. Whenever something goes wrong, our teammates are just as affected as we are, whether or not they are directly involved in the response or recovery. From our position in the trenches, we try to keep things that go wrong from becoming personal, but for our teammates, with little information or control over the outcome, it can be intensely personal. They wonder how a mistake, especially a costly one, might affect the security of their jobs. If it is a problem with a public profile, their families, friends, and their network of business relationships will check up on them, concerned about their safety or security. Don't let them get all their information through social or traditional media, or worse, the rumor mill. The same team that is invested in our achievements and success is profoundly affected by missteps and failures, even if they are not of our own making. Bringing them "into the know" will demonstrate your trust and concern for their well-being. Rumors, whether promulgated from the outside or spreading from within, can sap morale and be among the most damaging "sources."

That's why Cohen recommends leveraging your human resources departments when something goes wrong. As we are developing our messages to the media and the public, we should also be communicating in meaningful ways with our teammates. They will always be our best ambassadors to our partners. Much as senior executives are often the most natural and desirable spokespeople for delivering news to the media, so too are they the most appropriate people to communicate authoritatively with the organization-at-large. Without divulging confidential information that you would not share with the media or public, let teammates know what happened and what the organization is doing to fix or manage the problem.

Express confidence in the team's ability to recover from the challenge. Provide teammates with instructions on what they should do if contacted by the media. Tell them to refer all inquiries to a media relations executive or project team member, as appropriate to your organization. Let them know you will be updating them, and then be sure to follow up. If there will be a press conference or statement, let them know how they can see or hear it. If it's not broadcast live, your PR team can set up a dial-in or web conference so they can stay current with developments. Involve the HR department to be helpful as counselors to concerned employees, and to collect any remaining questions for later responses.

SEE IT COMING?
GET THE TEAM ON STANDBY

I work on a lot of outdoor events, and I take particular notice when I hear that thunderstorms are expected in the area. Some events don't operate at all in falling precipitation, like baseball games, car races, and many festivals. But, because of the deep economic ramifications of canceling or postponing, a lot more events do happen in the rain. So we sometimes get a bit soaked at football games and outdoor concerts.

Wet weather can make for a miserable experience for the participants and guests, but sometimes, it has resulted in some surprisingly memorable moments, like when Prince played *Purple Rain* in the rain at Super Bowl XLI on February 4, 2007. Or in 2004, at the post-game party for the NHL All-Star Game, when The Barenaked Ladies played outdoors in St. Paul, Minnesota, as falling snow piled up on the stage and was shoveled away by stage hands during the performance. "We're from Canada," announced lead singer Ed Robertson, brushing it all off. "This is nothing!"

Add in some random atmospheric electrical activity, however, and those fields, stadiums, and plazas filled with metal grandstands, lighting trusses, electronic gear, and people become very attractive to bolts of lightning. Although 90 percent of the people who get struck by lightning survive, you don't want to be a part of the 90 percent or the 10 percent. So, when a thunderstorm is on its way, seek shelter immediately because when lightning hits a tree, which can't take refuge indoors, the intense burst of heat can instantly vaporize the water contained inside and cause a mighty oak to literally explode from the sudden pressure.

I usually start to take note of the potential for thunderstorms three or four days ahead of an event, and my level of concern increases as the forecast becomes more short-term. Most outdoor venues subscribe to one or more commercial weather services, and some have their own weather station equipped with a local lightning detection system. We watch where, and how far away, the closest lightning strikes are, and whether they are heading in our direction. If lightning gets to within 12 or 15 miles and the storm's trajectory has it heading our way, we get our teammates into position, ready to stop the event, and to begin evacuating the outdoor areas of the venue.

When the lightning is within 8 miles and closing, we start clearing out the venue and encouraging people to seek shelter. The crew begins unplugging electronic gear. If there are strong winds that accompany the storm, we may take additional measures to secure equipment and materials that might literally blow away. Chances are, the lightning that passes through won't hit anything, but we are never going to take that chance. We have these protocols in place, just like the Pennsylvania State Police have theirs in place for managing crime scenes, because we know that thunderstorms are going to strike one of our live outdoor events at some point. And not to disappoint you, it's happened to me on multiple occasions.

We have discussed in detail the development of operational contingencies to be prepared for anything and how we should respond in the event the most likely things go wrong, like evacuating outdoor venues ahead of a thunderstorm. Preparing contingencies to plan how we would contact our various audiences when an incident occurs can be just as important. When the power went out in New Orleans at Super Bowl XLVII in 2013, it was vitally important to communicate as quickly as possible with the fans in the stands. This is why stadiums have battery-powered public address capabilities. If an outdoor event is going to be canceled or postponed, we direct people by public address announcement to leave and seek shelter, and we include instructions for guests to visit the venue's website and social media feeds for details on rescheduled dates, cancellation policies, and refunding procedures. With an electrical storm approaching, we don't want to delay their exit by engaging in question-and-answer exchanges, debates, or arguments.

If you become aware of a developing potential challenge that can disrupt operations for your company or project—from an emerging labor dispute, rumblings of a political protest, forecasted severe weather threat, a supply shortage, or literally anything that your intelligence (or even intuition) suggests is likely—add the need to prepare a communications strategy to your operational contingency readiness, as follows:

- Prescript key speaking points while you have time to be thoughtful.
- Identify who will deliver the message.

- Determine how to distribute the information before you are in the middle of a full-blown response.

Also, don't be too quick to press the send button to send anything you drafted ahead of time without reviewing it one more time to ensure that the information is relevant to what is occurring, or what has already occurred. Why should you start thinking about messages and dissemination ahead of time? If whatever happens is newsworthy, you can bet that the media will be on the story the moment it occurs. And, if it is predictable, they are probably ready even now.

STEP FIVE
EVALUATE

BREATHE. DEBRIEF. REPEAT.

February 4, 2013, the day after Super Bowl XLVII, now remembered as the "Blackout Bowl," was rife with speculation and conspiracy theories. Based on what happened in the second half of the game, it was at least somewhat understandable. When the lights cooled, so had the players. The Baltimore Ravens had built a commanding 28–6 lead early in the third quarter, but the momentum had definitively shifted when play resumed after the power was restored. First, Colin Kaepernick led the 49ers on an 80-yard drive to set up San Francisco's first touchdown of the night. Ravens quarterback (QB) Joe Flacco was later sacked by Ahmad Brooks, forcing the Ravens to punt from deep within their own end; it was returned by Ted Ginn, Jr. all the way to the 20-yard line. This set up a second unanswered score and narrowed the margin to 8 points, 28–20. The 49ers added a field goal before the quarter expired, bringing them to within 5 points of the Ravens, the team that had been ahead by 22 at the half. The teams remained separated by the same number of points when the game ended, 34–29. The Ravens' win avoided an upset, which might have more concretely entrenched the claim that the power failure was a purposeful effort to revive the 49ers and revitalize fan interest and sagging TV ratings for what had been to that point an undeniably lopsided contest.

"I'm not gonna accuse nobody of nothing because I don't know facts," said Baltimore Ravens Hall of Famer Ray Lewis, who was on the field when the lights failed. "But you're a zillion-dollar company, and your lights go out? No. No way," he speculated. "You cannot tell me somebody wasn't sitting there and when they say, 'The Ravens (are) about to blow them out. Man, we better do something,'" he surmised. "That's a huge shift in any game, in all seriousness. And as you see how huge it was because it let them right back in the game." Whether Ray Lewis really believed that or not, I cannot say. But, five years later he was sure to pop a reference to it into his 2018 Hall of Fame enshrinement speech in Canton, Ohio; it was a boisterous and entertaining monologue that was only one minute shorter than the blackout itself.

The 1997 Premier League Games: Conspiracy to Sway Games

Was a conspiracy to sway the game a total impossibility? There was a historical precedent. On December 3, 1997, a Premier League game between West Ham United and Crystal Palace ended prematurely when the stadium lights failed during a Monday evening game in London's Upton Park. In the United Kingdom, bets on the game had to be returned, but a group of speculators who wagered in Malaysia through a betting syndicate were paid on the score at the time the game was abandoned. Later in the month, on December 22, the lights inexplicably failed again at Selhurst Park, another English stadium during a match between Wimbledon and Arsenal. Evidently undaunted by the shrinking odds of remaining undetected, the betting syndicate allegedly targeted a third game, this time between Charlton and Liverpool. The plot was discovered when the local security guard who had been bribed to sabotage the game alerted the authorities, resulting in the arrest of four suspects.

WHAT HAPPENED TO THE SUPERDOME ELECTRICAL SYSTEM?

So, it is possible that a stadium's electrical system can be sabotaged. Did it happen that way in New Orleans? There is a prodigious mountain of evidence to suggest otherwise.

We didn't wait the six weeks it took for a forensic electrical engineer to complete a third-party investigative report before we got serious about how to avoid the career-ending possibility of a recurrence a year later. *It was an established fact that the relay opened.* Unless it was defective, that meant it detected an excessive increase in power consumption. Our own consultant introduced us to the concept of an *electrical budget*, a plan that is just like a financial budget, but one that evaluates how much power we need versus how much capacity we have, circuit-by-circuit, and minute-by-minute.

In New Jersey the following year, we would be hosting an even greater number of big events on game day at the complex than we did around the Superdome. So we began planning a test of the electrical system, simulating how it would respond to the uneven pattern of power consumption as parties and concerts ended, the game began, the halftime show unfolded, and the second half resumed. Although everything checked out fine, we still added four sets of backup generators to restore power in seconds if we still had to.

Meanwhile, the official investigation in New Orleans wrapped up. The new, upgraded electrical relay on the "A feed" did not appear to be defective. It did precisely what it was supposed to do and tripped when it sensed an increase in electrical current that was in excess of its *normal factory default setting.* Those last four words turned out to be the root cause of the power failure. As you might imagine, the Superdome is not a "factory default" kind of building and its electrical infrastructure would have tolerated a higher load. It's just that no one reset the relay to accommodate that essential piece of information.

Who should have known to recalibrate the relay for the stresses and strains of a major entertainment venue and the non-normal demands of a Super Bowl—the manufacturer, the utility, or the building? That may still be in dispute, but it doesn't really matter. Here's what does: the fast action of the Superdome operations team saved the Super Bowl from being canceled outright. You see, both relays— one on each of the feeds, "A feed" and "B feed"—were installed with the same factory settings. That means if the building staff hadn't immediately started to shut down the HVAC (heating, ventilation, and air-conditioning) system, the refrigerators, the nonessential lighting, and other power drains on the side of the building that did not fail, most likely the power would have gone out throughout the entire building, and possibly within seconds of the first failure.

I wouldn't have known to ask for the systems to be shut down, but I'm grateful that teammates who were both knowledgeable and empowered did when the heat was on and the lights were off. If they had not, my friends, it would have been "game over" for Super Bowl XLVII, a minute and 38 seconds into the second half. There was only one backup feeder. If the second one had failed, we would have been done for the night. Doug Thornton was right when he told me he couldn't guarantee it wasn't going to happen again, but he and his team had taken the steps that made it a whole lot less likely, and for my money, they are the unsung MVPs of Super Bowl XLVII.

There are a great many lessons to be learned after every Super Bowl—not just after the one when the lights went out; the one threatened by the protest against a new law; the one stricken with snow, ice, and unusable seats; or the one where everyone used the trains like we asked them to. In fact, there have always been lessons to be learned and improvements to be made after every project that I have worked on during my 30-year career of organizing and producing events. Even when things seem to go completely or mostly right, we commit to evaluating how we can make our projects more successful, profitable, and cost-effective; meet more of our objectives; or simply just make the customer experience better. And, when they go wrong, we thoroughly examine how we could have avoided that outcome, foreseen the challenges, been better prepared, or improved our response.

The Let-Down Effect

It is not always easy to get down to the serious business of evaluating how things went on a project, especially after a particularly stressful experience. Our bodies often undergo a curious physical rebound after being stoked by adrenaline, including a phenomenon called the "let-down effect." Once the source of the stress has passed, the evolutionary autoimmune response that protected us while we were unconsciously choosing between "fight or flight" reverses. We become more susceptible to the maladies we are as individuals prone to, from migraines and digestive discomforts to skin flare-ups and fatigue. That's why it is very common for us to get sick or feel discomfort after a particularly stressful time. There is, however, evidence that when we manage the stress we experience, we also manage the severity of physical let-down effects afterwards.

We can experience let-down effects after a pressure-filled, results-driven project, even when things have gone pretty well. When they haven't gone well at all, we can also feel disappointed, defeated, even despondent, professionally humiliated, and fearful for our jobs. The late NFL coach George Herbert Allen Sr., a veritable quote-machine, is credited as having said that losing the Super Bowl was "worse than death because you have to get up in the morning."

There's no two ways about it. Shaking off the lousy way we feel after we have invested our time, talent, and personal brand into a project that has, despite our best intentions, still spun a bit out of control, is tough. Maybe it was our fault that things went wrong, and maybe it wasn't. Perhaps we were successful in getting things back on track, or maybe we couldn't, but it was not for the lack of trying. We may have managed the issue to our best ability, or perhaps our own direct actions contributed to a result that could have been better. Coach Allen's sardonic quote reflected the stinging agony of having coached Washington in its Super Bowl VII loss to Miami on January 14, 1973. But the loss hardly made him a loser. When Coach Allen retired from the NFL five years later, he owned the tenth-best record in League history, with a .705 winning percentage, and he was enshrined in the Pro Football Hall of Fame in 2002.

I've never lost a Super Bowl, at least not on the field, so I can never fully comprehend the depth of Coach Allen's disappointment. But, I have woken up many mornings after feeling defeated and dejected by far less than ideal results. Some I can laugh about now, and some still hurt to think about. But I've learned that the keenness of the sting subsides. We can't go back and change anything we did, but we can own what happened, learn from it, share our learning with our teammates, and lessen the probability or the impact of a repeat occurrence. It seems trite to say: "Hey, stuff happens. Don't be too hard on yourself," and I can't remember ever feeling better after hearing it. It is entirely natural to be unhappy with failure and to be disappointed with a poor result. Endure the sting and own it, but it's what you do

WHAT TO DO WHEN THINGS GO WRONG

next that is essential, and that is to commit to being better prepared for next time. As Coach Allen also observed: "Winning is the science of being totally prepared. There is no detail too small."

PROJECT POSTPARTUM AND POSTMORTEMS

Thankfully, things don't always go wrong, and not all of us get sick or emotionally spent as our projects wind down. Many managers I have spoken with, however, share what I call "project postpartum." There is a bit of melancholy that our endeavor has been completed, and it seems that the longer we have been working on it, the deeper we have invested ourselves, and the greater the level of pressure we endured, the greater the sense of wistfulness. Part of this response is due to the sudden reduction of the stress hormones that had been coursing through our circulatory system, and part is due to the absence of the stimuli that precipitated their release in the first place. Suddenly, there seem to be fewer unrelenting deadlines, and just a little more room to breathe. By all means, take that breath whether things went predominantly right or mostly wrong, but not for too long. The project is not really over until we address a new set of self-imposed deadlines—our "project postmortems."

My former Radio City Music Hall boss, Barnett Lipton, hated that expression, and I understand why. *Postmortem* literally means "after death," and refers to an investigation into the cause of someone's demise. Once the project campaign is behind us, it's time to candidly evaluate *every* aspect of our performance. Did we meet our objectives, and if our metrics for success didn't measure up, why weren't the results as good as we had hoped? Were our original goals and expectations reasonable? In which ways did we succeed, and in which ways did we fail? How can we improve the outcome in the future? What should we keep doing, what should we stop doing, and what should we do better?

The After-Action Report Process

I always try to write up my own perceptions in an *after-action report* within a few days of completion. Setting that goal for myself provides me with a deadline that channels the "project postpartum," which I often experience after a major event, into a constructive continuation of the project.

My after-action report begins with reflections on whether our team accomplished the goals we set out to achieve. Most events I work on can be judged on relatively simple metrics—such as attendance, viewership, ticket revenue, and audience response—so I can evaluate our performance relatively quickly.

For businesses and projects that are judged on longer-term metrics—such as monthly revenue, customer satisfaction, or sales growth over time—an accurate assessment may require a more extended time period. Don't put off starting your after-action report while waiting for the numbers. Get started right away on everything else your report should analyze, like answers to these questions:

- What went right, and what did we do that worked well?
- What went right, but could have been done better?
- What went wrong, and how could it have been avoided or its impact lessened?
- Was our response to what went wrong effective and adequate?
- What would we do differently in the future to influence a better outcome?
- How did our team perform and how did they contribute to the result?
- What should we keep doing in the future, and what should we stop doing?

Writing my after-action report right away helps me to recollect more of the details before they naturally disintegrate with the passage of time.

Decay Theory proposes several reasons why memories may fade over time, but regardless of the cause, the longer we take to recall what we have learned, the more details are lost. It seems that the very act of quickly articulating our experiences in writing, even just by jotting down a key word or two, will help us better retain the information in our long-term memory. Our recollections will also be more comprehensive because we have begun to develop a written record.

We as project leaders are not alone in having leaky memories, of course. The same holds true for our teammates, business partners, and customers. When we get a survey from a hotel or airline, it is usually sent within a day of our stay or flight, so we can more accurately recall the details without interference and confusion with other travel experiences. Although I often ask teammates, both verbally and in writing, to send me postmortem comments, most never do, unless they want to share something that went particularly wrong. There is, however, an enormous amount of information on less consequential details—things that could have gone better—that if remedied can contribute incrementally to a more positive outcome. We just have to offer a forum to tease them out.

Postmortem Meetings and Sessions

Although I would always opt for a meeting, in person or by teleconference, to discuss the successes and failures of any project, sometimes it is difficult to coordinate availabilities due to the demands on the participants' time. Smaller, simpler projects can be evaluated with an internal survey or questionnaire, which can be answered at the respondent's convenience.

For bigger, more complicated projects, a formal postmortemprocess is essential. For many years, I had scheduled larger meetings, for up to two hours with 12 to 20 or more people, with knowledgeable teammates representing each business area. Everyone was to come armed with their notes, experiences, challenges, suggestions, and comments. But unless there was something that went egregiously wrong, it turned out that I usually ended up doing most of the talking and discussing the things that I felt could be improved. Or, one or two people dominated the conversation. Most of remaining teammates either felt their details were not worth the attention of everyone else, or they just didn't want to fall behind answering their e-mails during the meeting. It was simply impossible to engage everyone to share their points of view in a large, cross-organizational setting.

The year that everything seemed to go wrong at the Super Bowl, we knew there was an enormous amount of information and perspectives to collect. We decided to forgo the large meeting and replace it with a series of smaller, more focused sessions, scheduled for 60 minutes each, specifically dedicated to coming away with a deeper understanding of the experiences of one, or, at the very most, two related business units at any one time. Not only did we get more intelligence and depth in the more intimate setting, we discovered more things that went wrong EVERY year, but had never risen to a level of importance that resulted in our teammates sharing them at the larger meeting. It took a lot longer to conduct eight smaller postmortems than a single large one, but the investment of time was unquestionably worth it. In retrospect, though, I am sure that at least some of my colleagues were still holding back a little bit. Perhaps they didn't want to offend me or thought some of the issues they surfaced would be ignored and that it would be a waste of time to bring them up. There may have even been some distrust of me or of other teammates.

I hadn't even considered the last point until after I left the NFL. Neither had I understood the value of occasionally having objective, third parties conduct postmortems until the Indianapolis Motor Speedway asked me to host a companywide study of how the organization could work together more productively to manage their biggest and most widely viewed event, the Indy 500. We scheduled four solid days of individual department postmortem meetings, 90 minutes each, to explore how each business unit worked with others across the organization to stage "The Greatest Spectacle in Racing." I approached the assignment cautiously, with a list of prepared questions and conversation starters, and thought it would be daunting for participants to open up to a complete stranger. Instead, it seemed to be a liberating opportunity for the Indy team because they could share perspectives they had never articulated at other company meetings. One particularly memorable interchange vividly illustrated this for me:

"It is really difficult to work with *that* department," one manager offered when I asked the group about the biggest challenges they faced each year. "All of a sudden, they need something to happen, but they just don't understand how complicated it is to manage last-minute requests with everything else going on. This doesn't happen just once in a while, but all the time."

He was right, I agreed. Everything depends on everything else and one late change can have ripple effects that can impact many other things. "How do you think they feel about working with your department?" I asked.

"Hmmm . . . ," he had to take a moment to think about it. "They probably think we're really difficult to work with, too." Then, he added thoughtfully: "I'm sure they are just responding to a request from one of their partners."

Many more honest insights were gained during these department-focused postmortems in a setting populated with teammates who shared similar missions, concerns, and points of view. Most of the feedback was instructive and constructive, and helped to inform and sensitize management to the internal issues that were affecting the end product, interfering with progress and innovation, and impacting morale.

Schedule postmortems as soon as possible after the completion of a project. Whether conducting them yourself or through a third-party facilitator, be sure to craft and circulate a preliminary agenda ahead of time to give participants time to prepare thoughtful comments. When the time comes to meet, articulate your objectives and expectations for the meeting at the outset. Recognize the value of everyone's contribution, and welcome candor and criticism. Express your commitment to fixing problems and considering the group's recommendations. If there are specific things that went wrong, address them *directly* and encourage conversations on how to avoid them in the future. Add discussions that are relevant to that group's mission and their role in the project, but also leave time for the group to discuss their broader observations on topics and issues that are not necessarily related to their specific role or mission. You may be surprised at the diversity of opinion, insight, and information they offer about other aspects of the project. They may just be grateful that you asked, and more invested in the overall outcome because you did.

It's almost time to close the books on the last project, and to move on to the next one. We're more experienced and more prepared. This time every detail is sure to go completely right. Or will they? No, probably not.

CONCLUSION

A BULLET DODGED. FOR NOW.

Whatever things went wrong for whatever reason, they are now history and irretrievably anchored in the past. We may have worked tirelessly and taken extraordinary measures to imagine the wide range of places we could possibly fail. We planned meticulously and developed multiple contingencies to address the most probable things that could interfere with our project's success. We considered the complications of unintended consequences. We may have even pressure-tested our planning with a tabletop simulation of how we would respond should something fail anyway. It's a good thing, too, because despite our best intentions, it still did fail.

At that moment, we endured the reflexive jolt of adrenaline entering our bloodstreams and managed to resist our primeval reaction of "flight or fight." We and our empowered teammates confronted the problem, applying a broad diversity of expertise, experience, and perspectives to develop a methodical response in order to implement a reasoned solution. If the problem was not fixable within the time allowed to us, we sought to contain and manage its impact. We communicated quickly, clearly, and accurately with our customers, business partners, teammates, and the media, directly and on social platforms. Though the problem was solved or managed, it is usually not entirely behind us. A high degree of scrutiny may continue or even intensify within our organizations, in the court of public opinion, and in traditional and social media. Even if the problem was relatively minor and little noticed, from our own perspective we simply don't want whatever went wrong to go wrong again. The consequences of a repeat performance could be more damaging to both our company and to ourselves. There are certain steps yet to undertake, progressing our longer-term response through a series of phases: recover, review, learn, and revise.

RECOVER

We may have responded to the problem, capably corrected what went wrong, successfully attenuated the aftershocks, and, at minimum, took responsibility for the failure. What we do now is as important as anything we did before, and maybe even more so. As *Murphy's First Corollary* reminds us: *"Left to themselves, things tend to go from bad to worse."* We're not going to let that happen.

Our objective is now simple: whatever went wrong, we want it to never happen again. Our message to the outside world and our teammates is that we recognize the problem and regret the outcome. We are going to investigate what happened, fix what can be repaired, learn from our mistakes, and apply what we learn to do better in the future. There may be some unintended consequences still echoing from the original problem, and we will respond to those, too. We will continue to communicate and keep the appropriate parties apprised of our progress.

We continue to monitor and respond to negativity and dissatisfaction in the marketplace, and correct rumor and misinformation just as we did when the issue first surfaced. We gather data and customer sentiment proactively through direct conversations and social media. If we feel that the problem endangered the trust and business of customers and partners, we consider the use of surveys and focus groups to understand the extent of the reputational damage to the brand and to demonstrate our commitment to addressing the result.

Hopefully, what went wrong does not pose an existential challenge to the company, project, or to our own brands. Often, we can return to business-as-usual after we endure the ignominy of being the butt end of jokes around the water cooler, in the industry, on social media feeds, or even on late-night television. But when the problem is severe and the impact is serious, recovery can take a long time.

Making things right with customers and partners can cost money, perhaps a great deal of it. It can affect sales and it can be uncomfortable as our brand works to restore its reputation and rebuild trust. It can, in extreme cases, be litigious, a process that itself can extend the reputational and financial ramifications for years.

During the recovery phase, the best message to get out to the organization, and if appropriate to the outside marketplace, is that the company is committed to performing better, emerging stronger, and being better prepared. What is essential is that this is more than just a message. It should be a mantra. We have to mean it, believe it, and act on it. First, of course, we must get to the bottom of what actually led to something going wrong and how we handled things once it did.

REVIEW

Our objective during the review phase is to gather all the information we need to fully understand what happened and why, and to honestly evaluate the effectiveness of our response. Only then can we make the necessary changes in our plans, procedures, and processes to avoid a recurrence, and improve the outcome if it does happen again anyway.

We begin the review process immediately by recording our own after-action notes, requesting observations from teammates, disseminating internal surveys, and scheduling postmortem meetings. We then distill what may be a copious amount of input and turn it into a framework for learning and acting. As postmortems often bring issues to the surface that may not be directly related to the things that we already knew went wrong, it is helpful to group insights, good and bad, into categories: operational, organizational, financial, experiential, and other classifications specific to your project and business.

In the meantime, we have already begun the root cause analysis to ensure that we are treating the sources, and not simply the symptoms, of our identified problems. Independent third-party investigations may concurrently be underway, the results of which often provide great additional data for the review process. We and our teammates may be asked for input and perspectives as outside parties conduct their own inquiries, which we should, of course, provide with accuracy.

Third parties, however, are not guaranteed to be objective and may have been launched with their own specific agendas. Before participating in an independent inquiry, be sure to consult your legal team for direction and guidance. With their own timelines and priorities, the results of an external process can take longer to complete than we can afford as we progress through our own review process. Add their conclusions, or at least their perceptions, to your collection of data. Prepare your communications team for when their report will be released. If the findings are not accurate or objective, work with them to respond with corrections.

The most important thing we can do as we collect information is to LISTEN to everyone who provides it. As we make or respond to calls, e-mails, social media posts, and media inquiries, conduct internal postmortems, and participate in independent inquiries, we need to take the time to truly understand the comments, perspectives, and other feedback we hear. If what went wrong resulted in a poor experience for our customers or partners, we should put ourselves in their shoes. Appreciate the experiences they encountered and how they feel. Provide explanations of what went wrong and tell them what we are going to do to avoid similar situations in the future, but resist the urge to be defensive, deflect blame, or make excuses.

I've had occasions to reach out or make myself available to hear directly about lousy experiences from customers and partners. I let them tell their story and try very hard to be patient and not interrupt. It is not usually pleasant to listen to, but it is often appreciated by those who are given the opportunity to share their experiences.

If we acknowledge that we provided less than what we had set out to, it demonstrates that we care and this helps to promote the rebuilding of their trust with the brand, one partner and one customer at a time. We want to communicate that we empathize with any party who encountered inconvenience as a result of what went wrong, regardless of its root cause.

During the review phase, we must convey a consistent message that we are welcoming of any and all information—from inside or outside the organization—that can help us avoid a similar challenge in the future. We must express our appreciation for them as active participants in helping us identify problems. By providing feedback we can learn from, they are valuable contributors to our future success.

LEARN

Biologists classify common animal behaviors into two categories. The first, an *innate behavior*, is a genetically programmed reaction. It can be *reflexive*, like flinching when we see an object heading toward our eyes, or it can be *instinctive*, like a bird fulfilling the sudden urge to sing at the break of dawn. A *learned behavior*, on the other hand, is a change in how an animal responds as a result of an experience. An *experience* might be a personal event (I burned my hand on a pot because I wasn't wearing an oven mitt), one that is observed (I saw my mother burn her hand on a pot because she didn't use an oven mitt), or one that is taught (my mother told me not to touch a pot without an oven mitt). As a result, we learn how not to get burned when touching a hot pot.

Whether we experience something directly, observe it, or hear about it from someone else, we haven't really "learned" anything unless the information we have gathered changes how we approach a similar situation in the future. Our objective during the learning phase is to analyze the information and perspectives we have gathered and to identify not just the root cause, but all the contributing factors to what went wrong, and to apply that input to developing options for changing how we do things.

We have now identified the root cause and contributing factors, recognized the results and consequences, and assessed the sufficiency and appropriateness of our response. We have learned that changes are required to reduce the probability of a recurrence or to lessen the severity of the outcome. Was what happened something we should have imagined and for which we should now have a contingency? Were there things we could have done differently in planning and preparation? Should we make a change to our procedures, process, or organizational structure? Do we need to install or replace equipment that could have prevented the problem or improved our response? Recognizing our constraints, do we need to reallocate a portion of our budget to institute improvements or add people or skill sets to the process?

Was the problem a physical or system failure, a communications failure, or a response failure? Almost every story in this book relates to learning gained from a thorough review process:

- Our team learned about relays, what they are designed to do, and how they may react to wildly uneven patterns of power consumption in an entertainment venue.
- We changed our planning to include a rigorous test of the next host stadium's power infrastructure and added generators that would make up for some of the energy shortfall if there is another failure.
- We learned that we could improve the pace of good decision-making by changing how we empowered our teammates to work more directly with one another across the web of command, reducing the number of issues that needed to be elevated through layers of the organization.
- We learned that contingency plans related to redirecting the movement of large numbers of people could only be implemented if we added wayfinding signage, reassigned teammates to help guide guests, and had a way to quickly activate the change.
- Our friends in Hawaii learned that their Emergency Management System was far too susceptible to human error. Using the existing procedure made it quick and easy to send an urgent alert to the population, but it was equally easy to send a false alarm. It was also apparently more complicated to withdraw the warning than it was to send the alarm in the first place.

Repeating one of this book's common themes: "We learn more from things that go wrong than those that go right." Consider reaching outside your own project team to other organizations to see what they have learned from experience with similar problems. Unless they are a direct competitor, most will be pleased to share their own war stories and triumphs over adversity. As American humorist Sam Levenson (1911–1980) once said, "You must learn from the mistakes of others. You can't possibly live long enough to make them all yourself."

REVISE

We have now gathered and analyzed the information we have amassed, reached conclusions as to the root cause and contributing factors to what went wrong, and determined what needs to be changed, improved, or remedied. How we will do that is the objective of this phase.

Many times, there are multiple solutions from which to choose to be better prepared and to keep the same thing from happening again. The changes we can make can be simple or complex, cheap or costly, easy to implement or culturally challenging for the organization.

The Pro Football Hall of Fame Game

The Pro Football Hall of Fame Enshrinement Weekend is composed of several days of celebration in the host city of Canton, Ohio. The NFL's first preseason match, the Hall of Fame Game, is held in what is now known as Tom Benson Stadium. For many years, the game was the finale of the weekend. The stadium was also the site of the ceremony honoring the incoming class of football greats on the evening prior to the game, on an elaborate stage before a field filled with thousands of seats, broadcast positions, and technical equipment for the show.

In 2016, poor field conditions and a concern for player safety forced a last-minute cancellation of the nationally televised game. The decision to cancel was attributed to "congealed and rubberized" paint in the end zones and the center of the field, which resulted in an unsafe surface for playing football. The root cause was the haste in converting the field from a setting for a show to a venue for a game. In an effort to hasten the drying of the paint on the artificial turf, the grounds crew reportedly employed heaters that caused the paint to become gummy and the plastic turf to melt, resulting in a treacherous hard-as-concrete surface.

The revision the Hall of Fame proposed to the NFL was not based on an improvement to the conversion process or the painting of logos. It was made based on the right priorities. The chief concern for both organizations was to ensure the field for the Hall of Fame Game would be guaranteed to be in the best possible condition for the players, and the only way to do that was to play the game first, not last. The schedule was altered the following year so a fully prepared, groomed, and painted field would host the game on Thursday, and then be converted in time for the Enshrinement Ceremony on Saturday. Rearranging the preseason schedule may have been institutionally challenging for the NFL, but the risks of not making the change were deemed important enough to overcome the complications.

The Super Bowl Blackout

The root cause of the inability of CBS to provide audio coverage during the opening minutes during the Super Bowl blackout was because the equipment for the play-by-play team in the press box was reliant on receiving power from the building. The production truck could continue to broadcast when the lights went out because they were operating on their own power source. The network's procedures were changed in future years to ensure that the announcers' booth was also powered by a reliable external source.

False Ballistic Missile Attack in Hawaii

An investigative report, which was filed by the Director of the Hawaii Emergency Management Agency, offered 23 recommendations to address not only the root cause of the false ballistic missile alarm and the delay of issuing a correction to the public, but also a series of factors that could conceivably contribute to future errors or miscommunications. Among the recommendations included were changes in the system's software, such as adding a simple "cancellation" option, and a confirmation step that queried: "Are you sure you want to send a 'Real World Ballistic Missile Alert'?" Other recommendations altered the process, including a two-person confirmation requirement to eliminate the chance of an error by a single human.

Additional Information About Making Revisions

Most of these revisions may seem so obvious as to cause us to wonder why they were not imagined, anticipated, and planned for long before something went wrong. Of course, they seem obvious in retrospect, and we ourselves have probably experienced many things that have gone wrong under our watch that seemed so clearly avoidable. Why, then, were they not?

I have rarely been involved with a project for which there was no pressure of time. We simply have a lot to imagine, plan, execute, and to which we must ultimately respond. There may be ways we have done things that have not been updated in a while, things we do more out of habit and that were best practices once upon a time. It is always cheaper, faster, and easier to "dust off" an old plan, or at least elements of one, than to start a project from scratch, but things change all the time. We need to continually update, or even uproot our approaches from yesterday's best practices to the best intelligence, technology, and research that are available today.

Finally, be sure to communicate with your teammates that you are preparing to implement changes. They can provide a great resource to validate your thinking and their diversity of experience can better the chances that the changes you make will have fewer unintended consequences. It also can't help but boost morale because, after all, they have been wondering what you were going to do to make things work better since things first went wrong. Apply your teammates to testing, simulating, and reviewing the results of the changes. They are as invested in success as you are!

READY FOR THE NEXT THING TO GO WRONG?

I can assure you, if it hasn't happened to you—something going horribly wrong for you at work or in life—it just hasn't happened to you *yet*. And, if it has happened, it's going to happen again and again, despite your creative imagining, expert planning, and deft execution. Hopefully, it's not the same thing that goes wrong for the same reason. But if it is, you and your team are better prepared for it. Notwithstanding your calm, capable response when it does, there will be unnecessary second-guessing, Monday-morning quarterbacking, and very necessary reflection and self-evaluation. You will have to review, learn, and revise all over again. And again.

Despite years of experience that have contributed to making our preparations more informed and thorough, our execution better and more expert, and our skills in responding to challenges stronger and more effective, we never truly reach the ultimate level of expertise. Danish physicist Niels Bohr, for one, viewed an expert as someone who has made all of his errors in a very tiny area.

I've got plenty of mistakes still left in me, and you do, too. What we get better at is imagining more of the things that could go wrong, anticipating more of those that do go wrong, and, when they happen, managing a better response and recovery.

Getting back up on the metaphorical horse after a bruising fall because something went wrong is not easy. Our natural instincts encourage the development of a new learned behavior, making us a little more risk averse. Accept that what went wrong happened and take the responsibility to fix it. The behavior you will learn instead is that you can't eliminate the possibility that something will go wrong, but you can exert a great deal of control over the probability of the risks, and even more control over the response and recovery if the odds go against you.

There is apparently a right way to fall off a real horse, one that will make it more likely you'll be in better condition to climb back into the saddle after you've dusted yourself off. There is also a right way to fall off a metaphorical horse, one that will improve your resilience and make it a little easier to get back up when you next fall on your ass. First, forgive yourself for falling. You may have failed to stay squarely in the saddle, but gravity is always going to do the rest. You cannot control gravity, or most everything else around you, but you can learn how to fall. Each time you have fallen, appreciate what you've learned and integrate that learning to make you a better rider.

Walt Disney said: "All the adversity I've had in my life, all my troubles and obstacles, have strengthened me . . . You may not realize it when it happens, but a kick in the teeth may be the best thing in the world for you." I've gotten kicked in the teeth plenty. But, take it from me, it's harder to get kicked in the teeth if you get up and right back in the saddle.

REFERENCES

Chapter 2. Defining Disaster

Apple, Inc., "iPhone Battery & Power Repair," https://support.apple.com /iphone/repair/battery-power.

Associated Press, "Officer Gives His Version of United Flight Scandal, Says Passenger Injured Himself," *New York Daily News*, April 24, 2017, http://www.nydailynews.com/news/national/aviation-officer-version -united-flight-removal-article-1.3096121.

Chapter 3. Anything That Can Go Wrong

Burt, Bill, "Star-Spangled Career: Bruins' Rene Rancourt Reflects on a Life Defined by the National Anthem," *The Salem News*, April 6, 2018, https://www.salemnews.com/news/state_news/star-spangled-career -bruins-rene-rancourt-reflects-on-a-life/article_0b8ec8bb-9b87-50db -abe7-5b5e4eb46192.html.

Chandler, R. F., "Project MX-981: John Paul Stapp and Deceleration Research," *U.S. National Library of Medicine*, National Institutes of Health, 45: v–xxii, November 2001, https://www.ncbi.nlm.nih.gov /pubmed/17458737.

"Edward A. Murphy, Jr.," in *Wikipedia*. Retrieved October 26, 2018, from https://en.wikipedia.org/wiki/Edward_A._Murphy_Jr.

"G-Force," in *Wikipedia*. Retrieved October 26, 2018, from https://en .wikipedia.org/wiki/G-force.

"Murphy's Law Site: All the Laws of Murphy in One Place," excerpted from *The Desert Wings*, March 3, 1978, http://www.murphys-laws.com /murphy/murphy-true.html.

Chapter 4. It's a Matter of Time

Merriam-Webster.com, "Your Deadline Won't Kill You, or Will It?" Retrieved October 26, 2018, from https://www.merriam-webster.com/words-at -play/your-deadline-wont-kill-you.

Zarrett, E. Jay, "How Much Do Super Bowl Commercials Cost in 2018?" *The Sporting News*, February 4, 2018, http://www.sportingnews.com/us /nfl/news/super-bowl-2018-how-much-do-super-bowl-commercials-cost -nbc-coca-cola-hyundai/1qap05f9qd6hd1kn2i9lahwlk3.

Zinser, Lynn, "In Coughlin Time, You Can Be Early and Still be Late," *New York Times*, September 14, 2004, https://www.nytimes.com/2004 /09/14/sports/football/in-coughlin-time-you-can-be-early-and-still-be -late.html.

Chapter 5. Living in the Land of the Likely

BaseballAlmanac.com, "2002 All-Star Game." Retrieved October 26, 2018, from http://www.baseball-almanac.com/asgbox/yr2002as.shtml.

Glauber, Bob, "Super Bowl Officials Hope for Best Weather, Prepare for Worst," *Newsday*, January 22, 2014, https://www.newsday.com/sports /football/super-bowl/super-bowl-officials-hope-for-best-weather-prepare -for-worst-1.6852664.

"Major League Baseball All-Star Game," in *Wikipedia*. Retrieved October 26, 2018, from https://en.wikipedia.org/wiki/Major_League_Baseball _All-Star_Game.

Price, Bill, "Super Bowl XLVIII, Slated for MetLife Stadium—Home of the NY Giants and NY Jets—in 2014, Will See Freezing Cold Weather, says Farmer's Almanac," *New York Daily News*, January 24, 2013, http://www.nydailynews.com/sports/football/giants/freezer-bowl -metlife-stadium-super-bowl-blustery-14-article-1.1246452.

Schoenfield, David, "#TBT: The 2002 All-Star Game Fiasco," *ESPN.com*, July 9, 2015, http://www.espn.com/blog/sweetspot/post/_/id/60077/tbt -the-all-star-game-fiasco.

Sheinin, Dave, "Baseball Has Pace-of-Play Problems; Extra Innings Aren't One of Them," *Washington Post*, February 9, 2017, https:// www.washingtonpost.com/sports/nationals/baseball-has-pace-of-play -problems-extra-innings-arent-one-of-them/2017/02/09/fb61ae16-eeed -11e6-9662-6eedf1627882_story.html?utm_term=.f9795ab46d63.

Weather.com, Monthly Weather Forecast and Climate, Glendale, AZ, https://www.weather-us.com/en/arizona-usa/glendale-climate.

Chapter 6. The "BCD's" of Contingency Planning

BrainyQuote.com, "Top 10 Vince Lombardi Quotes." Retrieved October 27, 2018, from https://www.brainyquote.com/lists/authors/top_10_vince _lombardi_quotes.

Branch, John, "Ice and Injuries Mar Super Bowl Events," *New York Times*, February 4, 2011, https://www.nytimes.com/2011/02/05/sports/football /05dallas.html.

Cleveland.com, "Uncommon Dallas Show Shouldn't Affect NBA All-Star Weekend Events' Hope is All Players Get There," February 22,

2010, https://www.cleveland.com/ohio-sports-blog/index.ssf/2010/02
/uncommon_snowfall_in_dallas_sh.html.

"Dallas-Fort Worth Metroplex" in *Wikipedia*. Retrieved October 27, 2018, from https://en.wikipedia.org/wiki/Dallas–Fort_Worth_metroplex.

McCoy, Kevin, Doug Stanglin, and Michael Winter, "NYC Marathon Canceled Amid Criticism," *USAToday.com*, November 2, 2012, https://www.usatoday.com/story/news/nation/2012/11/02/new-york-city-marathon-bloomberg/1676883/.

Melnick, Meredith, "New York Marathon Canceled in the Wake of Hurricane Sandy," *Huffington Post*, November 2, 2012, https://www.huffpost.com/entry/new-york-marathon-canceled-sandy_n_2067241.

Profootballhof.com, "Super Bowl Game Time Temperatures." Retrieved October 27, 2018, from https://www.profootballhof.com/news/super-bowl-game-time-temperatures/.

Sherman, Ted, "How MetLife Scored Super Bowl 2014, Bringing the Big Game to N.J.," *NJ Advance Media for NJ.com*, January 29, 2014, https://www.nj.com/super-bowl/index.ssf/2014/01/how_metlife_stadium_scored_super_bowl_2014_bringing_the_big_game_to_nj.html.

St. John, Allen, "6-Minute Shuffle: How the NFL Sets Up a Super Bowl Halftime Stage," *Popular Mechanics*, March 11, 2010, https://www.popularmechanics.com/adventure/sports/a5307/4344900/.

Weatherworks.com, "2013–2014 Northeast Winter Stats," https://www.weatherworksinc.com/winter-statistics-2013–2014.

Wunderground.com, Dallas-Fort Worth International, TX. Retrieved October 27, 2018, from https://www.wunderground.com/history/monthly/KDFW/date/2011-2-1.

Chapter 7. Hope is Not a Strategy

Diamond, Dan, ed., *The Official National Hockey League Stanley Cup Centennial Book* (Toronto: McClelland & Stewart, Inc.), 1992.

Halekulani.com, "The Legends and the Uses of Ti Leaves." Retrieved October 27, 2018, from https://www.halekulani.com/blog/legends-and-uses-ti-leaves.

Murphy, Ryan, "10 Most Superstitious Athletes," *MensJournal.com*. Retrieved October 27, 2018, from https://www.mensjournal.com/sports/10-most-superstitious-athletes.

Chapter 9. Communicate or Die

Harris, Gardiner, "Peanut Product Recall Grows in Salmonella Scare," *New York Times*, January 28, 2009, https://www.nytimes.com/2009/01/29/us/29peanut.html.

Lake Champlain Chocolates, "How to Store Chocolates." Retrieved October 30, 2018, from https://www.lakechamplainchocolates.com/how-to-store-chocolate.

Lewis, Lauren, "Indianapolis Motor Speedway is So Big. These 8 Things Can Fit Inside with Room to Spare," *WRTV, Indychannel.com*, May 22, 2015, https://www.theindychannel.com/news/local-news/indianapolis-motor-speedway-is-so-big-these-8-things-can-fit-inside-with-room-to-spare.

Richtel, Matt, and Simon Romero, "The Blackout of 2003: Communications; When Wireless Phones Failed Because of Heavy Use, Callers Turned to Landlines," *New York Times*, August 15, 2003, https://www.nytimes.com/2003/08/15/business/blackout-2003-communications-when-wireless-phones-failed-because-heavy-use.html.

Wunderground.com, Tampa, FL. Retrieved October 30, 2018, from https://www.wunderground.com/history/daily/us/fl/tampa/KTPA/date/2009-1-27.

Chapter 10. Command and Collaborate

"Battle of Guam (1944)," in *Wikipedia*. Retrieved October 30, 2018, from https://en.wikipedia.org/wiki/Battle_of_Guam_(1944).

Kristof, Nicholas D., "Shoichi Yokoi, 82, is Dead; Japan Soldier Hid 27 Years," *New York Times*, September 26, 1997, https://www.nytimes.com/1997/09/26/world/shoichi-yokoi-82-is-dead-japan-soldier-hid-27-years.html.

Worthington, Daryl, "The Japanese Soldier Who Spent 27 Years Waiting for Orders," *NewHistorian.com*, January 24, 2017, https://www.newhistorian.com/japanese-soldier-spent-27-years-waiting-orders/7912/.

Chapter 12. Managing the Inverted Pyramid

Catlin, Kevin, "A Surgeon and Janitor Teach Us Leadership and Team-building," *Linkedin.com*, September 11, 2014, https://www.linkedin.com/pulse/20140911174208-16498332-line-of-site-leadership-and-team-building.

Kruse, Kevin, "What is Leadership?" *Forbes.com*, April 9, 2013, https://www.forbes.com/sites/kevinkruse/2013/04/09/what-is-leadership/#7395370b5b90.

Chapter 13. Building an Empowerment Culture

Anaejionu, Regina, "Why the Empowerment of Employees is Becoming Important in Organizations," *Chron.com*. Retrieved October 31, 2018, from https://smallbusiness.chron.com/empowerment-employees-becoming-important-organizations-11542.html.

Hamlin, Kristin, "The Pros and Cons of Empowerment in an Organization," *Chron.com*. Retrieved October 31, 2018, from https://smallbusiness.chron.com/pro-cons-empowerment-organization-13397.html.

Society for Human Resource Management, "Employee Job Satisfaction and Engagement: The Doors of Opportunity are Open," 2017. Retrieved October 31, 2018, from https://www.shrm.org/hr-today/trends-and -forecasting/research-and-surveys/Documents/2017-Employee-Job -Satisfaction-and-Engagement-Executive-Summary.pdf.

Chapter 14. Leading a Community of Problem Solvers

Yahoo.com, "Godzilla Joins Jaws, Alien, and the Blob in the Shy Monster Hall of Fame," May 19, 2014, https://www.yahoo.com/entertainment /godzilla-joins-jaws-alien-and-the-blob-in-the-shy-86214024547.html.

Chapter 15. Everything Affects Everything Else

Kahn, Chris, "'Drunkenstein' Planned Black Sunday at Super Bowl," *Associated Press,* February 8, 2008.

"Robert K. Merton," in *Wikipedia.* Retrieved on October 31, 2018, from https://en.wikipedia.org/wiki/Robert_K._Merton.

St. John, Allen, *The Billion Dollar Game: Behind the Scenes of the Greatest Day in American Sport, Super Bowl Sunday,* (New York: Doubleday, 2000).

Williams, Carol J., "9th Circuit Overturns Conviction of Man Who Made Super Bowl Threats," *Los Angeles Times,* August 24, 2010, http://articles .latimes.com/2010/aug/24/local/la-me-superbowl-plotter-20100824.

Chapter 16. Real-Time Management

Breech, John, "Retired Peyton Manning Finally Explains the True Meaning of his Omaha Call," *CBSsports.com,* April 12, 2017, https://www .cbssports.com/nfl/news/retired-peyton-manning-finally-explains-the -true-meaning-of-his-omaha-call/.

Kissel, B. J., "Breaking Down the Art of the QB Audible," *Bleacherreport .com,* July 26, 2013, https://bleacherreport.com/articles/1716979 -breaking-down-the-art-of-the-qb-audible.

McIntyre, Jamie, "Watchdog: Pentagon May Have Wasted $30 Million on Buying the Wrong Pattern of Afghan Army Uniforms," *Washington examiner.com,* June 21, 2017, https://www.washingtonexaminer.com /watchdog-pentagon-may-have-wasted-30-million-on-buying-the -wrong-pattern-of-afghan-army-uniforms/article/2626606.

Selig, Meg, "How Do Work Breaks Help Your Brain? 5 Surprising Answers," *PsychologyToday.com,* April 18, 2017, https://www.psychologytoday.com /us/blog/changepower/201704/how-do-work-breaks-help-your-brain -5-surprising-answers.

Chapter 17. Two-Minute Drill

Funk, Liz, "The Hidden Power in Trusting Your Gut Instincts," *FastCompany .com,* April 7, 2016, https://www.fastcompany.com/3058609/the-hidden -power-in-trusting-your-gut-instincts.

Massarella, Linda, "Accountants Fired from Oscars After Best Picture Fiasco," *Pagesix.com*, March 1, 2017, https://pagesix.com/2017/03/01/accountants-fired-from-oscars-after-best-picture-fiasco/.

Nicas, Jack, and Kris Maher, "Indiana Right-to-Work Bill Advances," *Wall Street Journal*, January 26, 2012, https://www.wsj.com/articles/SB10001424052970203718504577183224089135672.

Rock, David, "Easily Distracted: Why It's Hard to Focus, and What to Do About It," *PsychologyToday.com*, October 4, 2009, https://www.psychologytoday.com/us/blog/your-brain-work/200910/easily-distracted-why-its-hard-focus-and-what-do-about-it.

St. John, Allen, *The Billion Dollar Game: Behind the Scenes of the Greatest Day in American Sport, Super Bowl Sunday*, (New York: Doubleday, 2000).

St. John, Allen, "The NFL's Super Bowl Czar Shares Four Crunch Time Management Tips – and His Best Big Game Story," *Forbes.com*, February 2, 2014, https://www.forbes.com/sites/allenstjohn/2014/02/02/the-nfls-super-bowl-czar-shares-his-management-tips-and-his-best-big-game-story/#709996e71359.

Weinger, Mackenzie, "Daniels Signs Right-to-Work Law," *Politico.com*, February 1, 2012, https://www.politico.com/story/2012/02/indiana-right-to-work-by-super-bowl-072304.

Yee, Lawrence, Stuart Oldham, and Jacob Bryant, "New Photos Show PWC Accountant Tweeting, Mixing Envelopes Backstage at Oscars, *Variety.com*, March 1, 2017, https://variety.com/2017/film/news/oscar-best-picture-gaffe-brian-cullinan-envelope-1201999283/.

Chapter 18. Confronting the "Oops-Damn" Moment

Barker, Anne, "Hawaii: Here's What Would Happen if There Was a Real Nuclear Attack," *ABC.net.au*, January 15, 2018, https://www.abc.net.au/news/2018-01-15/hawaii-what-would-happen-if-there-was-a-real-nuke/9330162.

CNN Staff, "Timeline of the Hawaii False Missile Alert Shows How Drill Went Wrong," *CNN.com*, January 30, 2018, https://www.cnn.com/2018/01/30/us/hawaii-false-missile-alert-timeline/index.html.

Cohen, Zachary, "Missile Threat Alert for Hawaii a False Alarm; Officials Blame Employee Who Pushed 'Wrong Button'," *CNN.com*, January 14, 2018, https://www.cnn.com/2018/01/13/politics/hawaii-missile-threat-false-alarm/index.html.

Hawaii Emergency Management Agency Memo, "False Ballistic Missile Alert Investigation for January 13, 2018," dated January 29, 2018 from Retired Brigadier General Bruce E. Oliviera to Major General Arthur J. Logan, https://dod.hawaii.gov/wp-content/uploads/2018/01/report2018-01-29-181149.pdf.

Panda, Ankit, "False Alarms of the Apocalypse," *TheAtlantic,com*, January 13, 2018, https://www.theatlantic.com/international/archive/2018/01/what-the-hell-happened-in-hawaii/550514/.

Park, Madison, "Here's What Went Wrong with the Hawaii False Alarm," *CNN.com*, January 31, 2018, https://www.cnn.com/2018/01/31/us/hawaii-false-alarm-investigation-findings/index.html.

Quealy, Kevin, "How Much Would You Put Up with to Avoid United Airlines," *New York Times*, April 17, 2017, https://www.nytimes.com/2017/04/17/upshot/how-much-would-people-put-up-with-to-avoid-united-airlines.html.

Shen, Lucinda, "United Airlines Stock Drops $1.4 Billion After Passenger Removal Controversy," *Fortune.com*, April 11, 2017, http://fortune.com/2017/04/11/united-airlines-stock-drop/.

Shen, Lucinda, "United Airlines' Stock Has Recovered After a Doctor Was Dragged Off a Plane," *Fortune.com*, April 12, 2017, http://fortune.com/2017/04/12/united-airlines-stock/.

U.S. Geological Survey, "Earthquake Hazards Program." Retrieved November 2, 2018, from https://earthquake.usgs.gov/.

Chapter 19. The Crisis Within, The Crisis Without

Ankrom, Sheryl, "Anxiety Attacks vs. Panic Attacks," VeryWellMind.com, September 25, 2018, https://www.verywellmind.com/anxiety-attacks-versus-panic-attacks-2584396.

Bergland, Christopher, "Don't Panic! Stress is Contagious." *PsychologyToday.com*, June 29, 2016, https://www.psychologytoday.com/us/blog/the-athletes-way/201606/dont-panic-stress-is-contagious.

Cuncic, Arlin, "What Happens to Your Body During a Panic Attack?" *VeryWellMind.com*. Retrieved November 1, 2018, from https://www.verywellmind.com/what-happens-to-your-body-during-a-panic-attack-3024889.

Felman, Adam, "What Are Anxiety Disorders?" *MedicalNewsToday.com*. Retrieved October 26, 2018, from https://www.medicalnewstoday.com/articles/323454.php.

"Freezing Behavior," in *Wikipedia*. Retrieved October 30, 2018, from https://en.wikipedia.org/wiki/Freezing_behavior.

Li, Paul, and Jeannine Stamatakis, "What Happens in the Brain When We Experience a Panic Attack, *ScientificAmerican.com*, July 1, 2011, https://www.scientificamerican.com/article/what-happens-in-the-brain-when-we-experience/.

Remes, Olivia, "Surprising Ways to Beat Anxiety and Become Mentally Strong—According to Science," *TheConversation.com*, June 19, 2015, http://theconversation.com/surprising-ways-to-beat-anxiety-and-become-mentally-strong-according-to-science-77978.

Schaeffer, Charles, "How to Manage Panic Attacks," *Psychology Today.com*, August 4, 2016, https://www.psychologytoday.com/us/blog/women-s-mental-health-matters/201608/how-manage-panic-attacks.

Scott, Nate, "Refuge of Last Resort: Five Days Inside the Superdome for Hurricane Katrina," *USAToday.com*, August 24, 2015, https://ftw.usatoday.com/2015/08/refuge-of-last-resort-five-days-inside-the-superdome-for-hurricane-katrina.

Sissons, Claire, "What Happens When You Get an Adrenaline Rush?" *MedicalNewsToday.com*. Retrieved July 17, 2018, from https://www.medicalnewstoday.com/articles/322490.php

Smith, Melinda, Lawrence Robinson, and Jeanne Segal, "Panic Attacks and Panic Disorder," *HelpGuide.org*, September 2018, https://www.helpguide.org/articles/anxiety/panic-attacks-and-panic-disorders.htm.

Welsh, Tim, "It Feels Instantaneous, But How Long Does It Really Take to Think a Thought?" *TheConversation.com*, June 26, 2015, https://theconversation.com/it-feels-instantaneous-but-how-long-does-it-really-take-to-think-a-thought-42392.

Chapter 20. Right Has Left the Building

Associated Press, "Tostitos Commercial Dropped from Super Bowl After Bungee-Jumping Death," January 24, 1997, https://www.apnews.com/f7c31c881da45e2b24cb44ce6adfb538.

DePass, Dee, Judd Zulgad, and Dennis J. McGrath, "Metrodome Roof Rips, Collapses," *StarTribune.com*, December 13, 2010, http://www.startribune.com/metrodome-roof-rips-collapses/111748539/.

The Nielsen Company, "Super Bowl XLIV Most Watched Super Bowl of All Time," *Nielsen.com*, February 8, 2010, https://www.nielsen.com/us/en/insights/news/2010/super-bowl-xliv-most-watched-super-bowl-of-all-time.html.

Spera, Keith, "Stage Collapse Outside Super Bowl Stadium Injures Four," *NOLA.com*, February 3, 2010, https://www.nola.com/superbowl/index.ssf/2010/02/stage_collapse_outside_super_b.html.

Springer, Steve, "Halftime Performer is Killed in Bungee Jump in Superdome," *LATimes.com*, January 25, 1997, http://articles.latimes.com/1997-01-25/sports/sp-21917_1_bungee-jump-in-superdome.

Washington State Department of Enterprise Services, "Root Cause Analysis," Retrieved November 5, 2018 from https://des.wa.gov/services/risk-management/about-risk-management/enterprise-risk-management/root-cause-analysis.

"Super Bowl XXXI" in *Wikipedia*. Retrieved November 5, 2018, from https://en.wikipedia.org/wiki/Super_Bowl_XXXI.

"Super Bowl XL" in *Wikipedia*. Retrieved November 5, 2018, from https://en.wikipedia.org/wiki/Super_Bowl_XL.

Chapter 21. Managing Recovery

Burke, Timothy, "Watch CBS Herp and Derp Its Way Through the Super Bowl Power Outage," *Deadspin.com*, February 4, 2013, https://deadspin.com/5981464/watch-cbs-herp-and-derp-its-way-through-the-super-bowl-power-outage.

Guthrie, Marisa, "Super Bowl 2013: CBS Sports' Sean McManus on the Blackout and the F-Bomb," *HollywoodReporter.com*, February 6, 2013, https://www.hollywoodreporter.com/news/super-bowl-blackout-f-bomb-418419.

Ives, Nat, and Rupal Parekh, "Marketers Jump on Super Bowl Blackout with Real-time Twitter Campaigns," *AdAge.com*, February 3, 2013, https://adage.com/article/special-report-super-bowl/marketers-jump-super-bowl-blackout-twitter/239575/.

InternetLiveStats.com, http://www.internetlivestats.com/twitter-statistics/.

James, Matt, "React vs Respond: What's the Difference?" *PsychologyToday.com*, September 1, 2016, https://www.psychologytoday.com/us/blog/focus-forgiveness/201609/react-vs-respond.

Katz, Michael, "The Five Biggest Super Bowl Moments on Twitter," *USAToday.com*, February 4, 2013, https://www.usatoday.com/story/gameon/2013/02/04/super-bowl-2013-on-twitter-ravens-49ers/1890079/.

NOLA.com, "Super Bowl 2013 Blackout Caused by Faulty Relay Equipment, Entergy Says," February 23, 2018, https://www.nola.com/superbowl/index.ssf/2013/02/super_bowl_blackout_caused_by.html.

Scriber, Brad, "What Caused the Super Bowl Blackout at the Superdome?" *NationalGeographic.com*, February 5, 2013, https://news.nationalgeographic.com/news/energy/2013/02/130204-what-caused-the-super-bowl-blackout/.

Smith, Michael David, "John Harbaugh: "I Way Overreacted" to Power Outage," *ProFootball Talk.NBCSports.com*, February 4, 2013, https://profootballtalk.nbcsports.com/2013/02/04/john-harbaugh-i-way-overreacted-to-power-outage/.

Stampler, Laura, "These 13 Brands Totally Dominated the Super Bowl Blackout on Twitter," *BusinessInsider.com*, February 4, 2013, https://www.businessinsider.com/these-13-brands-totally-dominated-the-super-bowl-blackout-on-twitter-2013-2.

Chapter 22. Managing The Message

Argento, Mike, "Nickel Mines: 'What Could Be Done?'" *York Daily Record*, October 1, 2006, https://www.ydr.com/story/archives/2016/10/01/nickel-mines-what-could-done/91384216/.

Edelman, "2018 Edelman Trust Barometer, Global Report." Retrieved October 26, 2018, from https://cms.edelman.com/sites/default/files/2018-01/2018%20Edelman%20Trust%20Barometer%20Global%20Report.pdf.

Fox, Maggie, "Fake News: Lies Spread Faster on Social Media Than Truth Does," *NBCNews.com*, March 8, 2018, https://www.nbcnews.com /health/health-news/fake-news-lies-spread-faster-social-media-truth -does-n854896.

Harrington, Matthew, "Survey: People's Trust Has Declined in Business, Media, Government, and NGOs," *Harvard Business Review*, January 16, 2017, https://hbr.org/2017/01/survey-peoples-trust-has-declined-in -business-media-government-and-ngos.

Kessler, Luba, "Why Does Fake News Spread Faster Than Real News?" *PsychologyToday.com*, April 10, 2018, https://www.psychologytoday.com /us/blog/psychoanalysis-unplugged/201804/why-does-fake-news-spread -faster-real-news.

Kocieniewski, David, and Gary Gately, "Man Shoots 11, Killing 5 Girls, in Amish School", *New York Times*, October 3, 2006, https://www.nytimes .com/2006/10/03/us/03amish.html.

LancasterOnline Staff, "A Timeline of Monday's West Nickel Mines School Shooting," *LancasterOnline.com*, October 3, 2006, https:// lancasteronline.com/news/a-timeline-of-monday-s-west-nickel-mines -school-shooting/article_a7a69af3-5a16-5060-aa01-4db0c8a552b3 .html.

NationalGeographic.com, "Lightning." Retrieved November 5, 2018, from https://www.nationalgeographic.com/environment/natural-disasters /lightning/.

Norman, Jim, "Confidence in Police Back at Historical Average," *Gallup.com*, July 10, 2017, https://news.gallup.com/poll/213869/confidence-police -back-historical-average.aspx.

Chapter 23. Breathe. Debrief. Repeat.

Colino, Stacey, "The Let-Down Effect: Why You Might Feel Bad After the Pressure is Off," *USNews.com*, January 6, 2016, https://health.usnews .com/health-news/health-wellness/articles/2016-01-06/the-let-down -effect-why-you-might-feel-bad-after-the-pressure-is-off.

Curtis, Charles, "Gov. Christie Promises 'Bodies Will Be Strewn' if There is a Super Bowl Screwup" *NJ.com*, October 30, 2013, https://www.nj.com /super-bowl/index.ssf/2013/10/gov_christie_promises_bodies_will_be _strewn_if_theres_a_super_bowl_screwup.html.

Florio, Mike, "Ray Lewis Dusts Off Super Bowl XLVII Conspiracy Theory," *ProFootball Talk.NBCSports.com,* August 5, 2018, https:// profootballtalk.nbcsports.com/2018/08/05/ray-lewis-dusts-off-super -bowl-xlvii-conspiracy-theory/.

Greif, Don, "The Thrill of Victory and the Lessons of Defeat," *Psychology Today.com*, May 26, 2011, https://www.psychologytoday.com/us/blog /psychoanalysis-30/201105/the-thrill-victory-and-the-lessons-defeat.

Hughes, Mark, "The Floodlights Went Out; and an Asian Betting Syndicate Raked in a Fortune," *Independent.co.uk*, August 31, 2010, https://www.independent.co.uk/news/uk/crime/the-floodlights-went-out-ndash-and-an-asian-betting-syndicate-raked-in-a-fortune-2066133.html.

Hughes, Mark, "Superbowl Blackout: Investigation Under Way But Officials Don't Blame Beyonce," *Telegraph.co.uk*, February 4, 2013, https://www.telegraph.co.uk/news/worldnews/northamerica/usa/9848488/Superbowl-blackout-investigation-under-way-but-officials-dont-blame-Beyonce.html.

McLeod, Saul, "Forgetting," *SimplyPsychology.com*, 2008, https://www.simplypsychology.org/forgetting.html.

Murphy, Candace, "A Post-Stress Illness, the Let-Down Effect," *EastBay Times.com*, December 18, 2006, https://www.eastbaytimes.com/2006/12/18/a-post-stress-illness-the-let-down-effect/.

Patra, Kevin, "Ray Lewis: Super Bowl XLVII Blackout Was No Accident," *NFL.com*, September 1, 2013, http://www.nfl.com/news/story/0ap1000000237174/article/ray-lewis-super-bowl-xlvii-blackout-was-no-accident.

ProFootballHOF.com, "George Allen—Class of 2002," January 1, 2005, https://www.profootballhof.com/news/george-allen-class-of-2002/.

Thompson, Richard, "Super Bowl Blackout Report Blames Electric Relay Device, Cites Poor Communication," *NOLA.com*, March 22, 2013, https://www.nola.com/business/index.ssf/2013/03/analysis_of_super_bowl_blackou.html.

Zurawik, David, "Suggs Says Commissioner Goodell 'Had a Hand' in Lights Going Out at Super Bowl," *BaltimoreSun.com*, September 30, 2013, https://www.baltimoresun.com/entertainment/tv/z-on-tv-blog/bal-terrell-suggs-says-commissioner-goodell-had-a-hand-in-super-bowl-power-outage-20130930-story.html.

Conclusion. A Bullet Dodged. For Now.

Booker, Brakkton, "NFL Hall of Fame Game Called Off Due to 'Congealing and Rubberized' Field Paint," *NPR.org*, August 8, 2016, https://www.npr.org/sections/thetwo-way/2016/08/08/489168726/nfl-hall-of-fame-game-called-off-due-to-congealing-and-rubberized-field-paint.

Clay, April, "Regaining Your Confidence After an Accident," *HorseTalk.co.nz*, October 1, 2014, https://www.horsetalk.co.nz/2014/10/01/regaining-confidence-riding-accident/.

Country and Stable, "Tips for Recovering from a Fall Off Your Horse," December 20, 2017, https://www.countryandstable.co.uk/blog/tips-recovering-fall-off-horse/.

Winch, Guy, "The Essential Guide for Recovering from Failure," *Psychology Today.com*, July 16, 2013, https://www.psychologytoday.com/us/blog/the-squeaky-wheel/201307/the-essential-guide-recovering-failure.

Wolf, Morgan J., "The NFL's Hall of Fame Game Was Canceled Because the Crew Used Heat to Dry the Paint," *BusinessInsider.com*, August 8, 2016, https://www.businessinsider.com/nfl-hall-of-fame-game-cancelled-2016-8.

INDEX